Dear Masters

Daughters of Charity
of Saint Vincent de Paul

Civil War Nurses

D1230687

Extracts from Accounts by Sister Nurses

Edited by
Sister Betty Ann McNeil, D.C.

©2011 Daughters of Charity of Saint Vincent de Paul

Emmitsburg, Maryland, USA

Other titles about the Civil War are available for purchase through the Gift Shop of the National Shrine of Saint Elizabeth Ann Seton:

The National Shrine of Saint Elizabeth Ann Seton

Gift Shop
333 South Seton Avenue, Emmitsburg, MD 21727-9298 USA
301-447-7122 ▪ www.setonshrine.org ▪ Email: giftshopmanager@setonshrine.org

Requests for further use may be addressed as follows:
Archivist
Daughters of Charity
333 South Seton Avenue
Emmitsburg, Maryland 21727-9297 USA

Credits:
Consultation: Lori L. Stewart, Executive Director, Seton Heritage Center
Cover Design and Layout: Stephanie Mummert, Graphic Designer
Research & Technical Assistance: Daughters of Charity Archives,
Emmitsburg, Maryland: Bonnie Weatherly, Selin James, and Mary Anne Weatherly
Illustrations: Wayne R. Warnock

TABLE OF CONTENTS

ACKNOWLEDGEMENTS

Many individuals lent their time, talent, research, and editorial skills to locate missing data, clarify historical issues, and prepare the manuscript for publication. I would like to thank Wayne Warnock for his original sketches which illustrate the accounts presented in *Dear Masters*.

The Archives team and staff of the Seton Heritage Center have rendered timely and high-quality service in the production and design of this edition. I am grateful to Lori L. Stewart, Executive Director, for her creative insights, and to Stephanie Mummert, Graphic Designer, for her expertise and willing spirit. No request has been too minute for consideration.

Dear Masters represents a team effort which utilized the diverse experience of numerous persons who graciously reviewed and corrected several versions of this manuscript and provided constructive input: Sister Joan Angermaier, D.C., Sister Maria Gnerro, D.C., Sister Helen Gertrude Carroll, D.C., Rev. Michael Roach, Bonnie Weatherly, Mary Anne Weatherly, and Selin James.

I wish to express my appreciation to Sister Claire Debes, D.C., and the Provincial Council, who supported this initiative of transforming an idea into reality. I would like to thank the Daughters of Charity at Mother Seton House in Emmitsburg, Maryland, who provided me with much encouragement as this project unfolded. I am grateful to everyone who made *Dear Masters* possible, primarily the courageous sister nurses who recorded their experiences and Sister Loyola Law, D.C., for her compilation.

Betty Ann McNeil, D.C.

INTRODUCTION

Dear Masters highlights the mission and role of Catholic sister nurses who belonged to the United States Province of the Daughters of Charity of Saint Vincent de Paul, based in Emmitsburg, Maryland, during the American Civil War (1861-1865). Their property was also the site of the 1863 Union encampment. Today, the National Shrine of Saint Elizabeth Ann Seton located in Emmitsburg welcomes visitors to the beautiful campus where historic homes are open to the public, including the one in which Union officers conducted a war council immediately before the battle of Gettysburg. See www.setonshrine.org.

Under the capable leadership of Mother Ann Simeon Norris, D.C. (1816-1866, visitatrix [provincial] 1859-1866), and Rev. J. Francis Burlando, C.M. (1814-1873, provincial director 1853-1873), the Daughters of Charity accomplished their charitable mission at sixty sites in fifteen states and the District of Columbia. Their commitment required not only great personal courage and zeal, but also corporate flexibility and mobility which enabled them to boldly cross lines, caring for war victims from both armies with respect and compassion regardless of politics or religious persuasion.

One Sunday, Surgeon General William A. Hammond and General Franz Sigel visited the convalescent patients at Satterlee Hospital in West Philadelphia. The veterans eagerly crowded the halls except for one young man too ill to leave his bed. When the Daughter of Charity on the ward, conversed with him empathetically about being unable to be present for this official visit, the patient said simply with deep feeling that he would rather see a sister than a general because it was a sister who discovered him in an old barn near Gettysburg where he laid helpless. The sister dressed his wounds, gave him a refreshing drink, and saw that he received appropriate care. He was forever grateful for her kindness.

During the war years, no Daughter of Charity was mortally wounded in battlefield nursing although one sister contracted typhoid fever and died as a direct result of her military service.

Historical Background

The Sisters of Charity of Saint Joseph's was the first native sisterhood established in the United States. Founded near Emmitsburg on July 31, 1809, by Saint Elizabeth Ann Seton (1774-1821), also known as Mother

Seton.[1] Society of Saint Sulpice of Baltimore served as the ecclesiastical superiors for the Sisters of Charity. Historical developments after the French Revolution influenced the Sulpicians to arrange for the sisterhood to unite with the French Daughters of Charity of Saint Vincent de Paul in 1850. The headquarters for the new United States province of the Daughters of Charity remained at the founding site in Frederick County near Emmitsburg, Maryland.

The mission of the Sisters and Daughters of Charity was, and is, to seek out and serve the persons in need, especially individuals and families living in poverty, to teach children lacking educational opportunities, and to care for sick or dying persons.[2]

The distinctive seventeenth-century peasant attire, with its large white cornette (winged headdress) and blue-grey dress of the Daughters of Charity was a familiar symbol of charity.[3]

Some of the milestones in the expansion of the Daughters of Charity ministry in the United States include: the first free Catholic school (Emmitsburg, 1810); the first Catholic orphanage (Philadelphia, 1814); and the first Catholic psychiatric hospital (Baltimore, 1840).

The people of Paris named the servants of the poor of Paris "Daughters of Charity" after seeing the good they were doing and the respectful tenderness with which they cared for persons in need. The sisters' manner of serving persons among the poor, sick, and outcasts of society, flowed from their spiritual formation. The Daughters of Charity are a mission-driven society of apostolic life for whom the service of persons living in poverty is paramount. The principle of *leaving God for God* has permeated the sisters approach to service since the beginning. The co-founders, Saint Vincent de Paul (1581-1660) and Saint Louise de Marillac (1591-1660), taught the sisters that in cases of necessity they should give priority to serving persons

---

[1] See Annabelle M. Melville, ed. by Betty Ann McNeil, D.C., *Elizabeth Bayley Seton 1774-1821,* (Hanover Pennsylvania: The Sheridan Press, 2009).

[2] Daughters of Charity is used throughout this work although the terms "Sisters of Charity" and "Daughters of Charity" were used interchangeably in popular parlance until the middle of the twentieth century. Unless otherwise indicated, all sisters mentioned are Daughters of Charity as indicated by the use of the congregational initials following the first time a name appears. e.g., Sister Ann Simeon Norris, D.C.

[3] By this time, the Daughters of Charity had establishments in Philadelphia, New York, Baltimore, Frederick, Washington, D.C., Harrisburg, Albany, St. Louis, Cincinnati, Wilmington, New Orleans, Boston, Mobile, Detroit, Rochester, Milwaukee, Natchez, Buffalo, Syracuse, Santa Barbara, Norfolk, Richmond, and Chicago.

living in poverty over making their spiritual exercises and prayers, but if they planned well they would be able to do both.[4]

Foundational Values

Christian love, particularly for persons suffering, motivated his followers to respond to the welfare of those whom they served by "wishing them well."[5] Theirs was a spirit of charity afire. Saint Vincent taught that "if love of God is the fire, zeal is its flame."[6] He wanted his Daughters of Charity to be afire with the love of God and neighbor. The zeal of the seventeenth-century Daughters of Charity passed through time to their nineteenth-century American sisters and from them continued to spread around the globe.

Gospel values were and continue to be the root of the Daughters of Charity mission and ministries. Sister Rose Noyland, D.C. (1834-1909), succinctly described their spirit to a Protestant minister who regularly visited the hospital in Richmond, Virginia.[7] The minister inquired if she was ever tired. "I told him I was, very often." He replied, "you must get a large salary for what you do?" "I told him no less than the Kingdom of Heaven."[8]

In their nursing and also pastoral care the sisters transformed nursing technique into caring hands and hearts in the biblical sense "not in word or speech but in deed and truth."[9] There were challenges, especially when working with some Protestant ministers whose style was more competitive than collaborative, but the sick and dying expressed their own preferences. Concerned for body, mind, and spirit of the sick, wounded soldiers whom

---

[4] Conference 20. "Observance of the Rule," 22 January 1645, Pierre Coste, C.M., *Saint Vincent de Paul: Correspondence, Conferences, Documents*, ed. and trans. by Jacqueline Kilar, D.C., Marie Poole, D.C., et al, 1-12, 13a & 13b (New City Press: New York, 1985-2010), 9:190-92; Conference 4 "Fidelity to Rising and Morning Prayer," 2 August 1640, Ibid., 29. (Hereafter cited as *CCD*.)

[5] Conference 26. "On the Love of God," *CCD* 11:35.

[6] Conference 211. "On the Five Fundamental Virtues," 22 August 1659, *CCD*, 12:307-08.

[7] Sister Rose Noyland (1834-1909), served in care of orphans, schools, and hospitals in Maryland, Massachusetts, and Virginia for fifty-five years. During the Civil War, Sister Rose nursed in the Richmond General Hospital, Richmond, Virginia; General Hospital #3 and the Pest House, Lynchburg, Virginia, where she was the sister servant. Sister Rose's accounts of Richmond, Manassas, Gordonsville, and Danville provide insights into the courage and compassion of the sisters. Sister Rose is buried in the original community graveyard, St. Joseph's Cemetery at Emmitsburg.

[8] See ASJPH 7-5-1-2, #7 *Notes of the Sisters Services in Military Hospitals 1861-1865,* 122, Archives of the Daughters of Charity, Emmitsburg, Maryland. (Hereafter cited as *Notes.*)

[9] 1 John 3:18.

they nursed, the sister nurses followed what Saint Vincent had taught the first Daughters of Charity about rendering both corporal and spiritual care.

> We wouldn't, in fact, be doing enough for God and the neighbor if we only gave the sick poor food and medicine and if we didn't assist them, in accord with God's plan, by the spiritual service we owe them. When you serve poor persons in this way, you'll be true Daughters of Charity, that is to say, daughters of God, and you'll be imitating Jesus Christ.[10]

The sisters were concerned about both the spiritual and physical needs of those in their care but were responsive to the wishes of their patients in matters of religion. They respected denominational preferences and did not proselytize but their humble service gave abundant witness of God's tender and enduring love. Living the biblical exhortation of the prophet Micah: "Do what is good, and what the Lord requires of you: Only to do right and to love goodness, and to walk humbly with your God," by their presence, words, and deeds, the sisters were themselves a living testimony of their Christian faith: "For I was hungry and you gave me food, I was thirsty and you gave me drink, a stranger and you welcomed me, naked and you clothed me, ill and you cared for me, in prison and you visited me."[11]

When their patients asked questions about religious practices or doctrine, the sisters responded. When soldiers requested to see a minister of other clergy, read a religious book, or receive any of the sacraments, the requests were honored and arrangements made. Many patients, especially those who were dying or near death, requested baptism.

As apostolic women, the sisters believed that if they left prayer and Holy Mass to respond to urgent needs of poor persons they would be blessed because "serving the poor is going to God."[12] They strove to see God in whomever they were serving. They knew that they would see a great amount of misery which they could not relieve but they chose to be in solidarity with those who suffered while doing all they could "to provide them with a little assistance and remain at peace."[13]

---

[10] Conference 9. "Care of the Sick," 9 March [1642], *CCD* 9:50. See also Conference 24. "Love of Vocation and Assistance to the Poor," 13 February 1646, *Ibid.*, 196.

[11] Micah 6:8; Matthew 25:35-6.

[12] Conference 1. "Explanation of the Regulations," 31 July 1634, *CCD* 9:4.

[13] L 353, Louise de Marillac to Barbe Angiboust, 11 June 1652, Louise Sullivan, D.C., ed. and trans., *Louise de Marillac Spiritual Writings*, (New City Press: New York, 1991), 296. (Hereafter cited as *Spiritual Writings*.)

The Daughters of Charity in nineteenth-century America had imbibed the gospel-based teachings of their seventeenth-century co-founders. Their spirit consisted of love of Jesus Christ and service to the neighbor in a spirit of humility, simplicity, and charity. The practice of these virtues indicates the vitality of "the Company of Charity."[14]

Humility. The cornerstone of their ministry was humility which provided a lens to both personal talents and limits.[15] Embracing their human limitations empowered the sisters to put greater trust in God than themselves. They placed gifts, talents, skills, and knowledge at the service of others which connected them to suffering humanity. The sisters responded with compassionate care. Their service was a person-centered and value-based ministry of mutuality as they cared for their dear masters, the wounded soldiers during the Civil War years. They were considered angels of the battlefields.

Simplicity. Saint Vincent held simplicity, which he considered to be truthfulness or authenticity, in such high esteem that he called it his gospel. The Daughters of Charity strive to be genuine—to be transparent in word and deed—to speak and act without embellishment or guile.[16] The soldiers noticed the truthfulness and sincerity of the sisters, and therefore trusted them and had confidence in their nursing care, sometimes even more so than in the surgeons.[17]

Charity. Integral to the vocation of Daughters of Charity is charity which impelled them for service in ready availability to suffering humanity.[18] Their world view was universal. "A true Daughter of Charity is ready to go to any place, prepared to leave all to serve her neighbor."[19] Finding God everywhere—in the streets of the city, the wards of hospitals, and on the battlefield. The sisters understood the distinguishing aspects of charity— "to love God, to make no exception of persons, and to be indifferent to all places."[20] This frame of reference made the sisters flexible, mobile, and useful amidst the demanding and diverse circumstances of the war years.

Louise de Marillac, who had formed the first Daughters of Charity for service to poor persons, urged them "to be very courageous especially

[14] Conference 51. "On the Spirit of the Company," 9 February 1653, *CCD* 9:467.
[15] 556a. Vincent de Paul to Sister Jeanne Lepeintre, 8 November 1641, *CCD* 2:230; Conference 37. "On Humility," Ibid.,11:46.
[16] Cf. *CCD* 1:265; 9:476.
[17] Cf. *CCD* 1:264-5.
[18] 2 Cor 5:14.
[19] Conference 52. "On the Spirit of the Company," 24 February 1653, *CCD* 9:474.
[20] Ibid.

in perfecting themselves in the practice of true humility, gentleness, obedience, cordiality and support for one another."[21] These foundational values earned universal respect, admiration, and gratitude from both the Union and Confederacy for the Daughters of Charity. In his letter to Sister Mary Clara Trigant, D.C. (1818-1891), of Donaldsonville, LA, General Benjamin Butler wrote: "No one can appreciate more fully than myself the holy, self-sacrificing labors of the Sisters of Charity [sic].[22] To them our soldiers are daily indebted for the kindest offices. Sisters of all mankind, they know no nation, no kindred, neither war nor peace."[23]

Cause of Humanity

Twelve separate religious communities contributed the services of over six hundred sister nurses during the Civil War.[24] The Daughters of Charity were among the four communities which had previous hospital experience in the United States.

When Confederate batteries attacked Fort Sumter, the Daughters of Charity already had more than thirty years experience in American health care. They had served in three public hospitals and twelve Catholic hospitals. The sisters from Emmitsburg had a record of over fifty years of serving needy persons of all faiths and had opened foundations as far north as New York and Massachusetts and beyond the Mississippi as far west as California. In their institutions the Daughters of Charity were noted for developing and adhering to strict standards and quality controls. The Daughters of Charity were ministering in locations like New Orleans, St. Louis, Natchez, Norfolk, and Richmond in 1861. Sisters and citizens alike in these cities which would suffer from being surrounded by the dangers of civil warfare. The Daughters of Charity in New Orleans and Richmond were the first to become involved in military nursing.

---

[21] L.113b Louise de Marillac to My Very Dear Sisters [at Angers], (January 1645), *Spiritual Writing,* 123.

[22] Daughters of Charity.

[23] General Benjamin F. Butler to Sister Mary Clara Trigant, D.C., September 1862, published in Butler, Benjamin F., *Private and Official Correspondence of General Benjamin F. Butler during the period of the Civil War*, 5 vols., (Plimpton Press: Norwood, MA, 1917), 2: 215.

[24] See Mary Denis Maher, C.S.A., *To Bind Up the Wounds. Catholic Sister Nurses in the U.S. Civil War* (Louisiana State University Press: Baton Rouge, 1989), 37. See also Judith Metz, S.C., "In Times of War," Ursula Stepsis, C.S.A. and Dolores Liptak, R.S.M., eds., *Pioneer Healers. The History of Women Religious in American Health Care* (New York: Crossroad, 1989), 39-68; George Barton, *Angels of the Battlefield*, (Philadelphia: The Catholic Art Publishing Company, 1897); Ellen Ryan Jolly, *Nuns of the Battlefield* Providence, RI: The Providence Visitor Press, 1927).

Circumstances and events of the Civil War had a great impact on the Daughters of Charity and their ministries. In order to meet emergency needs of the sick and wounded, Daughters of Charity superiors withdrew sisters from schools, children's homes, and hospitals to staff ambulances for both armies. Almost one hundred sisters were assigned to Satterlee Hospital in West Philadelphia and many dozens more to other military hospitals, some being stationed at several successive locations.[25] A number of soldiers were treated in community hospitals and also veterans who required long-term care due to their war-related injuries.

The Confederacy. Sister Regina Smith, D.C., (1806-1864), a native of Grand Coteau, Louisiana, as the sister servant (local superior) at Charity Hospital, New Orleans, responded to an urgent plea for nurses and sent four Daughters of Charity from Charity Hospital to nurse sick Confederate soldiers in late March of 1861.[26] These sister nurses were among the first religious women to be engaged to nurse Civil War soldiers. In rapid succession Charity Hospital became a hub for nursing care and resources, all directed by Sister Regina. From there sisters were sent to Holly Springs, Mississippi, sites in Louisiana, namely, Camp Moore, and the Marine Hospital near New Orleans.

Confederate medical authorities requested the Daughters of Charity at St. Francis de Sales Infirmary to admit and care for their men in Richmond 16 May 1861. By July the sisters took charge of the "General Hospital," which they named St. Ann's Military Hospital.[27] Mother Ann Simeon Norris received telegrams from the Confederacy in May requesting sisters to nurse the sick and wounded soldiers in Richmond and Norfolk, Virginia. A band of nine sisters left St. Joseph's for Richmond 21 August 1861.

On 7 June 1861, Mother Ann Simeon received another telegram for sisters to nurse sick and wounded Confederates at Harper's Ferry, Portsmouth, and Norfolk, Virginia. Two days later additional sisters left St. Joseph's for Baltimore and Norfolk. During the Civil War the Daughters

---

[25] See Sara Trainer Smith, ed., "Notes on Satterlee Hospital from 1862 until its close in 1865," *American Catholic Historical Society Records*, 8 (1897):401.

[26] For a complete discussion of Charity Hospital and its significance, see John Salvaggio, M.D., *New Orleans Charity Hospital. A Story of Physicians, Politics, and Poverty* (Baton Rouge: Louisiana State University Press, 1992).

[27] What the Daughters of Charity called Saint Ann's Military Hospital was called the Alms House Hospital or Richmond General Hospital #1. For an informative discussion of the various sites where the Daughters of Charity nursed in Richmond, see Rebecca Barbour Calcutt, *Richmond's Wartime Hospitals* (Gretna, Louisiana: Pelican Publishing Company, 2005).

of Charity served as nurses in the following states of the Confederacy: Alabama, Florida, Georgia, Louisiana, Mississippi, Missouri and Virginia.

Urgent requests for sister nurses increased. Mother Ann Simeon and her council, in consultation with Father Burlando, issue the following stipulations for the sisters' service during the Civil War.[28]

1. That no ladies be associated with the sisters in their duties—such would be an encumbrance rather than a help.
2. That the sisters have entire charge of the hospitals and ambulances where they serve.
3. That the government pay the traveling expenses of the sisters, furnish their board and other actual necessities during the war; clothing also, in case it should be protracted.
4. That a Catholic chaplain be in attendance.
5. No compensation would be required by the sisters for their services.

The Union. Emmitsburg superiors responded to a request from the federal government by offering President Abraham Lincoln the services of approximately one-fourth of the community for nursing without the usual salary for lay nurses of twelve dollars per month. The sisters soon served with the ambulances, on the battlefield, in military hospitals, and in towns. On 5 June 1861, the *Washington National Intelligencer* reported:

> We learn that two hundred Daughters of Charity are ready to enlist in the cause of the sick and wounded of the army, at any moment the government may signify to them a desire to avail itself of their services, to take charge of hospitals, ambulances for conveying the sick or wounded, or any post far or near, where the cause of humanity can be served.[29]

A week later on 17 June 1862, Surgeon General Hammond called for one hundred or as many sisters as possible to serve as nurses on the hospital transports. The sisters were to report for duty the next day in order to sail in the transports to Fortress Monroe under charge of a medical inspector of the Army. They would serve as nurses in the vicinity of Fortress Monroe, White House Landing, and West Point, Virginia, and in Point Lookout, Maryland. Within a few months the United States government requested sisters to care for sick and wounded in hospitals in Washington, D.C. During the war years

---

[28] *Provincial Annals of the Daughters of Charity* (1863), 503. (Hereafter cited as *Annals.*)
[29] Sister Daniel Hannefin, D.C., *Daughters of the Church. A Popular History of the Daughters of Charity in the United States 1809-1987* (Brooklyn, NY: New City Press, 1989), 109.

the sisters served in the following hospitals in the District of Columbia: Providence Hospital, Eckington Hospital, Cliffburn Hospital, Lincoln Hospital, and the Washington Infirmary.

In addition to the District of Columbia, the Daughters of Charity cared for sick and injured soldiers or Civil War veterans in the following states loyal to Union cause or divided but where battles were fought: Maryland, Massachusetts, West Virginia, Illinois, Michigan, New York, and Pennsylvania.

Restoring Life

Sister servants received delegated authority to send sisters from their local communities on emergency missions on behalf of wartime relief. At the same time, they could recall and reassign sisters as circumstances changed and urgent needs emerged elsewhere. In the midst of their responsiveness, care of the sick and wounded was the primary concern rather than maintaining records of their good deeds. Rendering written accounts of their services came only after the war in response to a request of Father Burlando who asked the sisters to write "a full account of facts, circumstances and incidents in connection with the labors, hardships and privations of yourself and companions...in connection with the sisters' labors during the time of the last war."[30] He requested statistics on spiritual or pastoral care in addition to medical and nursing treatments. His purpose was to send a comprehensive report to general superiors in Paris.

During the Civil War years emergency local missions of the sisters were authorized to respond to new needs as they arose. For example, when a telegram arrived on 16 May 1861 from the Confederacy requesting sisters to nurse the sick and wounded in Virginia, particularly at Richmond and Norfolk, Sister Euphemia Blenkinsop, D.C. (1816-1887), informed superiors in Emmitsburg about the situation in which she found the sisters.[31]

The Daughters of Charity from France also had served as nurses in the Crimean War (1854-1856). The sisters also had a history of battlefield

---

[30] Rev. J. Francis Burlando to the Daughters of Charity of the Province of the United States, 30 October 1866, *Notes*, 1.

[31] Sister Euphemia Blenkinsop (1816-1887) was assistant to Mother Ann Simeon Norris during the Civil War and succeeded her in office (1866-1887). Due to the difficulties of Emmitsburg superiors in communicating with the sisters stationed in the southern states, the Council decided in November of 1861 to send Sister Euphemia as an authorized representative of superiors in the Confederacy.

nursing in Europe during seventeenth century while their founders were still living. At that time the sisters were told:[32]

> Men go to war to kill other men; and you, you go to war to repair the damage they do...Men kill the body—and very often the soul when those they kill die in mortal sin—and you go to restore life or, at least, to help to preserve it in those who survive by the care you take of them.[33]

Not only were the Daughters of Charity found at Civil War battlefield hospitals, improvised hospitals, isolation camps, but also on floating medical transports and with the ambulance corps wherever human misery existed there were sister nurses offering relief.

The larger hospitals where the Daughters of Charity nursed included: Satterlee Hospital, Philadelphia, Pennsylvania; Lincoln Hospital, Washington, D.C.; Military Hospital, Alton, Illinois; United States General Hospital, Frederick, Maryland; Military Hospital, St. Louis, Missouri; and St. Francis de Sales Infirmary, Richmond, Virginia. In the United States their service was characterized by flexibility and mobility as a real mission of mercy in multiple settings, including marine hospitals, prisons, temporary hospitals, and long-term care of veterans.[34]

Human Resources. The sisters first involvement in battlefield nursing and military service in the United States was during the Civil War and its aftermath.[35] When additional sisters were required to care for the wounded throughout the country, despite limited personnel, Daughters of Charity superiors sent as many sisters as possible even to the point of closing educational institutions in order to make personnel available for the war effort.[36] In one account the journalist commented on the scarcity of additional sisters at the Central House in Emmitsburg to meet emerging needs as the war continued. At that time there were already many sisters in the hospital in West Philadelphia Hospital, some in Washington, D.C., and at Point Lookout. Very few were available at St. Joseph's Central House to send elsewhere.

---

[32] Châlons, Sainte-Menehould, Sedan, La Fère, Stena, and Calais in France (1654-1660) and Cracow, Poland (1655).

[33] Conference 97. "Trust in Divine Providence," *CCD* 10:407.

[34] In their hospitals the sisters cared for veterans in Massachusetts, Michigan, New York, Pennsylvania, and Wisconsin.

[35] The Daughters of Charity also served subsequently in the Spanish-American War and in World War I.

[36] Sister Matilda Coskery, "Frederick" *Notes*, 140.

We Beheld Misery[37]

Union hospital tents soon appeared on the grounds of Providence Hospital, Washington, D.C., Sister Mary Carroll, D.C. (1836-?) and three other sisters began a general hospital for civilians 8 April 1861, and the sisters cared for both military and civilian patients. Private Leopold Charrier, of the 25th New York Volunteers was admitted there 2 June 1861. He was the first Civil War victim nursed by the Daughters of Charity at Providence. As a result of his war-related injuries, Charrier later became the first soldier to receive a military pension.[38] Some of the sisters at Providence soon served also at Lincoln Hospital. Sister Loretto O'Reilly, D.C. (1833-1869), the sister servant at Lincoln, became known as the "Guardian Angel of the Ambulances."

For those who witnessed the Daughters of Charity in the midst of the sea of misery surrounding them, their presence and endless hours of devotion to the sufferers was a "constant sermon."[39]

Sister Matilda Coskery, D.C. (1799-1870), served in nursing roles, primarily in Baltimore, Maryland, for over twenty years and was distinguished for her skills in psychiatric nursing.[40] William P. Preston, an attorney in Baltimore, spoke eloquently about Sister Matilda as "one who upon the bloody field of Gettysburg I saw bending over the dying and the dead, binding up with her own hands the prostrate soldier's wounds, or commending, with her earnest prayers, his departing spirit to the mercy of his God."[41]

---

[37] Archives of the Daughters of Charity (ASJPH), Saint Joseph's Provincial House, Emmitsburg, MD, USA. Biographical and Mission Records of individual sisters are taken from the following sources in the Rare Book collection: *Treasurer's Notebook of Sister Margaret George*; *Sisters/Daughters of Charity Catalogue [A-Z], 1809-1890*; and *Sisters/ Daughters of Charity Notes, A-Z, 1809-1890*.

[38] "Civil War," *Providence Hospital 1861-1961 Centennial Book*, (Washington, D.C. 1961), n.p.

[39] Gache, *War Letters*, 147.

[40] Sister Matilda Coskery (1799-1870) served primarily in health ministries of the Sisters/ Daughters of Charity in Emmitsburg and Baltimore, Maryland. Sister Matilda is buried in St. Joseph's Cemetery, the original graveyard of the community at Emmitsburg. See "Sister Matilda Coskery," *Lives of Our Deceased Sisters 1869-1875*, 10. See also *Enlightened Charity: The Holistic Nursing Care, Education, and Advices Concerning the Sick of Sister Matilda Coskery (1799–1870)*, Martha Libster PhD, RN, CNS, and Sister Betty Ann McNeil, D.C., (Golden Apple Publications, 2009). A brother of Sister Matilda was the highly respected Rev. Henry B. Coskery (1808-1872), Vicar General of the Archdiocese of Baltimore.

[41] Virginia Alcott Beauchamp, "The Mount Hope Case," *A Private War. Letters and Diaries of Madge Preston. 1862-1867*, (New Brunswick: Rutgers University Press, 1987), 242.

When she first became involved in Civil War relief, Sister Matilda was sixty-two years of age and on mission at Emmitsburg. She left extraordinary first-hand accounts of the sisters' courageous service at Harpers Ferry, Winchester, Frederick, Antietam, Boonsboro, Gettysburg, and others.

Sister Juliana Chatard, D.C. (1833-1917), served in educational and leadership roles from New York to Alabama for more than sixty years.[42] Sister Juliana distinguished herself in Civil War services in the capital of the Confederacy and wrote a first-hand account of her experiences. The sisters served in Richmond at St. Francis de Sales Infirmary, The Richmond General Hospital #1 (Alms House Hospital/Saint Ann's Military Hospital), and Stuart Hospital.[43]

Sister Rose Noyland, worked with Sister Juliana in Richmond. In her account Sister Rose recorded that Varina Howell Davis, the wife of Jefferson Davis, president of the Confederate States of America, frequently visited Union sick soldiers anonymously at Richmond General Hospital #1. She believed that the Confederates had more visitors and were well supplied.[44]

Sister Mary Gonzaga Grace, D.C. (1812-1897), supervised the Daughters of Charity nurses at Satterlee Hospital in West Philadelphia.[45] The hospital was still under construction but within two weeks the sisters reported for duty although only eight of the thirty-three wards planned to accommodate 75 patients had been completed.[46] Sister Gonzaga's account presents the experiences of the sisters at Satterlee, the largest hospital in

---

[42] Sister Juliana Chatard (1833-1917) served on missions of the Sisters/Daughters of Charity in Emmitsburg, Maryland, Richmond, Virginia, Mobile, Alabama, Philadelphia, Pennsylvania, and in New York at Utica and Troy. Sister Juliana was responsible for the formation of new members of the Daughters of Charity as seminary directress (novice mistress) from 1867 until 1882. Sister Juliana is buried in the original community graveyard, St. Joseph's Cemetery at Emmitsburg. See "Sister Juliana Chatard," *Lives of Our Deceased Sisters 1917-1922*, 28.

[43] ASJPH 7-5-1-2, #8, *Daughters of Charity in the Civil War*, 115.

[44] *Notes*, 122.

[45] An orphaned child who converted to Roman Catholicism, Anne (Agnes Mary) Grace (1812-1897) of Baltimore entered the Sisters of Charity in 1827 and received the name, Sister Mary Gonzaga. She served on missions of the Sisters/Daughters of Charity and she went on her first mission to the Free School and Asylum, Harrisburg and Philadelphia, Pennsylvania; New Orleans, Baton Rouge, and Donaldsonville, Louisiana; and Mobile, Alabama. Sister Gonzaga served as procuratrix for the United States province of the Daughters of Charity from 1859 to 1865. She is buried in Saint Mary's Cemetery in Philadelphia. See also Eleanor C. Donnelly, *Life of Sister Mary Gonzaga Grace* (Philadelphia: 1900).

[46] *Notes*, 394.

the Union.[47] Sister Gonzaga recorded an overview of what the sisters encountered shortly after their arrival when about 1500 sick and wounded soldiers were brought to the hospital.[48]

Sister Marie Louise Caulfield, D.C. (1821-1905), served in top-secretarial roles for the community.[49] When preparing to retire for the night on Saturday, 27 June 1863, she heard unusual noises and realized that Union troops were approaching. Sister Marie Louise recorded the hazards of the Union encampment at the sisters' central house in Emmitsburg, feeding "the ceaseless tide of famished soldiers," and nursing on the battlefield at Gettysburg.[50]

Sister Camilla O'Keefe, D.C. (1815-1887), recorded that the sounds, sights, and devastation the sisters met at Gettysburg were "beyond description."[51] Taking provisions for the wounded, bandages and other necessities, they passed hundreds of victims. Their driver had to be cautious to avoid bodies in their path. After the battle Confederate soldiers returned to the sisters seeking food as they headed southward after the battle of Gettysburg. "The roads were full of the retreating army, the fields were full; mud knee-deep everywhere; the tired and hungry soldiers ate and drank whatever was given them, the people were standing on the sidewalks with buckets of water." [52]

Confederate General Stuart led two brigades on the difficult retreat through unfamiliar and rain-soaked terrain in darkness. The Confederate cavalry of General Albert G. Jenkins' Brigade came through Emmitsburg

[47] Ibid.

[48] Ibid., 400.

[49] Sister Marie Louise Caulfield (1821-1905) served in Emmitsburg, Maryland, and also spent two years at the motherhouse of the Daughters of Charity in Paris. Sister Marie Louise is buried in St. Joseph's Cemetery the original graveyard of the community at Emmitsburg. See "Sister Marie Louise Caulfield," *Lives of Our Deceased Sisters 1906-1909,* 52.

[50] *Provincial Annals* (1863), 522.

[51] Joanna O'Keefe (1815-1887), entered the Daughters of Charity in 1836 and received the name, Sister Camilla. She served on missions in Martinsburg, West Virginia; Mobile, Alabama; St. Louis, Missouri; New Orleans, Louisiana; Buffalo, New York; Milwaukee, Wisconsin, and Emmitsburg, Maryland, where she died. Sister Camilla is buried in St. Joseph's Cemetery the original graveyard of the community at Emmitsburg. See "Sister Camilla O'Keefe," *Lives of Our Deceased Sisters 1880-1890,* 92. See Provincial Annals (1863), 533-46.

[52] Dr. Thomas C. Moore, "Reminisces 1860-1865," quoted in Mary E. Meline & Edward F.X. McSweeny, *The Story of the Mountain*, 2 vols. (Emmitsburg, MD: Emmitsburg Chronicle,1911),2:56. See also Silas Felton,"In Their Words: Reminiscences—1863-65, The Battle of Gettysburg," *The Gettysburg Magazine* no.43 (2010), 107-24.

about dawn July 5th. The 34th Virginia Cavalry led the advance into Emmitsburg where a skirmish occurred on the western side of the town. Afterwards General J.E.B. Stuart learned that Union General Hugh J. Kilpatrick and his cavalry had recently departed from the area.

Courageous Charity

The Daughters of Charity governing council at Emmitsburg decided to appoint Sister Euphemia Blenkinsop, provincial assistant, as the official community representative to sisters in the South.[53] In her role as acting visitatrix, Sister Euphemia, not only nursed the wounded whenever needed (Winchester and Frederick), but primarily she traveled within the Confederacy to support the sisters on the Southern missions during this time of crisis.

Almost two years later the Council again sent Sister Euphemia into the Confederacy to represent Mother Ann Simeon because they feared increasing difficulty in communicating with the sisters there.[54] At this time, the sisters also accompanied some boarders of St. Joseph's Academy back to their homes in the South. A journalist writing for the Provincial Annals conveys the courage of the eight sisters who departed with the pupils at that critical time.

> The travelers had to go part of the way by Flag of Truce boat, and for two days, and nights we were on this miserable thing. There was hardly sitting room...we took the cars [train] at Petersburg for Richmond. When we were about half way, the boiler burst, and the engineer was killed, several other persons were very seriously injured. We were in a deep swamp.[55]

Sister Mary Thomas McSwiggan, D.C. (1818-1877), the sister servant at Saint Mary's Asylum, Natchez, Mississippi, described their fears when shells passed over their child care institution during the bombardment of Natchez 2 September 1863. Some shells fell in the yard but providentially no one was hurt. Residents of the city sought shelter there with the sisters. William Henry Elder (1819-1904), bishop of Natchez and later archbishop of Cincinnati, came to help the sisters take the children out

---

[53] Council Minutes, 2 November 1861.

[54] Ibid., on 27 June 1863

[55] *Provincial Annals* (1846-1871), 499-500.

of the city about five miles to a safer area and gave general absolution to all because of the great danger. Weeks later the Union gunboat left the area.[56]

Culturescape Challenges

The American Daughters of Charity met many challenges during the Civil War. Sisters from Emmitsburg had been ministering in the South since 1830 when they first began teaching at the Poydras Female Orphan Asylum in New Orleans. By 1861 they were serving in other states which soon formed the Confederacy. The sisters also had missions in states belonging to the Union as well as California and the neutral states.

In spite of the national crisis, the Daughters of Charity continued to open new establishments during the war years while also contributing both personnel and resources to assist those wounded in combat. The year Confederate General Robert E. Lee gallantly surrendered to General Ulysses S. Grant at Appomattox also marked the highest number of entrants, ninety-seven (97), since the founding of the community in Maryland. During the war years, almost four hundred women entered the Daughters of Charity at an average rate of seventy-seven (77) per year. The community opened nineteen (19) new missions including some located far from Emmitsburg, e.g., California, Massachusetts, Louisiana, and Ontario.[57]

As Civil War nurses the sisters overcame significant sociocultural boundaries. Sisters reared in urban settings were subject to missions in rural areas. Those from mountainous areas worked in seaside settings and on the waterways. Crossing cultural, regional, and political boundaries brought different demands as did unforeseen climatic conditions which could be horrific at times. During their wartime ministry the sisters had to deal with security issues, develop emergency responses, devise strategic plans with new methods for communication and delegation of authority as their missions were being impacted by partisan politics and army movement.

The Daughters of Charity served in eastern and western theaters of the war. The sisters nursing mission carried them across military lines, requiring them to be flexible and mobile. Individual sisters served in different places according to changing circumstances. Sister Matilda Coskery, nursed at six sites successively in Virginia, Maryland, and Pennsylvania. Another

---

[56] Sister Loyola Law, ed., *Annals of the Civil War,* 3 vols. (Unpublished manuscript, 1904), 3:106-7. (Hereafter cited as *ACW.*) Elder had roots in Emmitsburg. He had attended Mount St. Mary's College and was related to the prominent William Elder family. Sister Helena Elder, D.C. (1802-1891) was his elder sister.

[57] *Catalogue [A-Z], 1809-1890.* See also, [Sister John Mary Crumlish, D.C.], *1809-1959,* 99-100.

example is Sister Felix McQuaid, D.C. (1812-1897), who left her mission in Albany, New York, to serve on the medical transports along the Virginia-New York route, then nursed in Frederick, Maryland, and West Philadelphia. Sisters born and bred in the South cared equally for Union and Confederate victims alike as did the sisters who sympathized with the Union cause.

The sisters had to adapt to regional cultures, social mores, customs, and food. As Sister Felix McQuaid recounted: "This morning we sat down as usual to tea or coffee without milk & dry bread & as a luxury pork & beans in one dish. Only Sister Bernard ventured upon this Yankee dish."[58]

The sisters served at the pleasure of governing authorities, dominantly male, most of whom lacked direct experience in human services or healthcare delivery. Often the officials underestimated the level of skill and commitment required to respond effectively to the misery caused by the War.

An account about Richmond, Virginia, illustrates the adaptability of the Daughters of Charity. The sisters were operating the St. Francis de Sales Infirmary for ill civilians when the war began but soon the facility was designated for the care of sick soldiers and the building was soon overcrowded.[59] The Confederacy then created another hospital in several large houses. The government officials thought their male nurses would be adequate to provide care but soon the surgeon and officers in charge came to the sisters and begged them to come to their assistance. The poor patients were in great need of their nursing expertise.[60]

Despite the usual comfort of ante-bellum Virginia, Sister Juliana Chatard recalled, "Our hospitals were often also extremely scarce of the necessities of life...For our own table, rough corn bread and strong fat bacon were luxuries, provided the dear sufferers were better served. As for beverage, we could not always tell what they gave us."[61]

Upon arrival in Winchester, Virginia, after a harrowing escape from Harpers Ferry at night, Sister Matilda Coskery recalled that the ladies of

[58] Betty Ann McNeil, D.C, ed., *Daughters of Charity in the Civil War,* (Unpublished Manuscript. 2002), 149. (Hereafter cited as *DCCW*). Sister Bernard Moore (1803-1907), born in Baltimore, had recently been on mission in Albany, New York, and La Salle, Illinois.

[59] St. Francis de Sales Infirmary may also be known as the Catholic Charitable Hospital. Sister Rose Noyland, Sister Juliana Chatard, and Sister Ann Louise O'Connell contributed to this account.

[60] *DCCW*, 115.

[61] Ibid.

the town had petitioned the Medical Director "not to have the Daughters of Charity serve the sick that they [the ladies] would wait on them."[62] The physicians ruled otherwise convinced that "those Ladies could never do for the sick as the Daughters of Charity would do."[63]

Safety and Security

At times the soldiers, who were used to the noises of cannon and shells, would ask one another why the sisters don't seem terrified or tremble. Their patients noticed that the sisters seemed to go about their daily routine as if nothing was disturbing them. When asked what they would do should the enemy reach us in triumph, the sisters responded simply that they would remain on duty at their post.[64]

The sisters carried out their duties despite spies posing as Daughters of Charity and fraudulent "nuns" in the fall of 1861.[65] Major General John A. Dix informed Francis Patrick Kenrick (1796-1863), archbishop of Baltimore (1851-1863), that the United States government had reason to suspect that Daughters of Charity were lending their trousseau to lay women who wished to pass into Virginia to further partisan political objectives.[66] Dix was incredulous and requested Archbishop Kenrick to advise the sisters so that they could exonerate themselves. The archbishop communicated directly with Father Burlando, who, along with Mother Ann Simeon and her Council, sent a signed statement to Major General Dix assuring him that

> at no time, under no circumstance, directly or indirectly, have any of the sisters belonging...gone to Virginia. or any other state for political purposes, or carried documents, or messages having political tendencies. The only object for which the Sisters were sent to Virginia was to nurse the sick and wounded soldiers.[67]

Apparently two women, who alleged to be from the South, were seen in Baltimore dressed similar to the Daughters of Charity. These ladies had also feigned a false identity claiming kinship to a congressman who

---

[62] *ACW,* 2: 52.

[63] Ibid.

[64] Sister Euphemia Blenkinsop, D.C., to Mother Gilberte-Elise Montcellet, D.C., 11 August 1862, published in *Deceased Sisters (1853-1869),* (Printed Privately), 1863: 25.

[65] *Mother Euphemia Blenkinsop (1816-1887)*, (Emmitsburg, Maryland: 1969), 36-39.

[66] Archbishop Francis P. Kenrick to Rev. J. Francis Burlando, C.M., Baltimore, Maryland, 17 December 1861.

[67] Rev. J. Francis Burlando, C.M., to Major General John A. Dix, Emmitsburg, Maryland, December 20, 1861.

had relatives in the community. When Sister Francis Liguori Everett, D.C. (1821-1895) and Sister Rose Genevieve, D.C. (1819-1893), nieces of the Honorable Edward Everett of the Commonwealth of Massachusetts, heard about the incident they were mortified.

In addition to being subject to martial law and military sentinels on their own property at Emmitsburg during the Union encampment in June of 1863, the sisters also dealt with security patrols in and around their buildings. In Richmond the sisters were told that they had received orders from their generals to capture Sisters of Charity [sic],[68] if they could, as the hospitals were in such great need of them. Fortunately, this did not happen. At other times the sisters crossed army lines, sometimes with passports, pass words, and counter signs, often at great personal danger. For example, when the Daughters of Charity were traveling to Harpers Ferry at the request of the Confederates, the sisters crossed the Potomac River on a bridge laden with kegs of dynamite prepared for the approach of the Union Army.[69]

Sometimes the sisters had not only the role of nurse but of peacemaker as in Winchester, Virginia, where they heard loud threats and angry jargon in the kitchen and found the cook and a nurse fighting. The sisters stepped between them and mildly but firmly requesting each man to calm himself.[70] Elsewhere at another time, "a patient tried to shoot the sister on his ward; he was arrested but later released at the sister's request."[71]

After the Battle of Gettysburg, Union authorities began using Point Lookout, Maryland, located at the confluence of the Chesapeake Bay and the Potomac River for incarceration of up to 20,000 Confederate prisoners. Since the Confederate captives were held inside wooden walled prisoner pens on the bay shore with only tents for shelter, many fell victim to exposure, disease, and starvation. One of the sisters on duty there at the Hammond Hospital complex described how a raging tornado and water spout tore a terrible path of destruction on the 6th of August 1864:

> Our poor little Chapel shook...doors and windows were blown down...Men sick, and wounded, were blown out on the ground, and the wards and cottages carried several feet from their base...Lumber and iron bedsteads were carried over the tops of cottages...the dead house [morgue] was seen

---

[68] Daughters of Charity.
[69] *ACW* 2: 52.
[70] *DCCW*, 136.
[71] *ACW* 3:106.

twirling through the air and the bodies...were not discovered
for some time after the storm...yet no one was seriously
injured.[72]

Some memories filled the sisters' hearts with anguish. "To lay the scene truly before you is beyond any human pen," wrote Sister Juliana Chatard about the Seven Days Battle around Richmond. [73]

The bombs were bursting and reddening the heavens; while the
Reserve Corps ranged about three hundred yards from our door...our poor
sisters in the [Richmond] City Hospitals were shaken by the cannonading
and the heavy rolling of the ambulances filling the streets bringing in the
wounded and dying men. The entire city trembled as if from earthquake.[74]

Goodness of God

A bronze relief panel set in stone memorializes the valor of Catholic sister nurses who served in hospitals, floating transports, and on battlefields during the Civil War. The Daughters of Charity are among the twelve communities honored. The *Nuns of the Battlefield* monument is located at M Street and Rhode Island Avenue, NW, across from Saint Matthew's Cathedral, Washington, D.C.[75]

Sister Loyola Law, D.C. (1834-1906), edited, extracted, and consolidated the manuscripts of first-person accounts submitted to Father Burlando and compiled them into three volumes, *Annals of the Civil War.* Some duplicate material appears in this work since Sister Loyola made extracts from accounts by different eye witnesses of the same circumstances—with neither word processor nor computer. Nevertheless, she organized her typescripts by service site (city or hospital). The *Annals of the Civil War* have been a rich resource for researchers for over a century. The *Annals* document the courageous compassion of the women who had given themselves to God in the service of poor persons and their enlightened charity.

Your chief concern, after the love of God...must be to serve the
sick poor with great gentleness and cordiality, sympathizing
with them in their sufferings and listening to their little

---

[72] *ACW* 1:24-25.

[73] *Notes*, 99.

[74] Ibid.

[75] Authorized by an Act of Congress approved 29 March 1918, the monument was erected
in 1924 by the *Ladies Auxiliary of the Ancient Order of Hibernians* who wished to
perpetuate the memory of heroic charity and compassionate care of religious women
to the public.

complaints, as a good mother should because they look upon you as their nursing mothers and as persons sent by God to assist them. So, you're destined to represent the Goodness of God to those poor people. Now, since the Divine Goodness deals with the afflicted in a gentle, charitable manner, so the sick poor should be treated as this same Goodness teaches you, that is, with gentleness, compassion, and love; for they are your masters.[76]

Dear Masters—The Daughters of Charity Civil War Nurses (2011), preserves the essence of the accounts of the *Annals of the Civil War* (Law, 1904) but presents the material state by state with annotations and corrections. I have taken the liberty to make minor editorial changes for stylistics, spelling, and format for the convenience of readers. Selected information has been added in brackets for clarification and identification of terms, e.g. "sister servant [local superior]." Every effort has been made to present the material in a comprehensible format for the modern reader.

Dear Masters engages readers in an epic of faith and service impelled by the love of Christ. The personal accounts of the sisters reveal their legacy of courageous charity. Their experiences as Civil War nurses whose experiences continue to inspire anyone who dares to care and make a difference for persons in need. The sisters risked all for the sake of their "dear masters" victims of war and disease.[77] Union and Confederate soldiers gratefully remembered their kindness and how the sisters cared selflessly for them displaying the same compassion, humility, respect and devotion to each person.

Betty Ann McNeil, D.C., Archivist

Daughters of Charity

Emmitsburg, Maryland

4 January 2011

---

[76] Conference 85. "Service of the Sick and Care of One's Own Health," 11 November 1657, *CCD* 10:267.

[77] Conference 21. "Observance of the Rule," Continuation of the Conference of 22 January 1645, *CCD* 9:173.

GEORGIA

The Army becoming more accustomed to hardships, became more healthy. There being no more fighting near Richmond, the sisters told the officer or surgeon in charge that there did not seem to be further occasion for them to be remaining longer. Therefore, if he would get them passports, they would return to Maryland.

He said that they [officials] could not consent to their leaving and that he knew they [the sisters] were needed in other places. The next day a letter came from Georgia, from the Military, begging for Daughters of Charity to be sent to their hospital there.[1]

MARIETTA

Five sisters left for this place [Georgia], 24 February 1863. Terrible fighting had taken place there. We were warmly received. We were, to many, a great curiosity, so much so that wherever we stopped, a great crowd gathered around us—men, women and children. On one occasion, having to wait two hours for a [train] car, the curious gathered around, examining us closely, saying, "What, or who are they? Are they men or women? O, what a strange uniform this company has adopted, etc. Surely the enemy will run from them!" Once or twice they pushed roughly against us to see whether we were human beings or not. A sister spoke to one, and many at this clapped their hands and shouted aloud, "She spoke! She spoke!"

On arriving in one of the towns, we did not know where to look for lodgings. Going to the Catholic pastor's residence we inquired where we might be accommodated. The dear old Father had never seen our costume, and everyday having impostors to avoid, he was reservedly cautious. He was unwilling to direct us to any house, but at last his pity got the better of his prudence and he said slowly, "I will show you where the Sisters of Mercy live."[2] He took us there. The good Mother received us with open arms, saying, "O, the dear Sisters of Charity![3] Oh! You are truly welcome!"

This Sister of Mercy had been kindly entertained some years before by our sisters in Baltimore, when some distressing community trouble had obliged her to ask a favor. The poor abashed Father had kept near the door,

---

[1] Possibly the Kennesaw House, built in 1845 as a cotton and remodeled before the Civil War to become the Fletcher House Hotel, which became a Confederate hospital and a morgue in Marietta, Georgia.

[2] This encounter probably took place at Savannah. The Sisters of Mercy distinguished themselves during the Civil War, both in Augusta and Savannah.

[3] Daughters of Charity.

fearing he had put trouble on the good Sisters of Mercy. When he saw our welcome reception, he brightened and approaching sister, stretched out his hand saying at the same time, "O, let us make friends! I thought you were imposters."

Continuing our journey, suddenly one night, there was a cry of alarm: "The cars have gone through the bridge and we are in the river!" We found ourselves still, but learned that the accident was with the train we were meeting. Except by the help of torchlight, nothing could be done until daybreak. Two sisters then crossed over and gave suitable attentions to the sufferers. None were killed or even in danger.

We reached by midnight a town, but no refreshments were to be had. The work of devastation had preceded us. Fortunately, our little basket prepared for five sisters afforded some support, but by this time our band had increased to eleven. These and several strangers with whom we also shared, ate, and truly our basket still was full.

At 9:00 the same evening, a poor soldier near us in the car said, "Oh! but I am hungry. I have not had one crumb of food today!" We gave him something and immediately others asked for food. The two following days we had six soldiers and ourselves to supply, but yet the generous basket was true to all demands! On the third day we reached our field of labor.

In this town of Marietta a fine building had been prepared for hospital purposes, and the whole place with its wants and workings were placed in our hands.

We were five weeks without Mass. At last, two sisters went to Atlanta where there were two priests, but the Army calls made all ordinary customs uncertain. The sisters begged that they might have Mass at least on Easter, which was near.[4] This was agreed on, and not only we, but many poor soldiers made the Easter Communion. We also renewed our Holy Vows at that time, it being the 25th of March.[5] We made an earnest appeal for a chaplain and headquarters appointed one, but before he arrived, orders were given to remove the hospital as the enemy [Union Army] was advancing.

We had just received many badly wounded men, and they grieved bitterly to see the sisters leave them. Oh! how much had been done there in these brief months for soul and body by the tender Providence of our good Lord. Now, we also grieved to leave any suffering behind us.

---

[4] Christians celebrate the Resurrection of Jesus Christ on Easter. In 1863 the date was April.

[5] The Daughters of Charity make private annual vows of one year. These are made each year on the feast of the Annunciation which usually is celebrated on March 25.

ATLANTA

On the 24th of May [1863] we reached Atlanta where all the houses were filled and only tents could be raised for our poor family. We had 500 in tents, wounded and sick, and others arrived daily. For ourselves, we had a little log house containing two small rooms. The mice ran over us at night, and the rain was so constant that through the day our umbrellas were always in our hands. Two sisters got sick and others seemed to be losing vigor. The Surgeon told us to keep in readiness for a move, but that the patients were so happy and doing so well under our care, that he could not think of leaving them.

In one of our temporary hospitals, one of the hospital officers was at first very bitter towards us, and made use of his leisure moments to take notes on the conduct and words of the sisters. He did not proceed very far before he asked for a book that would tell him of our Faith. The result was his own fervent entrance into that Church which he had so much despised. To see him later, before the tabernacle was really a sermon. When leaving the hospital he knew not how to thank the sisters, as the means his good God had used for his conversion.

A poor old colored woman, a domestic, said she always believed the Catholics were right and now as she had the chance, she wished to become one. She was soon a very grateful and pious Catholic. A little girl whose parents lived near us, heard the instructions given to this woman, whose daughter too (I forgot to remark), became a Catholic with her mother.

The little girl told sister that she had learned what she had taught the others. Sister showed the child some encouragement and she continued coming until at last she came jumping into the room one day, saying, "Sister, Sister, my Pa says I may be a Catholic! I want to be baptized in your church." "But, my child," said sister: "It is not enough to be baptized. Is your father willing that you be brought up in the Catholic Church?" "Yes, yes," she replied. "He says I may belong to the sisters' church." In a few weeks she was baptized by our good chaplain.

About this time some other sick and wounded were brought in which seemed to prove an obstacle to our closing this hospital. Among these there were several lying near one another. The conversation turning on the subject of religion, they were earnest in declaring their detestation of the Catholics. Sister passed among them, helping first one, then another. They, on their part were thankful, until at length she said: "How much you despise me! You say the Daughters of Charity are like pure gold, but the Catholics ought to be burned alive for their badness. The Daughters of Charity are Catholics, and if they were not Catholics, they would leave you to yourselves and go home and enjoy themselves."

"Oh! Oh!" they exclaimed, "You all cannot be Catholics! Oh! that is impossible!" She then explained a little the maternal teachings of our Holy Church. They really wept from shame and sorrow for having thought or said such hard things about such a Church whose children were lavishing a Mother's kindness on them, who were so destitute of all other care.

For some time they could not look at a sister without tears. In less than two weeks, five of these men died. The first said, "If any souls go to heaven, the Daughters of Charity will; and if their religion takes them there, it can take me there too." He received instructions and the rites of the Church, as did his four companions also who all died in very edifying dispositions. Two others of that band said, "When the war was over, they would become Catholics." The remaining number said they had learned to admire our Holy Faith, but had not courage to embrace it.

A poor, badly wounded man had been very cross and abusive in his words to the sister who served him, but she increased her kindness and seemed not to understand his rudeness. At last he became very weak. One day while she was waiting on him, she saw that he was weeping. She said, "Have I pained you? I know I am too rough, but pardon me this time, and I will try to spare you pain, for I would much rather lessen than augment distress in this house of misery."

He burst into tears and said, "My heart, indeed is greatly pained at my ingratitude towards you, for I have received nothing less than maternal care from you and I have repaid it with repulsive severity. O, pardon me, if you please! I declare I am forced to respect your patience and Charity." Sister felt very joyful at this change, hoping that she might after awhile speak to him again of baptism, but when she did, he refused the sacrament as he had done before.

She knelt and said the Acts of Faith, Hope, Charity and Contrition with some other prayers. These he listened to attentively but said nothing. Presently sister left a medal under his pillow, recommending to our Lady, the soul she felt so anxious for.

After some time, he sent for sister, saying to her, "Please say again for me those prayers you said this morning, and then baptize me, but do not leave me. Stay by me and pray until I am dead—until you are sure that I am dead." He died soon after with devout aspirations of faith, hope and sorrow.

In those temporary hospitals, God alone knows what and how the sisters endured, but He alone likewise could give the powers for such endurance.

Return to Richmond, Virginia. The Southern Confederacy seeing their cause likely to fail, resolved to concentrate their hospital families in or near Richmond. Upon our arrival here, we were immediately called upon. They begged us to take the hospital under our care and charge. Here again we recommenced our endeavors to save the immortal soul for God, by and while trying to revive the poor body. Here again, the Grace of a loving Redeemer was still abundant for the work.

ILLINOIS
ALTON
MILITARY PRISON HOSPITAL
FEDERAL GUARDS' HOSPITAL

Colonel Ware, who was then in command of the prisons applied to the bishop of Alton, Illinois for Daughters of Charity to attend the prisons in the above named place. Accordingly, Bishop Henry D. Juncker applied to the sister servant [Sister Florence O'Hara] of Saint Philomena's School, St. Louis, who immediately informed our worthy director [Father Burlando] of the demand for sisters.[1]

One of the officers [of the Daughters of Charity], Sister Procuratrix, was at that time in St. Louis at the Gratiot State Prison Hospital.[2] She received a dispatch from Father Burlando to go to Alton and take with her three sisters.

We started early the next morning, 16th of March 1864, and reached Alton about 9:00 a.m. There we were met by the Reverend Mr. Harty, (the Bishop being absent), who conducted us to the residence of a gentleman, a member of the City Council. He received us most cordially and we gladly accepted his hospitality.

Colonel Ware soon called to see us and accompanied us to the prison, which had formerly been called the Illinois State Penitentiary for Criminals. It had been vacated before the war for a more commodious and healthy locality. Before reaching the main entrance, we had to ascend a very rugged road, well protected by guards. We thought that they had never before seen the sisters from the manner in which they viewed us. Here a residence would have been provided for us, but we did not think it prudent to accept.

We passed through the yard which was crowded with prisoners numbering about four thousand Confederates and one thousand Federals. The latter being confined there for desertion or for faults committed in camp. The two parties were separated except in the hospital where we now entered. The poor sick were so delighted to see us that we heard, "Sisters!" reechoed in every direction, as some of them had previously known us at the hospital prison in St. Louis.

---

[1] Sister Matilda Coskery wrote the original account of the Daughters of Charity service at Alton.

[2] Probably Sister Baptista Dowds who had been named Procuratrix 27 June 1864.

It was said that they[patients] died here from six to ten a day. The place was too small for the number of inmates who were all more or less afflicted with disease. Some were wounded, others a prey to despondency, typhoid fever, diarrhea, and the smallpox. Consequently, the atmosphere of the prison was filled with the most noisome exhalations. Fortunately, the smallpox cases were removed to an island of the Mississippi as soon as they were discovered.

Arrangements were now made with the Colonel to visit the sick twice a day. As there were no accommodations for us to remain in the prison, we returned to the residence of Mr. Wise who had so kindly received us in the morning. He could not accommodate us but he procured lodgings for us in the house of his sister, where we remained nearly six weeks.

On return to the prison the next day, we found written orders of approval of our attendance by the government. We also met there the attending physicians who appeared glad to see us and said that they hoped to soon see an improvement in the condition of the poor sufferers, who had heretofore been so much neglected. On inquiring about the health of the patients we were told that four had died during the night.

A place was now allotted to us to prepare drinks and nourishment for the sick. It was an old workshop now used as the hospital kitchen, and in it we were in danger of falling through the rotten floor any moment. The attendants, who were prisoners, were exceedingly kind and obliging—so much so that they would even anticipate what we wished them to do.

Two weeks had scarcely elapsed before the sick began to improve. The doctors acknowledged that a change for the better was already visible. "There were fewer deaths," said they, and despondency had nearly disappeared. A look of commiseration, or a word of encouragement, soon made these poor victims feel that they were cared for, at least, by the lowly child of Saint Vincent [de Paul].[3]

The prison was frequently visited by a Catholic priest. While he was there one day, a poor man asked for Baptism. The good father was called to administer the sacrament but the sick man cried out, "No, I want sister to baptize me!" The worthy priest told sister to baptize him while he stood looking on. The man died soon after.

---

[3] Saint Vincent de Paul (1581-1660) along with Louise de Marillac (1591-1660) founded the Daughters of Charity in France 29 November 1633.

SMALLPOX ISLAND

Federal Guards Hospital and Smallpox Island. We also visited the Federal Guards Hospital and Smallpox Island at the request of Colonel Ware. We visited the guards once a day and patients at the Island only once a week. Even that consoled the poor patients, as we provided delicacies and the nourishment they mostly craved for at this place we were enabled to supply the wants of the body, but the poor soul was unprovided for, as we were not yet able to do anything for the sick in a spiritual way.

On the first of May, we were given possession of a house belonging to Saint Joseph's, Emmitsburg, that had been previously occupied as a school but was then vacant.[4] The United States Government took possession of it for a hospital and wished us to take charge of it. Consequently we repaired thither May 1st. We were now one mile distant from the prison but an ambulance was sent daily to convey us there.

The health of the sick Confederates improved rapidly as well as that of the Federal guards. Consequently it was not necessary to use our house for military purposes. At this period we baptized twelve; all of whom died.

Now, God, in the designs of his all wise Providence, suddenly changed the aspect of affairs. The Colonel, who had been so kind to us, was removed and the officer who succeeded him in the command of the prisons, was prejudiced and did all he could to displace us. We could no longer get what was necessary from the prison resources. New guards were likewise placed on duty, who refused to let us pass to the hospital. Some of the old ones happened to be looking on and saw the difficulty. They became indignant and stepping forward said, "These are not ladies or women, but Sisters of Charity!"[5] Thus were we permitted to go on without further trouble.

During the month of June, we baptized two who died after. We also had the consolation of seeing many of these poor men reading Catholic books while others evinced an eagerness to receive instruction.

On the first of July, we were notified that our services were no longer required at the prison. We could do nothing until our superiors were acquainted with our situation. Meanwhile the citizens were anxious for us

---

[4] The motherhouse at Emmitsburg, St. Joseph's Central House, and St. Joseph's Academy were located in Saint Joseph's Valley. The complex was frequently referred to as simply Saint Joseph's. The Daughters of Charity had begun the School of the Immaculate Conception in 1856, but it closed two years later due to low enrollment.

[5] Daughters of Charity.

to remain in Alton and to convert our house into a hospital. We received a letter from our venerated Mother Ann Simeon [Norris] with full permission to open a Civilian Hospital for the citizens of Alton.[6]

We were truly happy at the good we hoped soon to accomplish. The first object of charity that we received was a poor woman, who was brought to us in a dying condition with her two children. Her husband was a soldier and unable to support her. Her first request was to ask for Baptism which she received, and soon after she died. One of her children was likewise baptized and died. The child was buried with its mother.

One day a poor soldier, who was wending his way home, stopped with us and asked for baptism. He died soon after. A young man, accompanied by his father, came to us one day from the prison after being paroled. He desired us to baptize him, which we did, and at the same time he requested his father to be baptized. The father promised him that he would comply with his request as soon as he reached home. The young man died and the father left us, taking with him the remains of his son.

Some of the prisoners were permitted to visit the hospital on parole. One of them sent for us to go to the prison to see him. We went and gained admittance. While there we baptized him, and he died on the following day. Thus did our merciful Lord make us, in those frightful dungeons of horror and despair, the means of saving many souls who otherwise would have died in enmity with God, whom they knew not, and whom they now thanked for His many and signal favors for them.

On our return here [Richmond], we had at once a pious chaplain, and the Holy Mass four days in the week. For the first three years of the war, we had Mass only on Sunday and very, very often had only time for vocal prayers, then read the Meditation and hurried to the dying men. Thus passed the day, and after heavy battles, we could not retire until ten or eleven o'clock. We were called during the night, short as it was but we always rose at four o'clock. When the condition of our sick would admit of it, our blessed exercises were resumed with renewed fervor.

The [Confederate] Army having surrendered, set many prisoners free, and our poor sisters hailed the peace that seemed to dawn once more on a blood washed land.

---

[6] Mother Ann Simeon was head of the Daughters of Charity from 1859 to 1866. She and Burlando provided courageous and creative leadership which enabled the community to respond effectively to the national crisis of the Civil War. Flexibility and mobility characterized the sisters' corporate responsiveness.

LOUISIANA
MONROE

On the 5th of September 1862, three days after the bombardment of Natchez, [Mississippi] three sisters were sent from St. Mary's Asylum, Natchez, at the request of General [Albert Gallatin] Blanchard, who commanded the Post and Military [Hospital] in Monroe, Louisiana.[1] He was a good Catholic, and wished his soldiers to be treated with every care and attention. We were obliged to leave in the night, in consequence of a dispatch, which announced the approach of the Federal Gunboat, *Essex*, which might have prevented our departure if we had remained until the next day. We were compelled to cross the Mississippi River about eleven o'clock at night. The good Bishop of Natchez, [William Henry Elder] alarmed for our safety, determined to accompany us. He did so, together with the pastor of Monroe to the post to which we were destined. We crossed the river in a skiff, and happily reached the other side where we found an ambulance awaiting. We traveled the remainder of that night, and the two following days, over a very rough and dangerous road. We reached our destination safely on the Feast of the Nativity of the Blessed Virgin [September 8].

The General had a matron and nurses employed in the [military] hospital—the former he discharged, and made arrangements for the sisters to take charge the day after our arrival. The day we entered on duty we found a young man in a dying state—his father was sitting near him. He professed no religion and had never been baptized. After making some inquiries regarding the Catholic religion, he begged to be baptized, and died soon after in the most edifying disposition.

Another poor man was brought to the hospital soon after our arrival. We saw that he could not live long. Having learned that he had never been baptized, and that he wished to die a Christian, we sent for the pastor, who baptized him. Although he was suffering intense agony, he showed very edifying disposition, and died that night.

There was in the hospital a very rough, but seemingly kind-hearted young man, without any religion whatever and employed as a nurse. Whenever he saw a patient in a dying condition he manifested as much anxiety about him as a good Catholic could have done. If the sick person

---

[1] Sisters Geraldine Murphy, Emerita Quinlan, and Vincentia Conway served in the Military Hospital in Monroe, Louisiana. The Daughters of Charity opened Saint Mary's Asylum and School at Natchez in 1847.

resisted him, he would beg sister to come and speak to him. This nurse was taken sick, and appeared to be in danger of death. He was one, who was so solicitous about others that he merited a reward for his generous conduct. Our Lord would not let him die without receiving the Sacrament of Baptism. When he found that the priest was in the ward, he called to him with the greatest eagerness to come and baptize him. After receiving baptism in a most edifying manner, he expired. I regret that we did not take an exact account of all the edifying incidents that occurred in the hospital. However, one hundred and fifty received the Sacrament of Baptism.

A remarkable occurrence took place on the 8th of January 1863, which shows the protection of God over the Daughters of Saint Vincent. Sister Emerita [Quinlan] had in her ward a convalescent patient, who deemed himself of more consequence than the other men and was somewhat piqued at sister for not showing him special attention. However, sister kept him in his place and treated him only as she did the others. One day she went as usual to administer the medicines. As she was passing the ward in which he was, she heard him utter most terrible oaths. However she passed on. On her return, sister showed her displeasure at his disorderly conduct and he made every apology for his misbehavior. Sister proceeded on her way, having a bottle in each hand. At a very short distance from where this man was standing, she stopped to say a few words to one of the patients, who had been wounded. She happened to look back, and noticed, that the man, whose

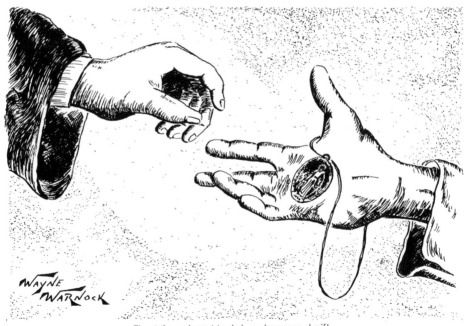

The Miraculous Medal—a treasured gift.

conduct she had corrected, put his hand under his coat, and at that instant a pistol exploded. The ball passed through the front of her cornette, within an inch or two of her forehead. The poor man whom she was addressing, thought he was wounded again. He jumped and clapped his hands on his old wound as if to assure himself of its escape from harm. Sister still held her bottles, and made her way through the cloud of smoke caused by the firing of the pistol and the crowd that gathered at its report. The man was arrested, but at sister's request, he was released. He said it was an accident. We discovered afterwards that he was a gambler, and that he had loaded the pistol to shoot an enrolling officer in town.

On one occasion as the sisters were on their way to visit a sick woman, they met the Mayor's wife, who was on the same errand. She was a Catholic, but had not practiced her religion for twenty years. This meeting had a good effect, for she took the resolution to return to her duty, trusting that the sisters would visit her when she would be in danger of death. She seemed to think that we visited none but good Catholics. She kept her resolution, and both she and her husband, who had not been to his religious duties for a long time, became good, practicing Catholics.

New Orleans

One evening there was a young man brought to Charity Hospital, who attended [the sick] in the Army as a physician. The officers paid great attention to him, particularly, a Methodist minister. At length, the [attending] doctors' skill being exhausted, there was no hope of his recovery. As yet, the sisters had not been able to say one word to him regarding his immortal soul, as the minister watched him so closely. They resolved to remain with the sick man, while the minister was at dinner. On entering the ward the young man made an effort to raise himself in bed, and when we approached him, he said: "Oh! Sister, I am so glad you came at this time. I know I shall soon die. I also know that the Catholic religion is the only true one. Please let me be baptized." I asked him to recite the Creed and the acts of Faith, Hope and Contrition with me. Fortunately the priest was in the hospital at the time. At the request of the patient, I asked the priest to see him. After a little instruction, he baptized him, and a few moments after the sick man fell into his agony and expired in the most edifying manner.

In passing through a crowded ward, I observed one, who appeared to be on the verge of eternity. I addressed him in an under tone, and inquired if he had ever been baptized. He replied in a thundering voice that he did not want to be dipped, and now he was too sick to think of such a thing. We prayed for him and placed him under the protection of our Blessed Mother. Just as we were retiring we heard loud screaming in one of the wards. Soon after the nurse announced that the man was dying, and wanted to be baptized. We went to the ward immediately, but when we reached there he was quite calm and said, "Oh! Sister, baptize me quickly, I am dying." After a few explanations on the Sacrament of Baptism, I baptized him, after which he calmly expired.

MARINE HOSPITAL

My first act, relates one of our sisters, on entering the ward, was to grasp a cup of water from a nurse, and baptize a poor expiring soldier. This poor man had expressed a desire for baptism the day previous, but as the danger was not pressing, the sister to whom he spoke, told him to wait until the next day, hoping to have him baptized by a priest.

It was the custom of every sister, before entering the wards, to supply herself with medals, *Agnus Dei* and scapulars.[2] Some would ask for a medal, through a spirit of curiosity, and examine it as if it contained a species of witchcraft. Our Blessed Mother was not to be mocked, and she conquered them by letting them see the goodness of her Divine Son, and they were nearly all converted. Some left the hospital with good impressions on their minds, and wished to retain the medal, at least they would say, "As mementos of the kindness of the sisters."

The same sister relates, that after endeavoring for a long time to get a cot for a very sick patient, who lay on the floor, reclining on his carpetbag, I succeeded and then seizing an opportunity, I persuaded a convalescent soldier to convey him to the cot. The patient was unwilling to go, as he was unable to carry his carpet bag and his boots. Not knowing whom to ask, he thought they would be stolen if he left them. He kept a watchful eye on them. The sister understanding the glances, and the reluctant movement of the patient, picked up the carpetbag in one hand and the boots in the other and followed. The poor man was very much struck at the humility and charity of the sister and said, that the soldiers wondered how the sisters could work so hard without pay. Our sister replied, "Our pay is in a coin more precious than gold. It is laid up in a country more desirable than earth." This little act of humility had the desired effect, causing the man to examine the religion which inspired so many deeds of Charity.

---

[2] Medals, *Agnus Deis*, and scapulars are Catholic devotional items or sacramentals which are blessed and may be worn by the faithful who seek God's blessing.

Blankets were used to shield the wounded from the sun.

Our sister also related that an old soldier had neglected his duty to God for many years, and who impatient under his afflictions, was continually murmuring against his Creator. At last through means of the Miraculous Medal, he was lead to better thoughts and determined to be reconciled to his God,[3] after which his countenance assumed a mild aspect, and he died in the most edifying manner.

During the first day that I visited the Marine Hospital, I saw a poor man (among the many who lay in the bleak passage). He seemed apparently weaker than the rest. I stopped to speak to him but he could scarcely articulate a word. I saw that he was dying. I offered him a drink, for which he faintly uttered, "I thank you." Tears of gratitude stood in his eyes. His strength reviving, I inquired if he had been baptized. He replied in the negative stating that he knew not what baptism was but would be very thankful to be instructed. I explained as briefly as possible the nature of the Sacrament and his obligations to receive it without delay as his moments were few. The poor man listened eagerly. I passed to another patient, leaving him to reflect awhile. I watched him, however, and saw his eyes follow me everywhere. At last he made a signal to me but could scarcely raise his hand. I hastened to him. He said in a broken voice, "I wish to be baptized. Make haste." There was no time to be lost. I baptized him and he soon breathed his last.

---

[3] The Miraculous Medal bears the image of the Blessed Virgin Mary and is usually worn around the neck with devotion and trust in God's loving care.

MARYLAND

ANTIETAM

A terrible engagement took place near the Antietam River [sic, Creek] in Maryland, not far from the Potomac, on the 19th [sic, 17th] of September, 1862. Not only were thousands on both sides killed, but as many more remained wounded on the field, [lying in] farm houses, barns, etc, [as] their only shelter. The fighting had been over a twelve or fifteen miles space. The towns of Boonsboro and Sharpsburg were hospitals [for the wounded].

The General in charge of the Maryland movement requested the people to aid the fallen prisoners, as the government provided for the North and would have done for all but had not enough.

Our good Superiors with the people of Emmitsburg collected a quantity of clothing, provisions, remedies, delicacies, and money for these poor men; and our overseer drove Rev. Father [Edward] Smith, C.M., [pastor of Saint Joseph's Church, Emmitsburg] and two sisters to the place in our carriage.[1] Boonsboro was about thirty miles distant [from Emmitsburg]. Our wagon of supplies bore us company. We reached the town by twilight. Two officers of the Northern Army seeing our cornettes by the lighted lamps shining on our carriage, one said to the other, "Ah! there come the Sisters of Charity [sic];[2] now the poor men will be equally cared for. No more partiality now."

We were kindly received at the house of a worthy Catholic physician, [Dr. Otho J. Smith], whose only daughter had been our pupil.[3] We were there but a few minutes when word came requesting the priest who was with us to come to the hospital. (There were in this town, four North hospitals and three used for the fallen enemy.) Father Smith went immediately, heard the poor man's confession, and he lived but a few minutes.

---

[1] Some other sisters contributed to this account by Sister Matilda Coskery.

[2] Daughters of Charity.

[3] Dr. Otho J. Smith (1810-1868) attended Mount Saint Mary's College (1828-1829) and graduated from the University of Maryland (1833). Jeanette Smith (1839-1868) of Boonsboro was enrolled at St. Joseph's Academy, Emmitsburg, Maryland, in 1855. She married (1865) Dr. John M. Gaines (1837-1914) with whom she had fallen in love when he was a Confederate surgeon prisoner of war taking care of wounded comrades after the battles of South Mountain and Antietam. The Smiths resided in a grey fieldstone home located at what is now 32 North Main Street when the family provided hospitality to the Daughters of Charity.

Next morning we set out for the battlefield, having Miss Janette, our kind hostess for pilot. We passed houses and barns occupied as hospitals, fences strewed with bloody clothing. Further on lay the wounded of both armies, still on the ground except some straw for beds, with here and there a blanket stretched by sticks driven in the earth at the head and feet of the poor man, to screen him from the burning sun.

Our first work was to finish roofing the six feet of earth they inhabited. We looked for an axe; then some fence rails fixing them as the others were, until every sufferer had at least a little shade over him. We distributed our little stores among them, though their wretched condition seemed calculated to destroy all relish for any food or drink. Unable to move or change their position, every filth surrounded them; add to this, vermin, maggots and stench. Bullets could be gathered from between them, that lay scattered around. One tried to raise himself as we approached, saying, "Oh! are you sisters coming to minister to us?" We consoled them all we could, but what to do or where to begin we did not see.

Many, many as in all other parts of the Armies, had never been baptized, and there were but two of us. Good Father Smith had to tell us at last to baptize them, and not wait, or expect him to serve all, seeing there would be too many left without in such case. If we stopped in one place, a messenger would be sent to call us elsewhere.

In a wagon shed lay many. One, [was] a good Catholic, mortally wounded. A Protestant officer called us to him, telling us of his bravery and valor, as "Flag Bearer," who had immortalized himself in their minds, in the bloody struggle. We spoke to him, telling him a priest was near who would see him presently. The poor fellow seemed to gain new life, but, if we left him, we would soon be called again by his kind officer, saying, "I fear he is dying; come to him; he has been so valiant, I wish to let his wife know that the Daughters of Charity were with him in his last moments." Father Smith came to him, heard his confession and prepared him for death. Poor Father was not allowed time to take any refreshment.

A neighboring encampment hearing a priest was here, sent for him, and telling us to continue, not waiting for his assistance, and he knew not when he would return, he went there.

About 2:00 p.m., the Medical Director sent a steward to tell us to come and dine with him. We sent our thanks, saying we had lunch. No refusal would do; a second message came. We joined him in an old shed that seemed to be a general depot. <u>Spoiled</u> pork and War biscuit the dinner, with tea in bowls large enough for bleeding purposes, and much we feared they were used for that purpose! The pork proved itself to more than one sense, so that we made a happy excuse for introducing our lunch basket and offering the kind director some nice ham and soft fresh bread. He pushed his plate from him, saying, "Ah! this is good."

Again to the poor men. A sister having baptized a man, he presently was seen by Father Smith who heard his confession, and some hours later he died. Passing again among them, she was called by one who had observed what had been done for his companion, and he said to sister, "What did you say to that man that died this forenoon, or what did you do for him? Whatever it was, I ask you to do the same favor, for, he died so peacefully that I wish to die like him." Sister told him what the other had received and, said she, "Did you see the gentleman in black with him also? Yes, well your companion made confession, too, to that gentleman." "Whatever it was," he repeated, "let me have; I wish to die as he did. Bring the gentleman and I will tell him all I ever did." He was gratified and died soon after. Father Smith exclaimed, "I believe that soul is now in heaven!" How happy to be thus employed; surely that soul went right to heaven!

Two wounded Protestant ministers lay among them—with one of these, Father Smith spoke a long time, while we were regretting the time he spent with him, but he replied to us in these words: "That poor man received all our doctrine as fast as I gave it to him and condemned his own. He will return to his neighborhood and may convert many, or do much good among those that you and I will never see. I repeat, therefore, baptize the men, yourselves, and I will do what I can." The other minister, calling a sister said to her: "I cannot tell you what a strange impression your presence gives me, sad and joyful at the same time, for I hear you are here only in the hope of alleviating our distress." "Yes," said sister, "but what should surprise you in this?" "Why," said he, "if your religion moves you to this, I have no faith in mine." This man also expected to get home, not being in danger. Sister told him that he was obliged to instruct himself, and not continue in doubt, or his salvation would be endangered. "Well," said he, "pray to God to enlighten me so that I may do what is right."

A Catholic steward told us he had seen our sisters at the Crimean War.[4] We spoke of confession, told him a priest was at a neighboring encampment, and when he returned he must see him. "Oh no," he replied, "we cannot attend to those things in times like these, though I have not

---

[4] The French Daughters of Charity served on battlefields during the Crimean War (1854-1856) in Europe.

been for seven years." Sister urged, but he seemed determined not to go. However, when the priest returned in the evening almost exhausted, and was just about taking some refreshment, the poor steward came and imploringly requested him to allow him to speak to him. Poor Father left his lunch and went with the penitent who was soon a peaceful, happy man, and told the sister before leaving, that, he was another man now.

A Northern steward and Southern surgeon disagreeing, one challenged the other to meet him in a retired spot, both withdrawing towards an old shed at the same time with loud, angry threats, etc. No man interfered but, one of the sisters followed them hastily, and speaking to them firmly and reproachingly, they separated like docile children, each retiring to his post.

Night drove us to our lodgings in the town before we were ready for it, but returning to the same field next morning, those we had assisted the day previous, were consigned to earth; and they that could not consent yesterday to receive baptism, now eagerly desired it. As soon as we arrived, some who were able to walk came to meet us, and the Medical Director, too, said: "You dine with me today, and," he added, "I will make arrangements for your accommodations here, if you will remain." But poor gentleman, a few hours later he was ordered elsewhere and we saw no more of him. In some barns the men lay so close together, that if one confessed, Father Smith had to lie just by the one, with his face almost touching his, and on rising, pick the vermin off his coat.

We were requested by an officer (Protestant) to attend the funeral of the brave Flag Bearer. It was now near dusk and on our way to the grave, about eight or ten [others] following. Reverend Father Smith and the sisters, also. We saw, perhaps, two hundred officers on horseback, war equipped, galloping towards us. One of these with a few, approached us nearer, all taking off their caps and bowing, said: "I am General McClellan and I am happy and proud to see the Daughters of Charity with my poor men. How many are here?" We said, "Two, General. We came to bring relief to the sufferers, and we return in a day or so." "Oh!" he replied, "Why can we not have more here? I would like to see fifty sisters ministering to the poor sufferers. Whom shall I address for this purpose?" Father Smith gave him the address. He then said, "Do you know how the brave Standard Bearer is doing?" We told him it was his funeral we were attending. General [George B.] McClellan was Chief in Command at this time of all the Northern Army.

About this time they began to move the wounded to Frederick City and Hagerstown, the mortally wounded having died. We went, during the

Sister Marie Louise observes the Union Army approach St. Joseph's.

six days we stayed, from farm to farm, trying to find those most in danger, but we cannot say how many were baptized. One poor man, old and gray-haired, was calling to one companion after another to assist him to rise, but one had one difficulty, another had some other, all maimed more or less. Sister then assisted him. She had been speaking to him in the morning, but he then expected to get well and go home. But now he no sooner stood erect then feeling faint, he exclaimed: "O, let me lie down, for I am dying." Sister said, "Do you desire baptism?" "Oh, yes!" She baptized him and he expired.

After our little delicacies were exhausted, we said to them, "we are sorry we have nothing to offer you but poor sympathy." "Oh!" replied a surgeon, "the sympathy of a Sister of Charity is a great boon to our soldiers at anytime."

Passing from farm to farm, through woods especially, we were in constant danger, as here and there unbroken bombshells lay, which only required a slight jar to burst, and our carriage wheels were rolling through dried leaves, straw, etc. The farms were laid waste, unthreshed wheat was used for roofing sheds for tents, or beds for the men. Fences that cannon balls had spared, were used for fuel. The quiet farm houses had none of their former inhabitants. Stock, that is, cattle of any description, as well as fowl seemed to have disappeared, even dogs were either killed or had fled the appalling scene. It was very remarkable also that on no battlefield during the war were any of those carrier birds seen, not even a crow; though piles of dead horses lay here and there, some half burned from efforts made to consume them by lighting fence rails on them—but this seemed rather to add to the foulness of the atmosphere than help to purify it.... Long ridges of earth with stakes here and there told: "So many hundred of the Northern Army lies here;" or, "So many of the Southern Army lies here."

Nearby lay General McClellan's Army, with arms stacked, shining in the sun like spears of silver; then the artillery, horses, etc., etc., looking all together most terrible and awful. We were told that just before the battle began, one Catholic soldier said to his comrade: "We expect battle, and there is a priest here; let us go to confession." "Oh," the other answered: "here are so many of our brave officers who do not mind these things I hate to do so." The one who proposed it went to confession, and in the early part of the fight, a piece of shell cut the companion's head in two.

A Northern surgeon was rebuking a "sympathizing lady" for her partiality towards the fallen Southerners, and he said: "How I admired the Sisters of Charity [sic], as to this matter when I was in Portsmouth, Virginia. They were called over from Norfolk to serve their own men,[5] the South, in the hospital, and labored with untiring charity, when a few weeks later, our men took the place and the same hospital was filled with the Northern soldiers, these good sisters were called on again, when they resumed their kind attentions as if they were the same men. This, he continued, was true Christian charity, and I would not fear for any human misery when they have control. And this, young lady, is what all you ladies ought to do."

The town of Boonsboro had very few Catholics, and the Holy Sacrifice of the Mass had never been offered in the place. Reverend Father Smith tried to get vestments, etc., from another town, ten miles distant, but did not succeed - the pastor of that place being absent.[6] However, the following day, Monday, he came bringing all that was necessary, and two Masses were celebrated in the parlor of the house where we stayed.[7] The convalescent soldiers hearing of it, came, went to confession, and

---

[5] The Daughters of Charity had operated St. Vincent's Hospital in Norfolk, Virginia, since 1857.

[6] The following towns could be considered to be about ten miles from Boonsboro: Hagerstown and Middletown, Maryland, and Shepherdstown, West Virginia. The Catholic parish at Hagerstown dates to 1790. At the time of the Civil War, Shepherdstown and other areas with few Catholic families were visited on rotation by itinerant priests.

[7] Dr. Otho J. Smith.

communicated with us. Even then the Catholics began planning as to how they might arrange for its being continued, until a small chapel would be erected. Since then they have Mass occasionally.

We left them on the 8th of October, having spent but six days among the poor soldiers, who had nearly all been removed before from this neighborhood.[8]

EMMITSBURG
ENCAMPMENT OF THE UNION ARMY
SAINT JOSEPH'S VALLEY

"It was a Saturday night," said Sister Marie Louise [Caulfield] in giving an account of the fact. "The sisters were all retiring totally unconscious of the approach of the army." [9]

Sister Marie Louise was at that time secretary of the community, and occupied the same sleeping apartment as Mother Ann Simeon [Norris] in the Southeastern part of what was called the "Gothic Building."[10] The secretary communicated by folding doors always left open, and was merely an extension of this room. The southern and western windows commanded a fair, open view, unobstructed as it is now by the academy building reared in 1872-1873.[11]

Mother Ann Simeon was in bed, Sr. Marie Louise not yet. She thought she heard unaccustomed sounds. She listened. They did not cease. She went to the window, and looked out. The confused sounds became clearer, the neighing of horses was distinctly heard and the flashing of lights seen here and there on the hill towards the tollgate.[12] Mother Ann Simeon

---

[8] President Abraham Lincoln paid an unexpected visit to Antietam on October 1. It is unknown whether any of the Daughters of Charity encountered the President during his three day visit since they probably were still in the vicinity.

[9] The unabridged account of the encampment on the property of the Daughters of Charity appears in *Annals of the Community* and not in the manuscript source for the *Annals of the Civil War.* ASJPH 7-8, 1863. This abridgement combines highlights of the accounts of Sister Marie Louise Caulfield and Sister Camilla O'Keefe.

[10] The Gothic Building, constructed in 1845, was demolished in 1964.

[11] The writer is probably referring to the building designed by Edmund George Lind (1829-1909) and Rev. J. Francis Burlando, C.M., and named for the latter. It is the first building on the campus not facing Toms Creek (south) but faced westward in Second Empire Style with a flattop-mansard roof, approached by a tree-lined road, later called "The Avenue." The structure has a cupola for observation. Today the building houses administrative offices at NETC and its library.

[12] In 2011, this is near the intersection of Route 15 and Business Route 15 by the fork of the Old Emmitsburg Road toward Mount Saint Mary's.

was up in a minute, and both dressed hurriedly. They knew the army was upon them. They came silently over to the academy building. There was no means of indoor communication, as there is now, and they came across the porches, ascending the exterior staircase that led from the lower porch up by the children's Infirmary. Entering that way they stole quietly up to the observatory over the music rooms, followed by sisters who had also been disturbed by unaccustomed sounds. There they stood, listening and watching through the dark the lights of the vast army encamping in the fields around St. Lazare's (the hill house; where the [Vincentian] Fathers lived).[13] The field opposite was in fine clover at sunset Saturday, but when the sun rose on Sunday was barren and bare as a board. The soldiers did not approach the house that night but went to our overseer's, Mr. Brawner's, then living with his wife in the small house between St. Joseph's and the tollgate and inquired whose farm that was. On being answered, "The sisters"—they asked the privilege of turning in their horses, and he knowing the folly of refusing had accorded the request.[14]

The next day being Sunday, they were coming in throngs to the house. One squadron succeeded another, and each squadron seemed more hungry than the last. Of course all were bountifully supplied. The General [Philippe Regis de Trobriand], a Frenchman, and probably accustomed to interaction with the community, stationed numerous guards around the house and over the premises. Here and there they were dotted, standing on guard two hours, fagged out with fatigue, and hungry as wolves. A sister approached one and asked him if he wouldn't like something to eat? "Glad to get it ma'am, but couldn't take it unless Captain of the Guard give permission." It was quickly obtained and he and his comrades dispatched bread, butter and coffee with astonishing rapidity.

About 4 o'clock in the afternoon came the troops, some on horseback, making their way up the road from the barn, some up the road from the hill, until the grounds around were actually covered with soldiers. Father Burlando was on the place to meet the generals. All seemed very kindly disposed, assured Father that the community should not be in the least molested, that the grounds should be full guarded and Emmitsburg be under Marshall [sic, martial] Law whilst necessary. An offering of refreshments to

---

[13] The Congregation of the Mission supplied chaplains and spiritual directors for the Daughters of Charity. These Vincentian priests sometimes stayed at the edge of sisters' property. They and the other Vincentian priests who ministered at St. Joseph's Parish resided in the town of Emmitsburg.

[14] The 5th Michigan Cavalry was part of the encampment on the property of the Daughters of Charity, 27-30 June 1863.

the men was very acceptable, the officers said that they had [nothing] to eat all day except something from the knapsacks, not having located anywhere until they reached Emmitsburg. Father offered the officers the use of the White House, which they gladly accepted. Dr. [William] Patterson and wife gave the generals very kind hospitality, the meals were prepared by the sisters and sent over to Mrs. Patterson. Then the supper or a good lunch for the men was got ready by the sisters, some set to cutting the bread, others making the coffee. Whilst the sister in charge of the bread in serving out so much said to the others, I fear we will run short for the supper and breakfast for the house...Well the poor men got a good supply of bread and butter, cold meats as far as it went, with good coffee. It was a pleasure for the sisters to be able to satisfy the hunger of so many, and oh, with what expressions of thanks did they not receive the meal from the hands of the sisters. The next thing was a soldier to be heard and interested with a pair of scapulars. Never did we witness such satisfaction as to see those poor men express their hope and confidence in the Mother of God that she would save their souls any way even if they should fall in the terrible battle that they were facing.

During the next few days the Army concentrated thickly in the neighborhood. There were encampments everywhere. A force was stationed in what we call "Pigs Park," the large and beautiful woods contiguous to our garden.[15] General Carl Schurz and staff occupied the Asylum (White House); Gen. [George] Meade [*sic*, Oliver Otis Howard] made the Father's house in town his headquarters; Gen. [Daniel Edgar] Sickles was at the Bridge; Gen. De Trobiant [sic, de Trobriand] at the Lady of the Field, he it was who placed guards; he had his "vivandiere" [and] left us a beef.[16] Private soldiers flooded the land, but were respectful and polite.

The Fathers got passes to go and return from town so exact was the Marshall [*sic*, Martial] Law sentinels were placed all around the buildings.

The place being under Martial Law they could hardly be otherwise. Many availed themselves of the opportunity and went to confession. Father [Angelo] Gandolfo, [C.M.], heard them in the Stranger's Chapel, Father Burlando in his room.[17] Poor fellows! It was the last chance for many of them. They never returned from Gettysburg whither their steps were tending.

---

[15] This area is now the wooded grove beside Sacred Heart Cemetery east of Saint Joseph's Provincial House.

[16] General Oliver Otis Howard was mistakenly identified as General George Meade who was then at his headquarters in Taneytown, Maryland. General Meade's location can be tracked and verified in the *Official* Records, V. 27, Parts 1 and 3.

[17] The "Strangers' Chapel" was a side chapel with a separate entrance for lay visitors.

A sister tries to stop a fight.

Sisters were engaged all day slicing meat, buttering bread, filling canteens with coffee and milk for the ceaseless tide of famished soldiers, and when were soldiers known to be in any other condition!

And now occurred a singular fact, worthy of record since it gives another instance of the sweet Providence of God ever watching over, and supplying the wants of our community when those wants grow out of the necessities of our Masters.[18] This fact is related by Sister [Mary Jane] Stokes, the sister then in charge of the farm. As squad after squad succeeded each other and all going away liberally supplied, she knew that the ordinary quantity of bread baked for the community could not suffice for such a disbursement and went to the bake house to see if anything was there for the sisters' breakfast. To her surprise "the baking of the day was yet untouched." The sisters had been feeding this vast concourse out of the ordinary portion prepared for themselves!

---

[18] "Masters" refers to the teaching of Saint Vincent's teaching to the Daughters of Charity. "That, then, is what obliges you to serve them with respect as your masters, and with devotion because they represent for you the person of Our Lord who said, 'What you do to the least of mine I will consider as done to myself.'¹ So, Sisters, Our Lord is, in fact, with that patient who is the recipient of the service you render Him." Conference 85 "Service of the Sick and Care of One's Own Health," 11 November 1657, *CCD*, 10:368.

Sister Mary Jane Stokes had charge of the farm and hands [workers] at St. Joseph's and related the following incident:

"The soldiers made their appearance here, as well as I can remember about three in the afternoon. We were going down to the barn, Sister Camilla [O'Keefe], the Treasurer, and I, to see about them there, when we turned around, and here was a whole pack of them at the house behind us. The poor fellows looked half-starved, lank as herrings, and barefoot. They were on their way to the Gettysburg battle. Well, the sisters were cutting bread, and giving them to eat as fast as they came for it, all the evening, and I was afraid there would be no bread left for the sister's supper. However, they had supper, and plenty. After supper as I belonged to the kitchen sisters, I went to Mother Ann Simeon, and told her I didn't know what the sisters would do for breakfast next morning, for they would have no bread. Then I went to see, and the baking of the day was there. I did not see it multiplied, but I saw it there."

Father Burlando remained at St. Joseph's overnight, not for one night but for successive nights, during those nights of deep anxiety, but it was not to sleep, although a lounge or some sort of resting place was prepared for him in the small room adjoining his office. One night as Sr. Marie Louise [Caulfield] and Sister Loretto [Mullery] were on their patrol, suddenly her companion was startled. In the gloom of the corridor she saw the outlines of a human figure. It was Father Burlando fully habited and hat on head, standing in his door. Sr. Marie Louise approached, and told him all was quiet and then urged [him] to take some repose, he needed all his strength to support the anxieties and surprises of the day. But he seemed restless & unwilling; then she invited him to accompany them to the community room, where they would sit & rest, which he did. And there, a little west of the door leading out on the porch, the three sat down and in the darkness, cheered each other's hearts, by companionship & conversation carried on scarce above a breath, that the sentries outside might not hear.

Before the fight at Gettysburg, while sentries or guards were placed around St. Joseph's, sometimes as many as nine at night, two sisters were appointed to do duty inside the house, and to patrol it from one end to the other.[19] All was kept dark after the usual hour of retiring that our [military] guards might not know there were also [sister] guards within. The beat was from the kitchen pantry to the church door. The sisters performed their duty in the darkness, without light. A dark lantern, with its one glass side placed inward was stationed on a window sill in the community room, the window

---

[19] Sister Marie Louise Caulfield, Secretary, and Sister Loretto Mullery fulfilled this duty.

which is now at the foot of the steps descending from the cells, but all that part of the building was then incorporated in the community room. All the windows were then furnished with inside board shutters, and the room dark as dark could be when they were closed. On one of these nights of deep anxiety, Sister Marie Louise [Caulfield] (secretary) and Sister Loretta Mullery were the two sisters appointed for patrol, the former, full of nerve and decision, the latter timorous to the last degree. About eleven o'clock or so, they had been to the pantry and found all safe on that side of the house, and saw the sentry on duty outside. They were returning through the old refectory, when just as they approached the door and two steps which led down into the passage way which ran between the Refectory and the Gothic building, there was uttered close by them in a deep, deep darkness, a frightful and unearthly yell, and then all was silent. In terror, Sr. Loretta clung to her companion, and it was a moment before either could summon courage to proceed. However, recovering nerve, Sr. Marie Louise insisted that they must continue, get the light, and return to investigate the cause of their alarm. Her determination controlled the fears of her companions, and together they returned with light and sought well, even descending the little flight of inside steps which led from the passage way, down to the ground beneath the porch, but not a living creature could be found. All doors were safely secured within, and the mystery was never solved.

A soldier was stationed at the foot of the little steps leading down from the kitchen by the "pantry;" another at the back porch of the Gothic building; another at the corner of the infirmary. Sister Marie Louise [Caulfield] stealing out noiselessly all shrouded in a black shawl to secure her from observation, heard from the upper porch a man's voice call out to the guard, "come farther out, you can't be seen there." It was the captain of the guard. She saw the soldier advance from the shadow of the building farther into the road.

"Let no man pass here tonight," continued the captain. He went on and a few minutes after she heard him say; "Let this man pass." It was one of our own men [who was employed by the sisters]. The guard repeated by call to next guard.

One evening there came a requisition from a Colonel, or somebody assuming authority, to have a certain amount of bread baked by a given time. The quantity was large, and the sisters were in consternation. Even though they sat up all night and baked, they could never prepare such a quantity of bread as was called for. Father Burlando applied to the officer occupying the

Asylum [White House] for a pass to town [Emmitsburg].[20] It was refused him until he stated with some decision that his house was in town, and he must go there.[21] He did not state however, that his object in going was to see the commanding general who had seized it, and from whom he hoped to obtain a retraction of the order.[22] Arriving in Emmitsburg with a loaf of bread which he took with him, he presented himself at his own door and asked to see Gen. Meade [*sic*, Howard]. His secretary answered the call saying the general was asleep, and could not be disturbed. On what business did he wish to see him? Father Burlando then made known the object of his visit producing the requisition. He considered it unjust; the sisters had been doing so much, and now such an order as that, taking the very bread out of their mouths!

"Well! The general would have nothing to do with it," responded the secretary, "would not act in the matter even if he were awake. But, the requisition was made without proper authorization, and if Father would go down the street to the Commissary, [John McAllister] Schofield he would obtain redress." He did so. Schofield, indignant at the sight of the paper, told Father not to fill the requisition; the person signing it had no authority; and moreover, told him not to furnish the soldiers with anything, for those who had been providing for them were amply supplied with stores.

As day came, a sudden order was given to strike tents and march for Gettysburg. In fifteen minutes it was done, and St. Joseph's Valley [and Emmitsburg] relapsed into quiet.

Father Gandolfo coming out [from town] early to say Mass, and unaware of the departure of the Northern Army was "halted" by some Confederate pickets. "But," protested the good Father, not knowing his [army] men [apart], "I am going to say my Mass at St. Joseph's. We have Gen. Meade [*sic*, Howard] at our house!" This profession of loyalty was not likely to advance his cause much. However, a few more words brought matters straight, and the gallant soldiers discovered probably [that] they might have met worse friends than good Father Gandolfo! The country [Emmitsburg area] now changed hands for a little time, and the Southern

---

[20] General Carl Schurz and his staff occupied the historic White House which was then used as an asylum for children. The original log building dates to 1810 and was home to Elizabeth Bayley Seton from 1810 until her death in 1821.

[21] This refers to the official community house of the Vincentian priests and brothers in the town of Emmitsburg, whereas the priests' house near toll-gate hill may be considered as temporary housing related to his office.

[22] General Oliver Otis Howard.

Grey swept round St. Joseph's, not in large force, but detachments of cavalry, picket men etc.

Father Burlando met some [Confederate soldiers] on his way from Emmitsburg one day, and was surprised by the salutation: "Good morning, Father Burlando! How is Jennie Butts?" "Jennie Butts" was his sister, a child from the South in the Academy.[23] Sister Raphael [Smith] and corps had difficulty when the Northern Army held the ground to force the children separated from their southern homes, and residents at St. Joseph's into something like civility towards our visitors [loyal to the Union]. She had greater trouble when the Confederates appeared to suppress all demonstration. This was sometimes more than she could do. One evening the young ladies set all rules and discipline at defiance when a few [Confederate] cavalry men approached, and called out from the avenue: "Give me a button. I'm from South Carolina!" Another: "And I'm from Louisiana!"

It was during these troublous times that Father Gandolfo carefully concealed a certain sum of money belonging to himself, or as some say, to the church in Emmitsburg where he thought it would be safe from discovery.[24] He chose a little culvert just within the graveyard. It was specie, in a box and placed securely beyond reach of harm or observation. Watching [carefully lest he be observed but] he must have been watched, for when the days grew less exciting and alarming, he went for his concealed treasure. It was gone! Mother Ann Simeon [Norris] pitying the good Father supplied the deficit.

One day several cavalrymen rode up, dismounted and entered. They were shown to the parlor, and Mother Euphemia [Blenkinsop] then the assistant went to see them, and what they wanted, if anything. As the Northern Army did so much in those days towards provisioning and clothing the Southern Army, one could not judge much by exterior apparel whom they had to deal with, and the sisters were very cautious. On the present occasion Mother was at a loss and her manner constrained. Finally one of the soldiers exclaimed: "Sister, I do believe you take us for Yankees!" "Well!" said Mother, "it is a little hard to tell. Wouldn't you like some refreshments?" The bread was just out of the oven, and the [Confederate] soldiers lunched gloriously on fresh bread, milk, etc.

The doors were all kept locked inside during the day as well as the night, by Mother Ann Simeon's orders. One day two little Seminary Sisters having occasion to go out for something when they came to return, found

---

[23] Virginia Butt was an Academy pupil from Norfolk, Virginia.
[24] Saint Joseph's Church was the Catholic parish in Emmitsburg.

The General expresses appreciation to the Sisters.

themselves locked outside.[25] On another, the venetian blind door used in the Seminary for the porch door was opened, and a soldier looked in. At the unaccustomed sight of all those little staid, demure, white capped creatures, he seemed dismayed, and left precipitately.[26] A regiment was passing one day between the Gothic building and the Asylum (White House), and a little cap, finding herself alone in the wash room peeped out at them. Suddenly she heard at her back the stern tones of the French Directress[27] ([Sister Genevieve] McDonough) who had entered unperceived: "My sister! what are you looking at?" "Soldiers, sister!" answered the frank Louisianan.

Before the arrival of the Army, the artillery passed up the road in its way to Gettysburg. Such a sight of canons was terrible. [During] the night [the soldiers went] off quietly about 4:30 a.m. The whole of [the] army was heard going off with their "quick steps" towards the road to Gettysburg. Not a vestige of the great army was to be seen anywhere around the place. All

---

[25] Seminary Sisters are women in the initial stage of formation as Daughters of Charity. This term is equivalent to novices among women religious.

[26] Seminary Sisters did not yet wear the cornette but a black dress with white fichu and cap making their appearance resemble the ad for the cleaning product *Old Dutch Cleanser*. At this period, sometimes these young sisters were called "little caps" or "white caps" because of their headdress.

[27] Sister Genevieve McDonough, D.C., was sent to Emmitsburg from Paris and was often referred to as the "French Directress." She served in Emmitsburg for five years until her death.

had trotted off towards the battle ground. Glad we were to get rid of them. Now for the great Battle of Gettysburg, the most terrific of the war.

FREDERICK
UNITED STATES GENERAL HOSPITAL

I was sent from the Central House to the U. S. General Hospital in Frederick City on the 4th of June, 1862, in company with two other sisters.[28] Ten sisters were asked for by the medical authority in charge of the hospital, seven of whom met us in Frederick from the different schools of Baltimore.

When we reached the hospital, we were received by an orderly who showed us our room in an old stone barrack, formerly occupied by General Washington during the Revolutionary War.[29] On entering, the sisters looked at each other and smiled, for it seemed quite too small for the number of occupants. There were ten beds jammed together, at the end of which was an old table and two or three chairs, the only furniture in the room with the exception of an old rickety wash stand and two affairs that seemed to be fixed up to ornament the place.

Meanwhile, the Chief Surgeon called to welcome us and hoped that we would be comfortable in our military quarters. He also said that we were to call upon the steward for whatever we wanted but, thank God, we had enough when we saw the condition of the poor wounded soldiers who were without food and nourishment enough, and even that was ill prepared. The medicines were plentiful, but badly administered by the male and female nurses who did not seem to attach much importance to the time or manner of giving them.

Our food consisted of the soldiers' rations, and not enough of them. It was served to us on broken dishes, with old knives and forks, red with rust. The patients often amused us at mealtimes by saying: "Sister, there is no necessity for the doctors to order us the tincture of iron three times a day; don't you think we get quite enough off our table service?"

Alas! We were only in the hospital a few days when we found that we were in the midst of a prejudiced community who did not want our

---

[28] This account is attributed to Sister Matilda Coskery who was the sister servant (local superior) of the sisters on mission at Frederick. In addition to Sister Matilda, the first group included Sisters Mary Alice Thomas and Sister Donata Bell.

[29] The Sisters made their home in one room of the stone Hessian Barracks. See Rev. Joseph T. Durkin, S.J., *Confederate Chaplain. A War Journal of Rev. James B. Sheeran, C.Ss.R, 14th Louisiana, C.S.A.* (Milwaukee: The Bruce Publishing Company, 1960), 26.

services. They had embittered the patients' minds against us so much, that often they would not look at us, much less speak to us. We had no delicacies to give them; the ladies had all; therefore, we could do little for the poor soul[s], while we had no means of nourishing the exhausted body.

At this time, we had a sudden and awful death of a Universalist, a death of total indifference to every Christian feeling. In vain were acts of contrition suggested; "Do not bother me; let me sleep" was the only response. O, how we prayed for him! He had never been baptized, and did not believe there was a hell! Every effort was vain; he slept about a quarter of an hour and awoke in Eternity.

July 4th, the day of the National Independence, brought us a reinforcement of sick from the field; about four hundred in number, the majority of whom had typhoid fever and dysentery. They came to the hospital unexpectedly; therefore, no preparations had been made to receive them; hence, these poor men had to lie in the open yard of the hospital for nearly a whole day, exposed to the scorching rays of the sun until beds could be prepared for them in the barracks. Thus were we doomed to witness a most distressing scene, without having it in our power to alleviate their sufferings; but the sister servant [Matilda Coskery], who could no longer behold such a spectacle, managed to procure some wine, which she multiplied prodigiously, and thereby gave all a refreshing drink which drew from the lips of these sufferers many a blessing and prayer on the Sisters of Charity [sic].[30]

Here our labors and fatigues commenced; we were up night and day. We did not even have time for our spiritual exercises, for the doctors wished us to administer the medicines at all times as the male attendants could not be depended on.

During this period, there were continual skirmishes in the Shenandoah Valley, [Virginia], from whence large numbers of wounded were frequently brought, so that in a short time the hospital was over-filled, and the Chief Surgeon was obliged to occupy two or three public buildings in the city as hospitals, where more sisters were asked for to take care of the wounded.

The Superiors [at Emmitsburg] sent a band of eight sisters who were divided among the various houses that were occupied as temporary wards until accommodations could be made at the General Hospital to receive all the worst cases. The sick and slightly wounded men were transferred to Baltimore, thus leaving the extra band without anything to do. However, the

---

[30] Daughters of Charity.

superiors sent word for them to go to the barracks where they could assist us until they would receive orders to return to their respective missions.

In this way our labors were lightened for a week or two when the sisters were recalled to resume their school duties they had left during the vacation months of July and August.

One day a young Quaker was brought to us fearfully crushed—one hand and arm mangled to jelly. Opening his poor eyes, he beheld a sister standing near him. A look of light succeeded the heavy expression of weary pain. "Oh!" he exclaimed, "I wish I were a Christian. I wish I were as good as a Sister of Charity, then I should be ready to die!" There was no time to be lost. We hastened to instruct him in what was necessary for him to believe, and baptized him, after which he calmly expired.

Often during our visits to the wards at meal times, we had much to suffer in listening to the complaints about the diet, which seemed rather to enrage the patients than appease them. In this state of affairs, what could we do but pray for them and silently share their misery? We tried to gain them by little acts of kindness or words of consolation, which apparently had no effect.

Things went on in this manner for nearly six weeks, leaving us in a most humiliating position. But, God, in his designs, saw that it was good for us, therefore in His own good time, He was pleased to change the aspect of affairs. To our great surprise the Chief Surgeon one day asked for a sister to superintend the kitchen; we immediately united to thank God for such a favor, as it would open a way to us to procure the food necessary for the poor sick.

Our good superiors hastened to "send a sister qualified for the charge." Her silence and gentleness soon quelled the turbulent spirit of the soldiers employed in her office, so that in a short time they became as docile as children.

Gradually the people began to tolerate us a little, and they were obliged to acknowledge that indeed, there was already a change in the hospital. The steward also said that for the short time the sisters had been there, their presence in the barracks had made a wonderful change in the men. "It has been observed" said he, "That they have become more respectful, and are seldom heard to curse or swear now." Even those few words consoled us and made us feel that perhaps the day was not far distant when our Lord by His grace, would enable us to do still more.

A patient, one day, sent a beseeching message that all the sisters might pray for him, "For," said he, "Ever since I saw the first of your white caps [cornettes], I have felt that there was something for me to do, but I don't know what it is."

Fortunately the corps of doctors then employed in the hospital were in our favor, and occasionally through their means we would be enabled to soften the prejudices of the patients, who saw the respect the doctors showed us by the attention they would give to any remarks it was necessary for us to make. And by degrees we gradually gained their confidence. Many of the soldiers were Catholics, but ashamed to acknowledge it, when they saw us so much disliked; but God, in his mercy, soon changed their hearts and we had the happiness of seeing them in a short time approach the sacraments and assist at Mass in our little room.

A sister was unexpectedly accosted one day by a convalescent who she had often noticed had viewed her with a surly countenance, and who took reluctantly from her whatever she offered him. He said, "Sister, you must have noticed how stiffly I have acted towards you, and how unwillingly I have taken anything from you, but I could not help it as my feelings were so embittered against you, so much so, that your presence always made me worse. I have watched you closely at all times since you came to the barracks; but when you came in late last night with the doctor to see the patient who lay dangerously ill, I noticed particularly that you did not come alone, but in company with a sister; and when you did all that was necessary for the patient, you retired. It was then my feelings became changed towards you, as I saw how clearly, how differently you acted from the female nurses who remain at night and at all times with the men. Hence, I reflected on the motives that seemed to actuate the Daughters of Charity and I could not help admiring them, and this has been the cause of my speaking to you today." He concluded by saying, "I thank you, sister, for all the kindness you have shown me, and apparently so disinterestedly." He was likewise happy to acknowledge that some of his prejudices had been removed, and that the Daughters of Charity had left impressions on his mind that would not easily be forgotten.

July 19, 1862, Feast of Saint Vincent de Paul.[31] The Director of the Jesuit Novitiate unexpectedly surprised us by sending an excellent dinner for the occasion. It was the first palatable food that we had tasted since our arrival at the hospital. Neither were we forgotten by the good superioress of

---

[31] Saint Vincent de Paul founded the Daughters of Charity along with Saint Louise de Marillac at Paris in 1633.

the Visitation Convent, who sent us cake and ice cream. Several Catholic ladies also visited us and sent us some refreshments for the day; but their kindness was short-lived as they were much opposed to our ministering to the Union soldiers whom they abhorred.

Hence, in such a place we had no one to befriend us. God alone, was our All, surrounded as we were by the Protestants on one side, who tried to entrap us at every step in order to have us removed, and on the other side, by the ladies who annoyed us all they could, by the misrepresentations they would make us to have us yield to their desires and thereby violate the regulations of the hospital. But, thank God, we did not despond, but renewed our confidence in Him, who alone could help us, and He did not fail to do so in His own good time.

There were a good many Germans in the barracks, and the band of sisters who were there only spoke English; consequently our superiors sent a German sister, who could speak to them and interpret for us. By that means we found out many Catholics who had heretofore been negligent of their duties, and were now eager to embrace the opportunity of approaching the sacraments. At our request, a Tertian Father from the Novitiate, who spoke German, came and heard the confessions. Thus were we able to assist many to regain the friendship of God, who had lost it for years.

We had a poor man in one of the barracks who caused sister some uneasiness. He was a patient sufferer, sinking slowly, day by day; but no kind word could move him to care for his perishing soul. He had a short way of changing the subject whenever God was named. It was only two nights previous to his death that the secret was disclosed. He was a careless Catholic! He had neglected his duties for many years. Now the moment of mercy came, and he consented to make his confession. Looking over his little effects after his death, we found a picture of Our Lady of Dolors, which had been treasured by the army child. It had been worn through many a desperate battle and had brought him safely through every danger. Who can say how much the heart of that Mother was touched, to behold that tattered image in the corner of the poor soldier's pocketbook?

On the evening of the 5th of September, 1862, we were suddenly alarmed by the unusual beating of the tattoo. We had all retired but the sister servant, who called to us to get up quickly and go to our barracks, that the Confederate army was in Maryland and would be here in the morning. All the patients who were able to walk, also the male attendants and the men employed about the hospital, would have to leave the place in about an hour. At the same time all the U. S. Army stores would be consigned to the flames. Imagine our feelings at such news! The hour passed like a flash. The soldiers had all disappeared except a few badly wounded, who could not be removed. The signal was given and in a few moments we beheld the entire city, as it were, enveloped in flames and smoke, so great was the conflagration of the military stores. O, my God! may we never again behold such a sight!

The sisters spent the remaining part of the night with the sick, who were left alone in the wards. The doctors who remained at their posts, carried their instruments, money and other valuables to the sister servant to keep for them, as they thought that whatever we had in our possession was secure, and therefore, they confided all they could to us without the least anxiety.

The next day was bright and beautiful but how sad a scene presented itself to our view, compared with that of the previous day! There was no one to be seen on the hospital grounds but a steward, the doctors (about four in number) and the sisters, who were going to and from the barracks to attend the helpless men left in bed.

It was then these poor creatures exclaimed in accents of gratitude and astonishment, "Ah, sisters! did you stay to take care of us? We thought you also would have gone and then what would have become of us?"

The scene just described was nothing in comparison to what had to come. About 9:00 a.m. the Confederates were discovered on the top of the hill, advancing rapidly towards the hospital.

Suddenly the advance guards appeared in front of our windows, which were under the doctors' office, and demanded without delay the surrender of the place to the Confederate Army under the command of Generals Jackson and Lee. The officer of the day then on duty, replied, "I surrender." The guards then rode off and in about fifteen minutes the whole Confederate Army entered the hospital grounds.

Oh! it was then we saw a mass of human misery; men, young and old, besides boys that were mere children, emaciated with hunger and covered with a few tattered rags that gave them the appearance more of dead men than living ones! After these skeleton looking beings had domiciled themselves in the respective barracks and tents, the sick, numbering over four hundred were brought in. Here again was another pang to the heart of the beholder! The majority were half dead and called for food and drink. They told us that they had been without anything to eat for thirteen days, except some green corn which they were allowed to pluck on their march into Maryland. Moreover, they swarmed with vermin that served to aggravate their misery.

Now was a field open to us to exercise charity and zeal in behalf of these poor creatures. But alas! a new trial awaited us. The U. S. Surgeon called upon the sister servant [Sister Matilda Coskery] and told her that we could not at that time give any assistance to the Confederates, as we were employed by the Union Government to take care only of their sick and wounded. But, he added that the Union Army was daily expected, and as soon as it would retake the city, that the Confederate sick would receive the same care and attention as the Union soldiers.

Thus were we placed in a dilemma. The Superiors could not be written to or consulted, as the city was under martial law, and no one was permitted to leave it or enter during that time; consequently we were in great distress for about six or seven days.

The citizens were now at liberty to do what they pleased; they flocked in crowds to the hospital distributing food, clothing, linen, etc., at their own discretion, which proved fatal in many cases as the diet they brought the patients was contrary to what their disease required.

Our only concern was for the dying, whom we could not assist. But our Lord in His mercy did not suffer them to die without the saving waters of baptism and the instructions necessary for them to enter heaven. Meanwhile the young scholastics of the Jesuit's Novitiate volunteered to nurse them and happily their services were accepted by the U. S. Surgeon who fixed accommodations for them to stay at the barracks. He also allowed us to give them their meals in our refectory to which they repaired an hour after the sisters repast.

It was truly edifying to see the zeal of those school boys whom our Lord made use of, to snatch so many souls from the jaws of hell. Our confessor, Father [Edward J.] Sourin, S.J., was likewise unwearied in his labors, and many were the souls he restored to the friendship of God. He deeply regretted the restrictions we were under, but at the same time we could not help admiring the wonderful ways of God in thus permitting these young scholastics to gain admittance to the hospital, to fulfill the mission of charity that we were so unexpectedly deprived of.

On the fifth day of the invasion, the sister servant [Sister Matilda Coskery] obtained a passport from General [Robert E.] Lee for two sisters to go to Emmitsburg and to return on the following day. Thus we were enabled to apprize our superiors of our situation.

The next day the sisters set out again for Frederick, but accompanied by sister assistant [Sister Euphemia Blenkinsop], one of the sisters remaining at home on account of ill health. On reentering the city, their astonishment was great, to see that the whole Rebel Army had disappeared. When they reached the barracks, the sisters informed them that they had left the city the preceding night, leaving only their sick who were unable to move.

Frederick was again in possession of the Union forces and we were now at liberty to exercise our duties in behalf of the poor sick Confederates who were now prisoners at the hospital. The doctors made no distinction between them and the Union soldiers; they lay side by side so that we had it in our power to give them equal attention. It was truly edifying to see the patience and harmony that reigned among them. Sometimes they would say, "Sister we are not enemies except on the battlefield." They would moreover express their gratitude for the care we took of them.

General McClellan was at this time in command of the Union Army. On one occasion he visited the barracks and was well pleased with the order that prevailed throughout. Before leaving, he expressed a desire to have fifty sisters sent to the front, but the scarcity of sisters made it impossible to comply with his request.

September 17th, the two armies met at Antietam and there one of the most bloody battles of the war was fought. The slaughter on both sides was terrific. Here again was opened to us a new field of labor. The hospital was too small for the number to be admitted. Hence the government ordered all the churches and public institutions in the city to be taken as hospitals for the wounded. The Catholic Church [Saint John's] was excepted. The Jesuits had to convert their Novitiate into a hospital, and the Nuns of the Visitation their Academy. Through a favor they were permitted to remain in their Monastery.

Here was a scene of carnage not to be described. The two armies who had so exultingly passed our windows but a few days before, now returned weltering in each other's gore. What a reflection for the human mind! Could man only comprehend the horrors of Fratricidal War, it would be enough to prevent him from engaging in it ever!

A reinforcement of sisters was now required to go to the various places then occupied by the wounded. The superiors could only send a few on account of the great demand for them throughout the different parts of the states; consequently some of the institutions were left to the mercy of the Protestants who failed not to exult in their privileges. Moreover, we had to divide our services between the barracks and tents, and yet it was impossible to do justice to all.

Thus were we occupied for nearly six weeks without any intermission of labor, except the few hours that we would occasionally take to repose, and even that was frequently interrupted. During that time our spiritual exercises were entirely omitted on account of the numerous deaths, which daily occurred. Yet we had a continual subject of meditation before our eyes, as well as the consolation of beholding many of those souls washed in the regenerating waters of baptism.

This was our aim, and only happiness. Therefore, we thought little of fatigue or bodily privations. Often we passed whole days without food sufficient to support us; but that was nothing to the pleasure we experienced in seeing our poor soldiers get enough. Often would we say to ourselves, "How happy we are to know that we are not better served than our dear sick!"

At this time we had about forty baptisms since the first [day] of September. We kept no account of the communions or administration of the last sacraments, although they were many.

The month of November brought us a little cessation of labor, yet we had much to endure from the severe cold of the season. The winter set in with heavy rains and deep snow to which we were constantly exposed. The poor patients had likewise much to suffer, from the badly constructed buildings, as the wind, rain and snow penetrated them, leaving the poor men in a most uncomfortable condition, until we called the attention of the Chief Surgeon to their pitiful state. He immediately gave orders for the dilapidated barracks to be repaired in such a manner as would contribute to their comfort.

During the Octave of the Immaculate Conception [December 8] we had the happiness of seeing the first solemn baptism in our little chapel. Another patient who had both eyes shot out, received Holy Communion, and after Mass a wandering sheep ended the infidelities of long years by a good confession.

We witnessed on one occasion the death of a child, although he was an enlisted soldier. We baptized him and he carried the innocence and simplicity of childhood with him to the grave. "I want to die because heaven belongs to me now," he said.

Soon after we had another baptism followed by another beautiful death. It seemed as if this favored soul had a foretaste of heaven. The precious name of Jesus trembled last on his dying lips.

Advent advanced and many of the poor Catholics were eager to approach the sacraments. All were anxious to know how they could get to church on Christmas day, as it would be impossible for so many to obtain leave to go out at once, and at so early an hour. Fortunately the steward who was a Catholic called on the sister servant [Sister Matilda Coskery] and offered to take them all in a band to the parish church on Christmas morning. They were delighted, and our happiness was inexpressible to see so many of them approaching the Holy Table on such a beautiful festival and to know that they were again the favored children of an Infant God.

The Protestant chaplain employed by the Union Government to visit the prisoners now began to receive the good effected, not withstanding his zeal; therefore, it made him a little uneasy to see that his loss was our gain, and consequently he commenced to censure our self-sacrificing Father Sourin, whom he thought should not be admitted to the hospital. He likewise remarked that the priest would never be able to accomplish all that he did if he were not aided by the Sisters of Charity [sic],[32] who did nothing to assist him in his evangelical labors.

Now he would not rest until he began to irritate the doctor against the priest and sisters, whom he thought should not be tolerated on account of the proselytes they made. Moreover, he would not be satisfied until the Chief Surgeon gave him an old vacated barrack for a meeting house, where he assembled all the soldiers he could get on Sundays, and also during the week, exhorting them to be beware of us and to pray that we might be delivered from the darkness we were in.

This was not enough. His zeal urged him to do still more. He appointed days in each barrack where he might hold prayer meetings for the sick.

Besides, the Protestant ladies would come and distribute bibles, tracts, etc., to envenom [poison] the minds of the patients against us. However, they continued to be satisfied with the care we took of them, and many were heard to declare that for the future there was no religion for them but the "Sisters' Religion."

---

[32] Daughters of Charity.

Although we had a thorny path to traverse, yet we were not discouraged, but renewed our confidence in God, who alone enabled us to accomplish our duties with a cheerfulness and patience as great as if we had no opposition to encounter.

Some of those poor soldiers were quite amusing with their grateful attentions towards us. A sister was asked one day if we ever wore any other color besides gray or black, "for," continued her interrogator, "I wish to present Sister N. with a new dress, she has been so truly good to me."

While speaking to a poor soldier on one occasion, we asked him if he had ever been baptized. He replied that he had baptized himself. "Baptized yourself? How did you do that?" "Let me tell you," said he; "the minister of our regiment promised to baptize all the men who wanted it, when we would get to a certain place. Meanwhile we were ordered to march to Gettysburg and I was very much afraid to enter the fight; so I took my canteen and filled it with water and dashed it over my head." The poor fellow died without any other baptism, as it was not in our power to do anything for him, as he was constantly attended by two Methodist preachers who took good care not to leave him in his last moments.

We were agreeably surprised by the U. S. Surgeon, who called upon our sister servant one day, and told her that he was pleasantly surprised to find the sisters so free from the political spirit that disturbed the times. He also remarked that our sentiments had been closely watched since our arrival in Frederick, as it had been rumored that the Daughters of Charity were all Rebels. However, he was glad to attest to them that our conduct proved that we took no part in politics.

It is thought that we had over one hundred baptisms from July 1862 until February 1863. We had many after that date, but kept no particular account of them.

July 1864. Frederick was again visited by the Confederates, but only by division of the army under General [James] Longstreet. When he reached the precincts of the city, he encountered a detachment of Union troops under General [Nathaniel P.] Banks. Consequently, a battle ensued which again filled the hospital with the mutilated victims of a bloody war.

It was truly heart-rending to see the mangled bodies of those poor creatures, many of whom were in their agony when brought to the hospital. Then great was our sorrow to see that their consciousness was not sufficient to permit us to offer them some few words of consolation, and to remind them to bear patiently their sufferings for the love of Him in whose presence they were soon to appear.

At this time we had about fifteen or twenty baptisms. The poor soldiers showed the greatest confidence in the sisters, whose advice they preferred before that of the physicians.

Among our patients was a very pious Lutheran who had consumption. The sister who had charge of him would say a little word to him occasionally, but he showed no desire to speak on religious matters and constantly read his Testament [Bible]. After three or four months we had the consolation of seeing him make his confession to our zealous little pastor. As he was sinking, the doctor sent for his wife who arrived a few days before he died. When asked if he did not want to get well and go home, he replied, that he wanted to die with the sisters.

General [David] Hunter had now received command of the Shenandoah Valley.[33] He paid a visit to the hospital and issued a regulation that all the prisoners should be placed by themselves in separate barracks, entirely apart from the Union men. Soon after, the U. S. Surgeon in charge of the hospital inspected all the barracks, and unexpectedly found one filled with Confederates and no sister to take care of them. The sufferings of these poor creatures touched him so much that he immediately went to the sister servant [Sister Matilda Coskery] and asked her to send a sister from one of the wards of the Union men, until the superiors [at Emmitsburg] could send one to replace her. In this way, the wants of all were pretty well supplied and their sufferings greatly alleviated.

On one occasion a patient was brought to us very ill; he was a Catholic, but had not approached the sacraments for thirty-five years. Sister spoke to him of confession but he answered that he was too sick and would have to wait until he was better. However, after a few days he consented to make his confession, after which he said to sister, "I feel so free and happy now." He died two days after.

The patience of these poor sufferers was the admiration of all. A worthy clergyman once remarked that, in his visits to the hospital he was always edified by their resignation, for never had he heard the least murmur escape their lips. "I think the intensity of their pains, both mental and corporal might, if offered in union of those of our Lord, expiate the sins of their whole life," said he.

---

[33] This meeting must have been shortly before General Hunter resigned his command on 8 August 1864.

Think then what must have been our anxiety, when we heard the condition of any one pronounced hopeless, who would not listen to anything but his recovery. Others, again, gave us much consolation.

A poor soldier sent late one evening for the sister who attended him. She went and found him sinking rapidly; his wound had bled anew and he was nearly exhausted from loss of blood. On seeing her, he exclaimed, "O, sister! I am going to die and I want to be baptized. Your religion is admirable —it is truly divine! I feel that without the pall of your church there is no salvation."[34] As his life was in imminent danger, sister concluded that his sentiments were sincere and told him to raise his heart to God to thank Him for the great and signal favor; after repeating with him the acts of faith and contrition, she baptized him conditionally, as he had no precise knowledge of never having been baptized. He expired the next day in the most beautiful manner; in fact, the interval of his life after baptism seemed to be one continual act of thanksgiving.

The deaths which occurred after our arrival had been deaths of frightful despair, or else death surrounded by a frightful mockery of religion, which would have drawn tears from the eyes of the angels: Universalists, Methodists, Presbyterians, etc., etc., dying unbaptized, with assistants around their beds singing of the "glory" into which they were about to enter, and depositing all the good and bad, in the peace of Father "Abraham's bosom." God has his own designs of mercy; hence the hearts of our patients were changed, and we had the unspeakable happiness of beholding many edifying deaths as well as conversions during our stay at the military hospital.

A young man was brought to us one day, who had a swelling on his knee. We did not apprehend any danger as he did not seem to suffer much. He told sister that he was a Catholic, but had not been to his duties for four years, during which time he had been in the army. In about a week after his arrival the disease left his knee and settled in his chest. Sister perceived that his malady would prove fatal and advised him to make his confession. The priest who was then in the ward also spoke to him, but he insisted on waiting until later. The next day he was much worse; sister spoke to him several times and each time he answered, "Tomorrow, tomorrow." Two other sisters went to see him, one of whom spoke his native language, hoping that would have some effect, but before they got near him, he cried out, "Tomorrow I will go to confession!"

---

[34] Cf. Isaiah 61:10. Possibly a reference to robe of salvation.

Sister then concluded to send for the priest, and if he would not consent to make his peace with God, she would not have anything to answer for on that point. After the messenger had gone, sister brought a medal of our Immaculate Mother; he took it, pressed it reverently to his lips and then said, "Sister, won't you send for the priest? I want to make my confession."

The good Father arrived to the great satisfaction of the sick man, who made his confession, and received the last sacraments. A few hours after, he calmly expired.

Thus in many instances, the Providence of our good God was manifested, for in afflicting us with so many annoyances and calamities, He chose in His mercy to make them a source of many blessings by bringing sinners to a sense of their duty, and imparting the light of Faith to those who before dwelt in the shadow of death. During the month of September, we were recalled by the superiors to the Central House; thus ended our labors at the United States Army General Hospital, Frederick City, Maryland.

POINT LOOKOUT

Point Lookout, Maryland, is situated at the southern extreme of Maryland, the Chesapeake Bay being the boundary on one side and the Potomac on the other.

On the 14th of July 1862, our Reverend Father Burlando with twenty-six sisters left Baltimore, and after twenty-four hours sail, reached this encampment. We were there but about two weeks when our Lord called for a victim of sacrifice, whereby to sanctify His work that Saint Vincent's children were to perform there. One of our band [Sister Mary Consolata Conlan] had contracted typhoid fever on the transport and was now called to her reward.[35] She gave up her whole being as generously as she had offered her zealous labors.

Our dear Father Burlando had returned to Baltimore, but a very pious priest came occasionally to the encampment, heard confessions, baptized the dying soldiers and gave us Mass in one of our little cottages. Our dear sister had, therefore, received the Sacrament of Penance and Holy Communion a day or two previous to her death, though no danger was then apparent. The priest being stationed twelve miles distant, could not reach us in time, after her symptoms became alarming, arriving only in time to perform the burial service.

---

[35] Sister Consolata Conlan (1842-1862) was nineteen at the time of her death. Her remains were transferred and reinterred after the war to Mount Olivet Cemetery, Washington, D.C.

Our dear sister was honored by every effort of the kind doctors and officers—they being pallbearers. All the soldiers, who had been buried, had only a sheet wrapped around them, as there was no lumber for coffins; but for our dear sister a white pine coffin was procured. The Authorities walked in procession, the soldiers playing a march for the dead. There on the bank of the Potomac rested the worn out Sister of Charity, but the prayers of our Holy Church, consecrated the spot, by the ministry of one of her faithful sons. A Martyr of Charity had become the base of that new mission.

Several cottages, tents, and wooden wards for the accommodation of thousands and thousands of sick and wounded, made this narrow strait a thickly inhabited place.

The poor men soon expressed their joy at having the sisters to attend them. Many of them were in a deplorable state from wounds, aggravated by painful removals, as the distance from some of the battlefields to this place was great.

We need hardly say that our holy founder's words were not forgotten: "In soothing the pains of the body, give them religion, drop by drop." For a symptom of danger was to all his daughters, the signal for the salutary inquiry concerning the blessed passport to heaven—baptism! Facts alone could convince us that so many redeemed souls seemed to know nothing about being saved or lost, eternally!

From the commencement of our labors, therefore, baptisms were very frequent, but we only handed in the reports to the good priest that he might record them with his own account, for as he often came on Friday and stayed until Monday. He was constantly engaged among the soldiers, instructing some, baptizing, hearing confessions, on Sunday mornings saying the first Mass at the encampment, and the second in our little chapel.

Our first Mass was said in a tent surrounded by soldiers. The captain of the guards being a Catholic, he marched his company to Mass on Sundays. At the elevation host a drum was sounded and all adored profoundly. Later, the [military] officers gave us more cottages, and by removing partitions we had quite a good sized chapel. The poor soldiers often kept up perpetual adoration there without being aware of it, from early morning until dark they would be there. Conversions were frequent and the zealous chaplain was very joyful at the success of his labors.

The doctors and officers were very kind to us, with some few exceptions. One of these is the following: A doctor who had always entertained prejudices to our holy religion now found himself in daily, even hourly intercourse with Catholics. He set himself to scrutinize every movement of the sisters, believing they would testify to the falsity of their religion.

For this purpose he complained of the sister in his ward, and seemed to wish that she would not go around with him to see the patients; he would give the male nurse all the directions and make his remarks to him, also. Our poor sister showed no disturbance, but recommending her little trial to our Blessed Lady, she quietly continued her attentions to the sick and wounded as best she could, omitting however, to go around with the doctor.

Things went on thus for some days when the doctor asked, "Sister, why do you not accompany me as formerly, when I go to the beds of the patients?" Sister replied simply that she thought he preferred that she would not do so. He slightly apologized and said, "Yes, he wished her to go with him." She resumed her duty and received his directions, faithfully complying with them as though no interruption had occurred. One day the male nurse said, "Sir, have you no directions for me?" The doctor answered, "Sister will give them to you." Sister wondered and thanked her Blessed Mother for helping her out of her trouble.

Sometime after, this doctor was removed to another ward; again he began to observe the works and manners of the sister there. He felt sure that the endurance of the sisters must fail in the end since he believed that a religion such as theirs was not capable of carrying them through all they had to suffer. Surprised each day, instead of seeing his expectations realized, he asked a Catholic gentleman in the Commissary to loan him a work on Catholic doctrine. He read, was enlightened, and went in search of the good chaplain for further explanations. Being fully satisfied, he asked for a furlough of a few days, using this time for a preparatory retreat at the residence of the kind priest. This being done, he returned to his post and was baptized in our little chapel, to the great surprise of the doctors and officers. He also made his First Communion, and joyful as was the chaplain and sisters, he the favored one, was the happiest and most grateful.

He used to tell the sisters that if he had lost everything this side of heaven by his change of religion, it would not have caused him any hesitation, and he would say, "Sisters, next to God, I owe my happiness to you, for I purposely tried you, to prove your religion; but your patience and humility gained the victory." This conversion gave us much encouragement.

A storm destroys the morgue as the wind whirls bodies hither and yon, at Point Lookout, Maryland.

It was also very consoling to see the influence that the presence of the sisters had over the soldiers generally. With some, swearing was a habit, but a check or two from a sister would be enough so that an improper word was rarely heard. Others who loved their glass [of liquor], feared only the sisters knowing it. Our kind doctors showing so much confidence, was calculated also to lighten their labors, and at the same time to enable them to do much good. As we have already said, there were some few exceptions. Upon one occasion a patient had asked for some information of our holy religion. Our sister having given him some knowledge of its doctrine, the poor man asked for baptism, having never been baptized. This he repeatedly asked, until sister said to him, "As you are not in immediate danger, let us wait for the chaplain who will be here tomorrow." When the priest arrived, the sister told the sick man who said, "Please bring him to me." He then asked the good Father for baptism. He was baptized and the priest finding such pious disposition, gave him the scapular as a protection for his faith.

A doctor who was also a minister of the gospel, hearing of this, was zealously angry and asked the sister, "<u>How</u> she could have him baptized a Catholic without <u>his</u> permission? He would report the sisters at Washington for their efforts to gain proselytes, etc." Sister said the man had asked for baptism under the Catholic form, that they had no objection that he should inform on them at Washington, and if similar occasions offered they would do the same, as in this instance. He was angry, pulled the scapulars from the sick man's neck and went to the priest, making the same threats and using abusive language, showed him the scapulars, saying that he would let them know at Washington what the priest was doing here.

Here, too, the poor minister met the same replies: "We fear not your threats but will do the same again if called on." "That he had no need of asking permission for performing his duty, etc." This good minister did go to Washington, but he returned quietly and gave us no further annoyance, and sometime after he was removed. Deaths, removals and the arrival of more wounded men would sometimes cause our wards to be emptied and filled again in the same day. And, oh how often would they die faster than we could explain the necessity of baptism to them, for often, upon the arrival of boat loads many of the soldiers had only life in them.

As soon as a boat would land, a horn was blown to let the sisters know that they must go to their wards where they would assign the place of each, as to bed, etc., then give a little broth or wine, as was best to each.

We should have remarked earlier in our account, that nearly from the commencement a band of philanthropic lady nurses had arrived, and showed surprise that the sisters were before them. They would have greatly annoyed us, but their duties were sufficiently apart from ours. They were as hostile to Catholicity as was the North and South to each other.

Many among the new arrivals were prisoners, Confederates; therefore, the officers were cautious as to who might be admitted among them.

About this time orders came from Washington that no female nurses were to remain at the Point. Our sisters were consequently making preparations for leaving when the doctor said, "Remain, sisters, until I hear from Washington, for we <u>cannot</u> dispense with the services of the sisters." He telegraphed and received as reply: "The Daughters of Charity are not included in our orders; they may serve all alike at the Point, prisoners and others, but all other ladies are to leave the place."

Then, truly there was a harvest of souls gathered to heaven for hundreds after hundreds were brought that seemed to have been sustained for the regenerating waters, dying as soon as these were applied. Some were so ignorant concerning salvation that much talk was necessary to let them know what they must do or be. If we could have poured the water on them, as on so many infants, we would hardly have reached them all. Some not in present danger would remain obstinate for weeks, but in the end would by the grace of God seem to make up for their delay by greater fervor and earnestness. With such our Blessed Lady was always the main resource for She could do what She pleased.

In one day we had the heartfelt joy of seeing one officer (formerly very bitter), one colonel, one captain, and two lieutenants ask for baptism in our little chapel, and two days later receive the Holy Eucharist.

A young man had seemed for some months to be approaching death by consumption, and occasionally asked some questions on our religion which sister tried to answer. One day he sent in haste for sister, saying to her, "Sister, I am nearly dying." Sister said, "You are very weak and you know that you are not baptized." He said: "For this cause I sent for you; so baptize me quickly before I die." Sister put a medal on him and told him to beg our Lord to bless him and prepare him for becoming His child, while she would go to get him a little wine. "O," said he, "come back quickly or I may die without baptism." As soon as she returned he exclaimed, "O, baptize me now!" Sister gave him a spoonful of drink and then baptized him.

He lay perfectly still, like one absorbed in prayer, and presently showed that he was stronger. In a few days he was walking around, and was prepared for his First Communion which he received. He, and the sisters also, attributed his recovery to the grace of the sacrament. His fervor was so lively that he converted his companions who asked for baptism, also; he, the one cured, standing sponsor for him. They were soon ordered elsewhere but promised the sisters to be faithful to the grace received. The second convert, being a married man, took books with him saying all his family should be baptized.

On the 6th of August 1864, we were at meditation in our chapel about 5:00 a.m. when suddenly a noise like thunder surprised us; upon looking out, we saw that the air was darkened with whirling sand, lumber, bedsteads, beds, stove pipes, roofs of houses, etc., etc. A raging tornado and water spout was tearing and destroying all in its way, taking us in its course, from the river to the bay. Our poor little chapel shook from roof to foundation, doors and windows being blown down, and parts of the walls giving way. Men, sick and wounded, were blown out on the ground, and the wards and cottages carried several feet from their base.

Two sisters who had not yet risen, being terrified at finding their lodgings falling to pieces, ran out. In their efforts to reach the chapel they were struck down by the falling boards, etc., and as often raised from the earth by the violent wind.

The sisters were too stunned with surprise to know what to do, although truly nothing could be done for they would only have left one part of the chapel to go to another, when the part that they had just left would be blown away.

In one of these breaks a sister seized hold of the tabernacle [from the chapel], fearing that its next place would be in the bay. The altar was the only spot in the chapel that the angry elements seemed to respect.

Lumber and iron bedsteads were carried over the tops of the cottages. The wards had been nearly full of patients, and several of these wards were leveled to the ground. The men who were able to move about were running in all directions for safety, many of them only half-dressed. The dead house was seen whirling through the air, and the bodies which were in it were not discovered for some time after the storm.

The fervor of our sisters during this time was very ardent. Everyone seemed to have a cry or aspiration of her own. One threw herself before the statue of Our Lady and said, "Am I not thy child, and will you suffer me to be crushed to death?" Another crying to Saint Vincent said, "O, our blessed Father, have you not said that your daughters shall not meet such violent deaths as now threatens them? Are you indifferent to our distress?"

The storm lasted but ten or fifteen minutes, but in this time heavy matters were carried through the air like so many feathers. As soon as the wind was quiet enough, we carried the tabernacle, with lighted candles, from the ruins of our chapel to one of our cottages which remained uninjured. Oh! how tremblingly did we bear this Sacred Ark to our own poor dwelling.

The poor priest was deeply afflicted when he arrived next morning; though death had seemed imminent every moment, yet no one was seriously injured, and great as our confidence in our good Lord had been tested, it was now very much augmented so that we hope to never fear again.

New difficulties were the consequences, for it was some time before all could be repaired and the poor patients must be cared for. The sisters would stand by the stove with their saucepan of broth in one hand and an umbrella in the other, too happy that they were relieving the suffering men.

The sisters going to the provost one day on some business, were told that a deserter was to be shot the next morning, and they would do well to call on him. They went to the prison but the man showed no desire to see them, and they came home, but the thought of his awful death caused them to appeal to our Blessed Mother in his behalf.

Later the prisoner regretted not having seen them and asked to have them sent for. The kind provost sent an orderly, telling the sisters of the poor man's desire. It was now dark and the sisters said that the prison was too far off, and being dark they could not go. The orderly soon returned with a note from the provost, saying, "I, on horseback will be your pilot to the ambulance I will send for you. I will show the driver safely through the little woods we must pass and I will conduct you home safely. I think circumstances require your corresponding with the desires he expressed, for they are very earnest."

They were soon at the prison, but found a minister of the prisoner's persuasion with him, and he continued his interview with him, for an hour or two after the sisters' arrival. The sisters, not knowing whether the minister had prepared him for death, hardly knew how to commence after the minister had left. [They] were taken to the prisoner who apologized for not seeing them [the sisters] earlier. Speaking of his fate, sister said, "You have not been baptized, I suppose?" "No," said he, "never."

Then sister informed him of its necessity and advantages, and also of the terrible consequences of its omission. This gave opening for other points of our holy doctrine, and as soon as they were laid down, they were believed and adopted by the attentive listener. "Oh!" he would exclaim, "why have I not known you sooner!" This he would repeat most fervently, "well, if you can baptize me, do so, I beg you. Oh! why did I not know you sooner?"

They remained with him some hours, giving him such exhortations as his condition required, then after baptizing him they continued to speak of the holiness of our holy religion. At each new impression made on him, the same regret would be expressed: "Why have I not known you sooner?"

The sisters said they would be pleased to bring the good priest to him, as he occasionally visited the prison. The man, too, desired it and asked if he could not be sent for. The provost, looking at his watch, said, "He could not be here in time; it is now late and the execution must take place in the morning."

The young man resigned himself fully to his fate, saying, "I deserve death and freely pardon anyone who will take part in it. I know that I must die by the hand of one of my company, but whoever it may be, I forgive him." Then he would return again to his devotions with so lively an appreciation of the mysteries of our holy faith, as to leave the sisters nothing to fear for his salvation. They really felt that God was his Light and Strength. They bade him adieu, promising to assemble before the holy altar, in his behalf, when his hour of trial drew near, and remain in prayer till all would be over with him.

The kind provost now made all ready for their return, and said, when leaving the prison, "May I have such help at my death, and die with such dispositions." At the dreaded hour, the sisters knelt before their humble altar most fervently imploring our Divine Saviour to receive the soul of their poor friend. They continued there long after the sound of the fatal fire had told them that his eternal destiny had been decided. The soldiers remarked that everyone on the Point was present at the execution, but the sisters who had retired to pray for the poor deserter.

A young man with typhoid delirium was brought with other sick soldiers. He had brothers who were Catholics, but he was without religion. He had a bushy beard when he came in, and he was pointed out to the priest, but his delirium prevented his receiving any spiritual attention. Before the priest left the Point, the sick man was shaven and placed in another ward, and the good Father making his rounds again looked everywhere for him, but to no purpose.

The sister told him to what ward he had been taken, and he went again but did not now recognize him without his beard. But our good Lord knew him with or without his beard, and just as Father was passing his bed, coming to himself he cried out, "Where is the priest that I may be baptized?" The good father then asked him his name; overjoyed and thankful to God, he disposed him for baptism, after receiving which, the man died.

When the Reverend Father found that he could have Mass in the barracks of the encampment, which at that time had about one thousand men, sick and wounded, a large space was cleared and an altar arranged, decorated all around with flowers and branches of green trees. The first Mass caused great excitement, as well as joy, to many. Twenty soldiers served the Mass, one hundred received Holy Communion, and all attended. Probably one half of the patients present had never before seen the ceremonies of our holy religion.

Of the thousands who were under the sisters' care, we are able to assure you that nearly all were, not only well pleased, but also most grateful for the attentions given them by the sisters. They who at first spurned our kindest efforts, would tell us afterwards that our religion was so calumniated by those who were ignorant of it, that they had looked on us with horror until they saw for themselves what Catholics were.

Thus you see, we had many, very many occasions of making the virtues and character of our religion better known where it had been until now, either a matter of indifference, or it had been hated, really hated. Without being able to detail evidences of having benefitted these poor men much, yet, with rare exceptions they venerated and respected our religion, and many believed that it was the only right one, the <u>only</u> religion. Many died bearing with them saving fruits of this, their newly received faith.

Peace being declared, preparations were made for a general removal, but, Oh! how many went to their Eternal home, while picturing to [themselves] their tenderest wishes, their earthly homes, friends, etc.

The doctors desired the sisters to remain until all the sick and wounded had gone. This done, they too left the Point. This was August, 1865. Our dear Valley with its many blessed boons was a most delightful contrast with our last three years.

MISSISSIPPI
NATCHEZ

On the 2nd of September, after three o'clock adoration, we heard the first shell booming over our heads, without a moment's warning.[1] The reality seemed to fill everyone with consternation. The scene that followed is beyond description. Women and children rushing through the streets screaming with terror. Immediately our asylum [Saint Mary's] was thronged by persons of every description begging just to be admitted within its walls, as they would feel secure under the protection of the sisters. I can never forget the anguish I felt at the sight of mothers with infants in their arms, begging us to preserve the lives of their infants, without a seeming thought about their own safety. At the sound of the first shell our good bishop hastened to the asylum, to assist us in placing the children out of danger of the shells about five miles beyond the city.

The bishop was surrounded as soon as he appeared and nothing could be heard but cries of, "Oh! Father, hear my confession. Bishop, please baptize me. Do not let us be killed without baptism." The bishop kindly went into the confessional but soon perceived that he would be detained there too long. Therefore he requested sister to assemble all in the chapel, and he would give a general absolution as the danger was so imminent.[2] Immediately, their cries and sobs were suppressed. Our Honored Bishop, after a few most touching words, commending us to the protection of our Immaculate Mother and urging us to raise our hearts with faith, love, and confidence to heaven, bade us remember that not one shell could harm the least one, without the divine permission, etc. He then directed all to make an act of fervent contrition aloud with him, after which he gave general absolution to all present.

The shells passed over our heads in rapid succession while we were kneeling in the chapel. Some fell in the adjoining yard yet not one [person] was injured. The stillness of death reigned. No sound was heard but the fervent aspirations of our Holy Bishop, and the suppressed sobs of the small children. Then giving a last blessing, he told the sisters to get the children off as soon as possible. When all were in readiness, each child, with a bundle of clothing, passed out of the Asylum, with the thought that they were never

---

[1] The Daughters of Charity have traditionally offered a prayer at 3:00 p.m. in remembrance of the Crucifixion of Jesus at that time.

[2] General Absolution is forgiveness imparted by a priest in the name of God for the faithful who repent from sin and who are in the face of grave danger such as going into battle.

to enter again its loved walls. Five of our sisters accompanied them and the babies, with two sick children following in a market wagon, the only vehicle that could be procured. While sister was placing the smaller children in the wagon, a shell passed over the horses heads, so near as to frighten and cause the horses to start but it fell some distance without exploding. Our poor children had to run five miles without resting, so great was the danger. This scene would have softened the hardest heart. After remaining some weeks in the country and addressing the most fervent supplications to the Blessed Virgin our prayers were heard. The authorities compromised and the gun boat left the city without doing any further damages. The good bishop announced the "Forty Hours" devotion [would be held] in thanksgiving.[3]

---

[3] The Forty Hours refers to a solemn Catholic devotion in which continuous prayer is made by the faithful for forty hours before the Blessed Sacrament exposed in a monstrance on the altar.

MISSOURI
ST. LOUIS

Prompted by a sense of duty, I will try to give you some of the most edifying particulars of the Gratiot and Myrtle Streets Prisons.

The sister servant [local superior, Sister Catherine Mullen] of the St. Louis Hospital received an order from the Provost Marshall August 14, 1862, to send sisters to the above named prisons. Consequently three sisters were appointed to perform this duty of charity.[1]

Our first visit to the prison was by no means welcome. Prejudice greeted us everywhere. The patients would not even speak to us, though bereft of every consolation of soul and body. However, we were not discouraged but persevered in our work of mercy. We prepared at our hospital the broth and other delicacies that the poor sick stood in need of and which we carried every day to the prisons at twelve o'clock. It was then that the "porridge pot" was hailed by the poor prisoners and caused many of them to bless God.

Now that they looked on us with confidence, they would flock to us like children around a mother, to make known to us their little wants, which Providence never failed to supply to their great astonishment. They would frequently ask us how we could provide for so many. We replied that our Lord made the provision.

We had to work with great prudence in the beginning in order to avoid misunderstandings. We gave [what was needed] to those only who were sick in the hospital and with permission, sent [provisions] by others to those who were confined in quarters. After some time we were allowed to visit the sick in the quarters. It was there indeed that we beheld misery, as these poor creatures were destitute of every attention.

The [military] officers now clearly saw the good that was about to be effected and they endeavored to carry it out by planning a hospital ward that would contain about one hundred beds. The Sanitary Commissions also began to approve of the good work and proposed to give us a place where we could remain day and night to attend more leisurely to the wants of the sick.

---

[1] Sisters Othelia Marshall, Mary Agnes Kelly, and Melania Fischer cared for sick prisoners of war. Sister Florence O'Hara contributed to this account.

God, in the designs of his mercy, now enabled us to begin the work of charity towards those benighted souls who groped in the darkness of sin and death.

One day a sister met an eminent physician walking rapidly up and down one of the passages. She saluted him and saw directly that he was excited. She immediately discovered that the minister was preaching. The doctor exclaimed, "Let him keep away from me. I want to hear none of his doctrine!" On a previous occasion while the minister was making his rounds through the ward, he found the doctor reading a Catholic work, at which he expressed surprise. The doctor replied, "Would to God that you would read it and let me explain it to you as you read!" This same doctor also said, "Sister, I never knew what the world was until I came here. My eyes have been opened and I am resolved to become a Catholic, but I will wait until I leave the prison as many would say that I became a convert on account of the sister." He left the prison, instructed himself more fully in the truths of our holy religion, received baptism, Holy Communion, and confirmation, and was also the means of converting his whole family. Strange to say that in 1849, this same doctor [had] desired to walk knee-deep in Catholic blood!

It was truly edifying to see many of those poor men, whilst awaiting the sentence of execution, instructing themselves in the knowledge of the true faith. Two were to be executed, but the worthy priest who daily attended the prison obtained the pardon of one, while we obtained that of the other. We had also the consolation of seeing them become fervent Catholics.

When a sick doctor in the prison was about to leave for home, we provided some Catholic books for him to take with him, but he said: "Sister, my wife and daughters will not believe what they contain or what I will tell them about Catholics, for they are under the impression that they all, including priests, nuns, and all religious orders, wear horns!" Sister said: "Well, do you see my horns?" "Oh, no," he replied. "It is only prejudice on their part, and I can truly say that the only kindness received in the prisons has been from Catholics and Sisters of Charity."[2]

On another occasion a poor man was sentenced to be hanged, but before his execution, we gave him a catechism to study. There was another gentleman in the room with him who had become a Catholic a few days previous, and in whose care we left him. On our return the gentleman told us that the Methodist preachers had been there several times. One of them took the catechism out of his hand and told him that it contained lies and

---

[2] Daughters of Charity. See note 2 above in the *Introduction*.

The old stone barracks in Frederick, Maryland.

not to believe it. The poor fellow was determined not to give in to them. Therefore he paid no attention to what they said.

There was an elderly gentleman confined in the prison hospital, whom we noticed always evinced great pleasure in seeing to the wants of his companions. He told us that it made him feel so happy to see them get what they needed most. He obtained his release and afterwards sent us fifty dollars to supply the wants of the suffering sick.

His son became a Catholic and was afterwards executed. His remains were given up to his family and his father requested the Catholic clergyman who attended him before the execution to preach his funeral oration. He obliged but in a Baptist church where his hearers were all Baptists.

A poor boy whom we had been preparing for death sent the Protestant doctor after us that we might go and baptize him, "for," said he, "I want to go straight to heaven when I die." Another poor fellow whom we had prepared for death happened afterwards to hear the minister preaching. He cried out at the top of his voice: "Stop him, and call in the Sisters of Charity! Where are the Sisters of Charity?"[3]

All who were in danger of death, we baptized ourselves. The others were left to the chaplain who daily visited the prison and where he was allowed the privilege of preaching on Sundays to a crowded assembly.

[3] Daughters of Charity.

During our stay at the prisons there were about five hundred baptisms. We kept no account of them but sent the names of all to the church of the parish in which the prison was located.[4]

Many were the difficulties we had to encounter but aided by the grace of God, we were enabled to surmount them. We hope that we thereby accomplished the work of Charity and Mercy that God in His [Goodness] called [us] to fulfill on behalf of those poor creatures who were the victims of a bloody war.

House of Refuge Hospital (St. Louis Military Hospital). This hospital in the suburbs of St. Louis was established on 12 of August 1861 by Major General [John C.] Fremont, at that time commanding the Department of the West. Several battles had taken place and the hospital was filled with sick and wounded. The general justly desired that every attention should be paid to these soldiers who had exposed their lives for their country. He visited them frequently and perceiving that there was much neglect on the part of the attendants, applied to the sisters of St. Philomena's School for a sufficient number of sisters to take charge of the hospital, promising to leave everything to their management.[5] He desired us to go as soon as possible. He went the next day to visit the hospital. No delay to apply to the superiors for permission was necessary as Father Burlando, during a visit made a few months previous, foreseeing the probability of such an occurrence, had given us directions to guide us in such cases. The presiding surgeon at the hospital received us kindly. The ward masters, stewards, etc., were not at first pleased to have the sisters over them, but finding that they were not disturbed in their duties became reconciled and satisfied. The sisters had the superintendence of everything relating to the sick, as they were not a sufficient number to undertake it, the number of patients being generally 700 and at times over a thousand.

Though most of the soldiers and attendants were Protestants and knew nothing of Catholics or their religion, they treated the sisters with every mark of respect, wondering at first at their strange dress and appearance. One asked if they were Free Masons. They soon began to appreciate the kindness and service of the sisters and to show their gratitude by listening attentively to their instructions and advice. The respect was such that not an oath or disrespectful word was heard in the hospital during the three years that the sisters were there.

---

[4] Probably the parishes were the Old Cathedral of Saint Louis, King of France, the mother church in St. Louis located near the waterfront, and Saint Vincent de Paul parish in the Soulard district.

[5] The Daughters of Charity opened Saint Philomena's School in St. Louis in 1846.

The hospital was visited every other day by the Ladies of the Union Aid Society who could not help admiring the almost profound silence observed in the wards. They could not understand the influence which the sisters exercised over the patients, both sick and convalescent, who were as submissive as children to every wish of the sisters. The latter however were not without trials and hardships. The devil raised many obstacles to the good work he could not prevent, but the difficulties were not as numerous as might have been expected and were easily overcome.

The Archbishop of St. Louis [Peter Richard Kenrick] was delighted that the sisters were asked for at the hospital and provided a chaplain, who said Mass every morning in an oratory arranged in our apartment, and after Mass visited every ward, instructing, baptizing and reconciling sinners to God. We had the happiness of being allowed to keep the Blessed Sacrament in our little chapel.

The labors of the priest and sisters were well repaid by the immense amount of good they were enabled to perform. An exact account was not kept by the sisters, but the number as near as we can ascertain is as follows: baptisms (700); conversions of Catholics who had neglected their faith (500); many had only been baptized, others had lived years in sin, a great number made their First Communion. The greater number of those who had been baptized died in the hospital. Several who recovered asked on leaving for medals and catechisms to instruct themselves and families. Some of the sisters had kept notes of some remarkable and interesting events and conversions which took place in their respective wards, but most of them were destroyed. The hospital was closed at the end of the war and the sisters returned to their former homes [missions and ministries]. It should be mentioned that though the officers of the hospital were Protestants, they were glad to see a priest visiting the patients and sick every morning. An ambulance was sent four miles for his accommodations and the same for his return to the city. A salary was paid to the minister who had applied to the government for it. The priest did not ask it and bestowed his service *gratis*. We were fortunate in having ministers appointed who did not interfere with us. The first was rather zealous but sister prayed him out. The second and last was a politician. His religion, if he had any, varied with the times. His subjects of discourse were President [Abraham] Lincoln, General [Hylan Benton] Lyon, and other heroes. He was very affable towards the sisters, saying to them "do all the good you can, sisters, I do not wish to interfere with you."

The sisters employed in the hospital wrote the following notes which give details of the religious conversions and spiritual care of their patients.

Ward ___

Mr. Fisk. The first remarkable incident was a man named Fisk. This poor man was quite sick when brought to the hospital and so prejudiced that he accepted the attention of the sisters with the utmost indifference. In spite of all our care he became more prostrate every day, but his mind was strong and his intellect perfectly clear. He had the disease of the lungs. I think it must have been gangrene for the smell was so offensive that in a short time he saw himself forsaken by all, except the sisters and good Father Burke. There had not been a word said to him about religion or death so far, but the sister placed a medal under his pillow and left our Immaculate Mother to do the work. Soon grace was visible. A few mornings after, just as the minister had gone his rounds, giving his tracts to everyone, the poor old man called one of the sisters and said, "Well, sister, it is done, I am converted. That old minister comes along here forcing his childish trash on me and trying to persuade me that he had only my eternal welfare at heart, but I tell you, sister, that it is that almighty twelve hundred dollars salary he has most at heart. How different with your good priest, he gets nothing for his services and yet he is indefatigable and the same with the sisters. They have devoted themselves for life to the service of poor creatures like us. Is that so, sister? Is human nature capable of all this and are you never to return to your friends again?" "No," replied the sister, "We have given ourselves to God to serve Him in His suffering members, the poor and our religion teaches us that what we do to them He will accept as done to Himself." "I see," said the poor man, "by their works you shall know them." Very good, said the sister to herself. The Immaculate Mother has done [her work], and so it was in a few days after he asked her for a priest, was baptized with the most lovely sentiments of faith and love, receiving at the same time Holy Viaticum and Extreme Unction.[6] Nothing could exceed the happiness of this poor man, his very countenance seemed radiant with holy joy. "I suffer much, sister," he would say, "But I feel that I will go to heaven." "I have the truth and the truth has made me free. Oh! My God, how have I been tossed about by every wind of doctrine." He died soon after in these beautiful dispositions and promising to pray for all those who were instrumental in leading him to the truth.

---

[6] Holy Viaticum (Communion) and Extreme Unction (Anointing of the Sick) are sacraments, in which the priest and those present commend those who are ill or dying to the suffering and glorified Lord, that he may raise them up and save them.

A Young Methodist. Another striking instance of divine grace was that of a young Methodist whose conversion was obtained through the power of the Miraculous Medal. This young man was brought to the hospital in a very weak state. The doctor entertained no hope for him. The sisters, perceiving that he had but a short time to live and having learned that he had never been baptized, endeavored by every possible means to make the patient aware of his danger. The poor man, although thankful for every attention to his body, yet refused to hear anything about death or eternity, and said many times, "If I had been brought here when I was first taken sick and had you sisters to take care of me, I would have been cured long ago." The poor man thought only of his body and not of the danger he was in of losing his immortal soul. He did not think baptism would do him any good. He believed in Jesus and thought that was all he had to do to be saved. The sister, seeing him getting weaker, became still more anxious for his poor soul, remaining near him and offering many fervent prayers for his conversion without any apparent change in him. The priest who visited the hospital saw him daily. One day, after remaining with him longer than usual, he told the sister there was no hope for him except in prayer. The poor man was sinking rapidly, seemed aware of his danger and waited death with greatest calmness. Nothing seemed to trouble him except the thought of leaving his poor mother and of dying so far from home. There was one of his comrades in another ward whom he requested to be sent for as he said he wished him to be with him in his last moments so that he might be able to tell his mother of his death. He was in his agony. The sisters remained with him until twelve o'clock. Seeing there was no hope of doing anything for his poor soul, we left him with his friend and the nurse who was to watch during the night. But before retiring, sister placed a medal of our Blessed Mother under his pillow saying with confidence that the Blessed Virgin would not let him be lost. Our hope was not in vain. The following morning at an early hour, we went in haste to the ward, but were met by the nurse who exclaimed, "Come quickly and see the man who died and has come to life again." She then stated that the man having apparently died, she and the man who sat up with him had washed and dressed him. The assistant then went to bed in the same ward leaving the nurse alone with the corpse. The latter was about tying up the jaws when to his great surprise the man who had been laid out opened his eyes. You may imagine the joy we felt on hearing this news. We did not pay much attention to his account then, but hastened to the patient's bed and found him breathing, and with eyes fixed on us said, "I am so glad to see you." The first words we addressed to him was to exhort him to be baptized, adding that our Lord had saved him through the intercession of

His Blessed Mother. He replied, "Sister, I desire to be baptized." We told him that the priest would be here soon. He answered, "Oh, it will then be too late," and entreated us not to delay, fearing that every breath might be his last and [hearing] the earnest entreaties of several of his companions who had now awakened and were gathered around his bed. After making for him the acts that all might see with what ardor he desired to receive this most holy Sacrament, he tried to repeat them aloud. Then with his hands clasped and eyes raised to heaven, while the sister baptized him, he made the most beautiful aspirations of gratitude and love, and said, that he saw a crowd of beautiful ladies dressed in white with crowns on their heads and heard most beautiful music. In half an hour afterwards, he ceased to breathe and went to join the procession and sing forever the praises of her who has never been invoked in vain. The man confirmed all that the nurse had said with regard to his apparent death and everyone who witnessed it pronounced it as an evident miracle.

Mr. Nicholson. The priest, having one day been called into attend a poor Catholic soldier, he heard his confession, anointed him, and gave him holy viaticum. It was the first time that our Lord had deigned to visit our ward. We tried to receive him in the best way we could. All the Catholics who were in the ward, having assembled around his bed while those who were not Catholic remained, but all kept strict silence. The poor man received the precious body of his God, with the most lively faith and humility and died soon after in the most edifying manner, invoking the aid of Mary. His last words were, "Holy Mary, Mother of God, pray for us sinners, now and at the hour of death." Just after the priest had left, the ward master who was a Catholic, came in the greatest excitement and said, "Sister, I am going to find the officer of the day to have Nicholson (this was the man's name) put in the guard house. He then told us that this miserable creature had ridiculed everything the priest had done. Having placed himself where he could see everything that was going on, I tried to calm him by telling him not to mind, but pray for the poor soul that he might be brought to know God. After reasoning with him a long time, he said, "Well, I will do as you wish, if you get the doctor to discharge him, for I could not remain in the same duty with him a day longer. I told him that would not be the way to imitate the example of our Lord who was all powerful and could have punished him at the moment he was insulting him. He promised at last to forgive him. For a week after, the poor man was taken sick and in a few days was at the point of death. Every effort was made to bring the poor man to a sense of his duty but no impression could be made on him. His sufferings were intense, he could not sleep day or night, nor remain scarcely five minutes in the same position. It was distressing to look at him. He had never been baptized. Several of his comrades who had been in the ward for some time and had witnessed the changes caused in many of their companions by the reception of the sacrament of baptism came to ask the sisters to try to persuade him to be baptized, thinking it would make him quiet. Many prayers were offered for him and a medal placed under his pillow. Many said his sickness was a visible punishment sent from God for his impiety. He would not mention the name of God in any way and implored the doctor most piteously not to let him die. Four days had passed in this manner without the least change when one of his companions who seemed more interested than the rest, came with tears in his eyes saying that he felt so sorry to see him die without any hope. The sister, thinking that it might be human respect that made him refuse to show any marks of repentance, asked his companion to speak to him of his danger and to persuade him to make his peace with God. He did so and it had the desired effect. He returned soon saying, "Sister, he wishes to see you." Having gone to him he said, "Sister, I will do whatever you wish me to do." I then told him what was necessary to do. I was soon convinced that he was sincere and asked him whom he wished to baptize him. He replied, "Whoever you wish to send for." Thinking he might mean a minister, I asked if he wished to have the priest who attended the ward, he said that was the one he meant. There was no time lost. The priest was sent for and we had the inexpressible happiness of seeing him received into the fold by the same priest whom he had but a short time ago treated with contempt. Soon after he died. Before his death he became perfectly calm and expired invoking the holy name of Jesus.

A Scottish Presbyterian. We had the happiness of seeing a Scottish Presbyterian received into the church, who when brought to the hospital was a very bitter Protestant and who held all Catholics and religious in abhorrence. Priests and nuns, he thought, were the worst people in the world. After his conversion, he acknowledged that he had often watched the sisters to see if they treated all the patients alike. Seeing there was no distinction made between Catholic and Protestant, he began to conceive a favorable opinion of them. He had never been very sick and, therefore, did not require much attention from the sisters. He was taken with the smallpox and had to be removed to the Island which was some distance from the hospital. He requested the sisters to give him some Catholic books, saying that he intended to become a Catholic, if he got better. I gave him a catechism and some other instruction books. In a few months afterward, he returned to the hospital and wished to see the priest to be received into the church and before leaving for his regiment, made his First Communion. There were many of

The wagon of supplies arrives from Emmitsburg, Maryland.

these poor sufferers that hardly knew there was a God. As for baptism, they never heard of such a thing. They were entirely ignorant of the necessity of it. When the sister spoke to them of the goodness of God in instituting a sacrament, that through it we might be made the children of God and regain the little we had lost by the sin of our first parents, they did not harden their hearts to the voice of God but would shed tears. One said, "Sister, do not go away. Stay and tell me more of that God I ought to love. How is it that I have lived so long and never heard anything or anyone speak to me that way before? What is it I will have to do to become a child of God?" Sister said, "Only believe and be baptized." "Well," he said, "cannot you baptize me?" But I told him since there was not much danger of death that night, I would get Father Burke to do it in the morning. He said that he did not like to wait so long, that he was then so weak and if he would die without it he could never go to heaven. To satisfy him I told him I would watch and if I saw the least change that I would baptize him. Then he said, "Now I am satisfied and will depend on you to open the gate of heaven for me, for it is through you that I will enter there." There was not any change in him that night and the next morning Father Burke baptized him. He had beautiful sentiments. When the crucifix was placed in his hands, he kissed it and said, "Oh my God, I have never known or loved you till I came to this hospital." "Sister," he said, "I forgot that paper you told me to say sometimes," I then repeated it with him, "Father, into thy hands I commend my spirit. Servant Jesus, receive my soul." While the priest was engaged with him, his companion in the next bed called me and said, "Sister, what is that old gentleman doing to that patient?" I replied that he was baptizing him, then he asked, "What good is that? Will it keep him alive longer?" I told him it might and that it was also to prepare him for a happy death. I inquired if he had ever been baptized. He said no, so I told him of the necessity of it. He listened very attentively to all I had to say and then said, "Sister, to what religion do you belong?" I answered that I was a Roman Catholic. That seemed to surprise him for a moment and he said, "Sister, I have always had a horror of the Catholic religion, but all that hatred has gone since I came to this ward. Of what religion is that old man?" I replied that he was a Roman Catholic priest. He asked me if his form of baptism was my belief. I said yes. "Then I would like to speak to him for I want to be baptized." He was baptized the same morning and died a most edifying death. These were companions on earth and were also to be united in heaven.

Other Patients. I could never have believed there were so many poor souls that knew not that there is a God. When we received new sets of patients, it was amusing to see them. On entering the wards they would stare so hard at our dress. It appeared so strange to them. Some had never seen a sister before and would say, "I do not want to stay in this ward for I do not like the looks of that woman who wears that bonnet." He would be answered by another that he had nothing to fear for she was a Daughter of Charity. When they would get very sick, we would procure for them all that was necessary for them, whether Catholic or Protestant.

There was in the ward a patient who was very sick. When he first came in, he was there only a few days when he became very low. Then I spoke to him of baptism he replied, "Sister, whatever you say I will do, for I know whatever you tell me to do is right." He was baptized and then said to me, "Sister, you are more than a sister, you have done what my mother would never do." In the evening he called me and said, "Sister, I want you to stay and say some prayers for me. It will not be long for I feel as if my days in this world are at an end." Then I will pray for you, and in a few hours he breathed his last.

The evil one could not rest any longer for he saw that there were too many souls snatched from his grasp. You could see him almost visibly working in the person of his ministers. We labored during the day, but they during the night. Sometimes in the evening when we left the ward, we would have one or two patients prepared for baptism with most beautiful sentiments, but to our great surprise, in the morning we would find them entirely changed. What were we to do? To give up? We could not think of such a thing! When everything else would fail, I would show them the cross on my [rosary] beads and say, "Ungrateful soul, do you see what your sins have cost? Will you refuse to be baptized?" And they have died edifying deaths. The devil did not stop here and tried new means, since the former had failed. There was a patient who was very bigoted against the Catholic religion but he liked the sisters for he said he did not consider them Catholics. They were too good. They were self-sacrificing women, and he had often heard of such people but had never seen them before. He became very sick and sister did not know what to do for he was so much opposed to Catholicity. Sister would make acts of Faith, Hope and Charity, although he would not repeat them with her, yet he paid every attention while she recited them, particularly the Act of Contrition. He thought that a beautiful prayer. One day he was a little better disposed to listen to me than on former occasions so I thought I would profit by this opportunity. I inquired whether he had ever been baptized or not. He said he had not and he did not intend to be either. This part of the conversation was not as agreeable as you might expect. He said, "Baptism would never save a man that had always lived in sin." He did not believe in any baptism much less in Catholic baptism. How often was I under the necessity of leaving the poor sufferer with a sad heart. I would go the second and third time, but with as little satisfaction as the first. He would tell me to go away, that I was killing him by inches. There was little time now as life was sinking. I asked Father Burke to speak to him. He did so but it was of no use. When all things had failed, I placed a medal under his pillow and begged our Blessed Mother to intercede with her Divine Son for this poor soul. The next morning the attendant, when making the bed found the medal. He wanted to bring it to me thinking that I must have dropped it but the patient would not give it up and told him to ask sister if he might keep the little image that he found on his bed. I told him, yes that he might keep it. He was very much pleased and would keep it in his hand all the time. He got worse that morning and I remained up with him, but he was too sick to notice anyone. He called one of the attendants and told him to go and tell sister that he wanted her. From what a burden was I relieved for I knew our dear Mother was going to do something. I went to him and he said, "Sister, you told me some time ago that I could not be saved without baptism. Now I want to be baptized for I want to be saved. Whom are you going to get to baptize me?" I told him that I would get the priest to baptize him. He was very well satisfied. After Mass the next morning I told the priest that our poor patient wanted to be baptized but he would not believe it and said he would not go up that morning. After much persuasion, I induced him to go to the ward. When the poor sufferer saw him, he said, "Father, I was waiting for you. Why did you stay so long? Have you come to baptize me?" "I want you to do it now." The priest baptized him. He died a few hours after.

There was also another man in the same ward who was very low at the time and would not hear of baptism. He did not have such a horror of Catholics as the former. He said he had never heard of such sisters till he came to this hospital and that he knew there were no such women in the world. He thought that there must be something good in the Catholic church to have such good members, although he would not like to join it. He became worse and I spoke to him again of baptism, but he would not listen to it. He said when he would get well and go home, he would join some church but it would not be the Catholic church. I was distressed to see him die that way and I knew it was not well to annoy him too much. I said some prayers with him before I left the ward and told the nurse that if the patient got worse, to come for me, but he rested very well that night. The next morning at four o'clock I went up to the ward. He seemed to be resting very well. I then left, but during morning prayers I was called and told that the patient was worse. I went to him as quickly as possible and found that he was entering his agony. What was I to do? I knew not! I spoke to him again about baptism. He said that he was too far gone. I assured him that there was time enough yet if he would only profit by it. I spoke to him frequently of the love of God. I asked him if he would continue to be ungrateful to so good a Father—he had imitated the wandering of the prodigal child long enough, now it was time that he should imitate him in his repentance. I had hardly finished speaking when he began to weep and said, "Yes, sister, I have imitated the prodigal in his wild conduct and I want to imitate him in his return. Will you get me baptized?" The priest was coming to say his Mass and I assured him that he would baptize him. The time appeared so long that he would frequently say, "Sister, do you think he will be here soon?" I replied in the affirmative. When the priest came and was told that the patient wanted to be baptized, he could not believe it, for he had sent him away from him the morning before. He went, however, to the ward and baptized him. He died a most edifying death.

Ward A[7]

William Let. The first conversion that took place in ward A after I began my duties there was that of a poor soldier named William Let. He was about twenty years of age and knew nothing about his God or about

---

[7] The following accounts are dated 9 December 1866.

religion. Seeing him growing weaker every day, sister thought that while she lavished her care and attention on the wants of the body, the poor soul was in a state yet more sad. She began to speak to him of God and of his immortal soul. She saw that her words had made an impression on him and was encouraged by it to continue, and after she had explained to him the truths of our holy religion and recommended him to the intercession of our Immaculate Mother, she felt convinced that he would not be lost. In a short time he called for a priest and was baptized, and died shortly after, showing beautiful sentiments of piety and repeating the acts of Faith, Hope, Charity and Contrition, and recommending his soul to the protection of our Blessed Mother.

William Hudson. Indeed it was too much consolation for the sisters to snatch these poor souls from the evil one, for they were almost within his grasp. We counted our labors and fatigues as nothing. The joy of seeing one soul return to God more than repaid us for all. It was really astonishing to see the change of some of these poor rough soldiers. I could scarcely believe it if I had not witnessed it. When they were brought to the hospital, with regard to religion they were more like Indians or Africans than persons brought up in a civilized country. Some of them hardly knew that there was a God, and yet in these the grace of God was most visible. There was a poor young man brought in, named William Hudson, who would not at first hear of baptism. He held out a long time, saying that he did not consider it necessary to his salvation; still sister did not despair, she put a medal around his neck recommending him to the intercession of our holy Mother. He soon became more docile and sister profited by every chance to speak to him of the judgments of God and the danger of dying in sin, observing that he listened with the greatest attention. She explained to him the Sacrament of Baptism and the necessity of it. A little while after, he called her and asked, "Who is that old gentleman that comes here sometimes?" meaning Father Burke. Sister replied that he was a Catholic clergyman. Our Blessed Mother finished the work she had commenced. He was baptized shortly after, and died a most beautiful and edifying death. A few moments before he died, he repeated the Acts of Faith, Hope, Charity and Contrition and invoked the assistance of our Blessed Mother by whom, I cannot doubt, his soul was conducted to heaven.

About this time several others had been prepared for death, the incidents of which I do not remember, except one poor soldier who was a Catholic but only in name and who did not practice his religion. When sister gave him a medal and asked him to wear it, he did not know what it was and asked her if it was a check for his trunk. Sister explained to him what it was and after instructing him sufficiently in the sacraments and in the mysteries of our Holy Faith of which he seemed almost ignorant, he received the Sacraments of Penance, Extreme Unction and the holy Viaticum, expressing beautiful sentiments of Contrition.

Mr. Huls. Mr. Huls, a man about thirty-five years of age, would not at first consent to be baptized. Although he believed in baptism and said he would not die without it, yet he kept putting it off from time to time. As I saw that he had not long to live, and as I knew that in the beginning he was not very well disposed toward Catholics, I did not like to offer him a medal but I put one under his pillow and left our Blessed Mother to take care of him. Next morning, I went to his bed as usual, and after giving him a drink and saying a few words to him, I was returning when he called me back saying, "Sister, what must I do before I leave this world?" I told him that he must be very sorry for all the sins of his past life, because sin was a great evil and had been the cause of the sufferings and death of our Lord Jesus Christ who is so good, and notwithstanding our ingratitude is ready to pardon us even at the last moment, if we sincerely return to him. I told him to cast himself into the arms of His merciful Father who impatiently awaited his return and who was ready to open for him the gates of heaven, etc., adding that it was absolutely necessary to be baptized. He believed all with a firm faith, repeated with me the Acts of Faith, Hope, Charity and Contrition, and some other prayers to implore the mercy of God, saying that he was ready to give up all since such was the holy will of God. His constant prayers were "O God, be merciful to me, a sinner,"; "Lord, into thy hands I commend my Spirit." A little while after, as I saw that he was entering into his agony, I baptized him. No sooner was the water poured on his head than he seemed to understand all the grace of the sacrament. He revived a little and began to pray of himself, and made, unassisted, the most beautiful aspirations of love and gratitude to God; of resignation to the divine will and repeated Acts of Contrition as if each word was whispered by his good angel. As I remained by his bed, helping him sometimes to pray when I would stop, he would say, "Sister, I am able to pray longer and in these beautiful sentiments he gave up his soul to God as if he was going into a peaceful slumber."

William Barrett. William Barrett, a young man about nineteen years of age, was brought to the ward very low. After I had prepared every comfort possible for the poor body, I began to inquire gradually into the state of the soul. I found it most deplorable, not indeed for having been guilty of any great crimes, but with regard to the error and ignorance in which he had been raised. He knew nothing about religion, never said a prayer and scarcely knew that there was a God. When I spoke to him of God or of his immortal soul, he did not at first relish it much because he did not understand it, but after some explanation he became greatly moved and wished to hear more, but when I told him of the love of our dear Lord in becoming man for us, and how he suffered to save us; he could not retain his tears. "Oh!" he said, "Why did I not hear anyone talk in that way before?" I then explained to him the Sacrament of Baptism and entreated him not to despise the grace that our Lord now offered him, telling him what a favor our Lord granted him in bringing him to the hospital where he could prepare for death, etc. He understood all and more than I could tell him, grace indeed had touched his soul. He was truly penitent. He said, "Oh! I wish to love God but I am so miserable. I wish to pray but I do not know how, sister, will you pray for me?" I told him that I would and that I would engage the Mother of God to pray for him, if he would consent to wear her medal, at the same time presenting him one which he gladly accepted, put it around his neck and repeated the prayer. "O Mary, conceived without sin, pray for us who have recourse to thee," and some other prayers, begging the Blessed Virgin to obtain for him the grace of a happy death. Then he asked if I wanted to take him to the river. I said no, that baptism was given by pouring water on the head of the person, etc. "Well," he said, "I want to be baptized." I told him then to try and prepare during the time that remained to receive it worthily, because it was a sacrament instituted by our Lord Jesus Christ to wash away sin and that it would open for him the gates of heaven, provided he was truly sorry for his sins.

"Sister," he said again, "I want to pray. I don't know how. Will you pray for me?" I told him that I would. "Well," said he, "Come nearer so that I can hear you." I said some prayers for him and he prayed, himself, with all the ardor of his soul. Then I told him that the priest would be there the next morning to baptize him. "Oh!" he said, "I will be so glad if I live until then." He did not wish anyone to trouble him or to talk to him but the sisters. The attendants went to ask him the address of his friends. He said to them, "Do not talk of my friends now, the sisters know their address. I want nothing but to pray and be baptized." He repeated almost without interruption, "O God, be merciful to me, a sinner." As he was very low that night, we were afraid to leave him, so we remained with him until three o'clock in the morning. Then as we feared that every breath would be his last, sister baptized him. Still he did not die. The priest came at six o'clock. As all the Protestants around heard him ask to be baptized the previous evening, they expected to see the priest coming to the ward, and seeing no signs of him and the danger of the sick man, they asked me if the priest had not come yet. I answered that he would be there soon, and as I thought it better not to tell them that sister had baptized him for fear of scandalizing any of them, I asked the priest to come and see him. He came and talked with him a long time and said some prayers with him. The poor man was failing very fast, still he kept his mind fixed on God. He could not thank Him enough for the graces he had received. He poured forth his whole soul in gratitude. He prayed continually, although he could scarcely breathe. He asked several times what time it was and at what time we thought he would die, so impatient was he for the moment that was to unite him to his God. Sister repeated for him the little hymn, "Jesus, Saviour of my Soul," he repeated the two first verses with her and calmly gave up his soul. The Protestants were standing around and one of them opening his book said, "Sister, there is the hymn you repeated for him." Another said, that if he had been baptized, he would have died last night, as much as to say that our Lord had prolonged his life till the priest came. All said that they had never witnessed a more beautiful or edifying death. Even the priest, who had been speaking to him a few moments before, said that he had no doubt that that man would go straight to heaven, that he had never witnessed more beautiful sentiments.

A few days after his death, his poor old Father came to the hospital but finding that his son was dead, was inconsolable in losing him. He said he had lost all, he was the staff of his old age, there never was a better son. The poor old gray headed man wrung his hands and could not be comforted, till they took him to the grave and had the coffin opened. He would have buried himself in the same with him, if it were possible. However, he became more reconciled when he had seen the decent manner in which his son had been laid out and buried. It showed, he said, that he had been cared for, although far away from his home, and on his return from the grave he came and thanked me for it, and on leaving the hospital he took some books with him to study the religion in which his dear son had died so happy. And is it possible, they would ask each other, that these people are Catholics? Is it possible that they are they whom we have been taught to despise? There was one poor old man who told me, himself, that in his neighborhood the people were prejudiced. They would not give a night's lodging to a traveler if he were a Catholic. As for himself he never knew anything about them [Catholics] till he came to the hospital but that what he had seen there was enough to convince him of the truths of the Catholic religion. He had seen there what did not exist among Protestants. He, himself, was a member of the Presbyterian church, but that he would be a Protestant no longer and asked for a catechism. I gave him one and some other books, and he studied very diligently. When he found himself getting weak he asked me to send for the priest to baptize him and prepare him for death. As he had a large property, he said if it were the will of God, he would like to live and enjoy it longer, but if the Lord willed it otherwise, he was ready to give up all. His constant prayer was "Not my will, Lord, but thine be done." He tried to profit by every moment he had to prepare for death. The day on which he felt able to read, he employed his time in studying catechism or his prayers. When he was too sick to read, he prayed and meditated continually. A few days before he died, I went to his bed to give him a drink. He pulled out his medal, "Oh," he said, "There is my Mother," and as the big tears of gratitude rolled down his cheeks, he kissed it, saying, "I kiss it every hour." When he was no longer able to eat or drink, or sleep, he was still able to pray. One day, being very much fatigued after the attendant had turned him in bed, he fainted away and was near gone. They ran to me and said he was dying. I succeeded in forcing a few drops of wine down his throat. After a few moments, he breathed again and as soon as he was able to speak, he said, "Sister, Why did you not let me go then? I was going so nicely." Afterwards he said to the attendant that he supposed sister would not let him die for another month. He died, however, a few days after a most beautiful and edifying death, perfectly conscious to his last breath.

Mr. Nelson. Mr. Nelson would not consent to be baptized. He said he did not think it would do him any good since he never had any religion. After I had explained to him as well as I could the necessity of the Sacrament of Baptism, he burst into a flood of tears. "Ah sister!" he said, "I am afraid it is too late," and he covered his face with his hands and shed tears in abundance. I told him it was not too late, that our Lord was at that moment more disposed to pardon him than he was to ask pardon, etc. "Ah!" he replied, "I am twenty-two years of age and never have I done anything for God, for the salvation of my soul. Oh! if I die now I shall go to hell." I reminded him how our Lord had lived thirty-three years on earth in humiliations and sufferings, how he ended his life by dying on the cross for his salvation and that of all poor sinners, of His goodness to pardon the good thief the moment he turned to Him on the cross, etc. I had scarcely finished when he began to pray like the Publican, and with as much humility.[8] He repeated over and over, "O God, be merciful to me a sinner." He repeated also the Acts of Faith, Hope and Charity with all the fervor of his soul. He asked to be baptized but he said he did not think the priest would satisfy him, that he would prefer a Baptist or Methodist. Well I told him to prepare till next morning and if the priest did not satisfy him on every point, I would

---

[8] Cf. Luke 18: 9-14.

send to town and get whoever he wished. He put on a medal and asked me to pray that he might live till morning, saying again that if he should die now he would go to hell. I told him that he must have more confidence in the goodness of God, that as soon as a person is disposed to do what Jesus Christ demands of him and is truly sorry for his sins, that is all that is required of him; that I had no doubt that his sins were already pardoned, and that there remained for him only to be baptized, to be in the friendship of Almighty God. He then felt more calm, he prayed and asked me to pray for him during the night. As soon as the priest came next morning he baptized him and was so pleased with his dispositions, he said he had no doubt but that he would go straight to heaven. After he was baptized, I went to him to ask if he was satisfied. He could not restrain his transports of joy and gratitude. He could not sufficiently thank the Lord for the graces He had granted him in receiving into His fold such a sinner as himself and in his humility referred all the glory to God and acknowledged in all but his goodness and mercy. He died two days after, a most beautiful and happy death. Six more were baptized and died in the same good dispositions.

Mr. Haynes. Mr. Haynes, an old man about fifty years of age, who had been a long time in the hospital and a constant and close observer of the actions of the sisters, was converted and baptized. He had been a member of the Baptist church before his conversion. A few days before his death, a minister came to him to give him some consolation. The sick man said to

The battlefield at Gettysburg.

him, "Sir, I do not need your services. I have been baptized and prepared for death by a Catholic priest—that is sufficient. I am happy." He showed great signs of repentance. He tried to pray continually, begging our Lord to show him mercy and to pardon the errors of his past life. Often during his illness did he express to others, particularly to the priest his surprise and admiration at the devotedness of the sisters which he said was the cause of entering into himself and examining the articles of the Catholic Faith, and finally of his conversion. He told the priest that fourteen years before, he had made a vow never to see a priest or minister, even on his dying bed, but that the kindness and devotedness of the sisters had gained him.

Another was baptized and was dying near him. I asked him if he was trying to be very good, to love God and to raise his heart often to Him. "Oh yes, sister," he said, "I am trying; I wish you could stay here with me one hour and teach me how to pray and to love God." He repeated the Act of Contrition, O Mary, conceived without sin, etc., and then expired. About the same time, five more were baptized and died in the same beautiful dispositions.

There was one who appeared to be about sixteen or seventeen years of age; he was very innocent and good but did not want to be baptized till he went home to his mother because he said his mother was so good to him and he knew it would be a great satisfaction to her to see him baptized. He held out a long time, still he believed in the necessity of baptism and said he would not like to die without it. He became weaker every day and I saw that he had not long to live. I told him that he would soon appear before our Lord and advised him not to defer his baptism. "Well," he said, "You have been a good friend to me. I will do whatever you think best." He was baptized and a half hour after he was a corpse.

These are a few of the conversions that have taken place in ward A. I am sorry that we cannot remember all but it is now three years since we left there. There have been also a great many Catholics brought back to their duties, and a great many even who made in the hospital their first confession and first communion.

One poor man, after he had made his first confession and communion, said to me, "Well, sister, you have accomplished in a short time what my wife has been all her life trying to do." He then told me that his wife was a very good Catholic, that she had often implored him with tears, but could never get him to go to his duty. "How delighted she will be," he said, "When I write and tell her." He was about thirty-five years of age and was a pretty hard case. As he was slightly wounded, he kept around the premises most all the time, and we had to watch when he came in the ward to get his meals to speak to him of his duty.

When a strange doctor would come to the hospital, it was from the poor patients that he would learn to appreciate the value of the sisters. At one time a big country doctor came to Ward A. He was so rough in appearance that I was almost afraid to look at him; he went around the ward talking to the patients. He found one poor man very low and suffering very much. He tried to encourage him by telling him that he would go to sister and get her to make him something nice. "Ah! said the poor dying man, I know that anything sister will make will be nice for she is the nicest person I ever met with in my life, but I do not want anything now. Sister has left nothing undone for me." The doctor opened his large eyes and took the direction in which sister was. That same evening he picked up courage to speak to her saying, "Excuse me, sister, we are not yet acquainted, but I came to introduce myself, etc." I afterwards found him very agreeable as long as he remained in the hospital.

When the patients would return to their regiments, they would say to their sick companions, "If you go to St. Louis, try to get to the House of Refuge Hospital (St. Louis Military Hospital). The sisters are there, they will make you well soon."

One day we were going through the wards of one of the hospitals in the city which we were requested to visit. A poor soldier half raised himself up in bed, saying, "Ah, sister, how glad I am to see you. Ah! if you were here to take care of us, that poor boy," pointing to one of his companions who was dying in the next bed, "would be well long ago." Some of them looked upon the sisters as superior beings. They said they could not understand how persons could live in the world and not care for the world. One man expressed himself thus (and he was a non-Catholic) that the Daughters of Charity were like gold tried in the fire.

One evening one of the sisters went to the ward after night prayers, to see that nothing would be wanting to the sick during the night. She found one poor man suffering intense pain in his forehead and temples. He had taken cold in camp, the inflammation went to his eyes so that he became entirely blind, and the pain of his forehead and temples was so intense that he thought he could not live till morning. She asked him to let her bind up his forehead with a wet bandage. "Oh sister," he said, "It is no use to do anything for me. The doctor has been bathing my head with spirits of ether and other liquids, but nothing will do me any good. I cannot live till morning. My head is splitting open, but you may do so if you like." She took a wet bandage which unknown to him she saturated in a little chloroform, bound up his head and left him. Early in the morning I went to ask him how he spent the night, "Oh sister," he said, "I have rested well from the moment you put your hands on my head. I experienced no more pains." He never thought of attributing his relief to the chloroform because he did not know it and she left him in his ignorance.

Ward C.

The first conversion that took place in ward C was that of a poor Catholic who had not been to confession for seventeen years, nor did he wish to go. When sister would speak to him of his duty he would say that he was an old soldier who had been in many battles and that he had not been killed yet. Still he had faith in our Redeemer and the Blessed Mother, saying that she would not let him die on the battlefield. As he was walking about quite well the sisters feared that he would be sent to his regiment. They redoubled their prayers and persuaded him to wear a medal of our Blessed Mother. At first he did not want to do it, fearing it would put him under some new obligations. He took it, however, and in a short time afterward he made his confession and his peace with God. It was done in time, for in a day or two after he took suddenly ill, became unconscious almost immediately and died the same night.

A Young Universalist. A young man about twenty years of age, a Universalist in belief, was brought into the ward quite sick. At first he did not wish to hear anything about baptism, believing, as he said, that all would be saved at the last day. He would contend that there was no hell. He believed that God had created a heaven. No matter how wicked a person was God would permit him to be only slightly punished and then he would take him to heaven. I put a medal under his pillow and from time to time gave him a few drops of holy water by way of medicine. Shortly after, he asked me if I would come and read for him. I did so. Then he asked me to explain to him our purgatory.[9] He paid the greatest attention and said that was his belief but that he believed in no other hell. Almost every time I went to him he would have some explanation to ask of some part of our worship and he began to relish it more and more. There was an old preacher who came to him every day to convert him. He annoyed him so that in the

---

[9] Purgatory is the process of purification necessary for one to enter into full communion with God whereby every trace of sin is eliminated and every imperfection in a soul corrected before entrance into Heaven.

The Sisters provided emergency care in St. Francis Xavier church, Gettysburg.

end he would not listen to him. One day he sent him away altogether. The poor preacher came to me and complained that the patient would not listen to him. I promised that I would [speak to the patient], and so I did, but it was not to the preacher's advantage. He [the patient] was satisfied with the explanations of the mysteries of our holy faith. He had never viewed them in that light before. He convinced himself of the truth and shortly after called for a priest to baptize him. When the priest was beginning the ceremony, the sick man fearing yet that he might be one of the ministers of some other creed said to him, "Sir, stop one moment," "Do you belong to the holy Catholic Church?" "I do," replied the priest. "Do you," he asked again, "belong to the same church of that lady with the white bonnet?" "To the very same," replied the priest. "Well then," he said, "you may baptize me." After his baptism he kept his mind united to God by prayers and by the most beautiful aspirations. Sometimes he would ask me to help him thank God for the lights and graces he had received. When he was alone, he prayed continually, himself. If the preacher went to trouble him, he would turn his head from him and say, "Leave me, I have long enough listened to error. It is time now that I should begin to relish truth. I have the sisters to instruct me and a Catholic priest has baptized me. That is all that is necessary." He lived several days after but they were days of edification to all around him, of merit to himself, and his death was most beautiful and edifying.

There was one patient, who had been very sick but like his companion had no religion whatever and also was quite careless about having any religion. Twice sister attempted to speak to him about the necessity of baptism, but with very little success at first. Placing a medal around his neck, the Blessed Virgin soon did her work. In a short time the change was visible to all. He would pray of his own accord and also beg others to pray for him. He then asked to be baptized and the priest wishing to satisfy himself got him to repeat the creed. The priest said, "I believe in the holy Catholic Church." The patient surprised by these words said, "Stop, sir! I believe in the holy Roman Catholic Church and it is the only one that I wish to have anything to do with, and if you do not believe in that, I wish to have nothing to do with you. I wish to be baptized in the Catholic faith." The good priest hastened to tell him that he was a Catholic. "Ah then," he replied, "Please baptize me," which he did, and he died a most happy death.

Another who had been in the hospital some time, became very sick, but would not listen to anything concerning baptism because he said that he did not think it necessary to salvation. I placed a medal under his pillow, gave him occasionally some drops of holy water and recommended him to the intercession of our good Mother. In a few days he not only begged to be instructed, but also asked to have prayers recited frequently for him and asked for the priest to baptize him. The priest was so pleased with his dispositions that he thought it proper to also administer to him the Sacrament of Extreme Unction. The poor man who had not been instructed in this sacrament did not wish to receive it without my approval, but as soon as I gave it he was disposed for all and manifested beautiful dispositions, and died a very edifying death.

Mr. Saunders. Mr. Saunders, a person professing no religion of any kind, remained sometime in the hospital, but was not very sick. He was, however, a close observer of the actions of the sisters and seemed to take notes of everything. When he was returning to his regiment, he came to thank me for the kindness he said I had shown him and the services I had rendered him. Although I had done nothing, judging him well disposed, I thought that I would profit by the occasion to offer him a medal and a little book called the *Catholic Instructor* which he accepted with gratitude and left the hospital. One year after, he returned and related to me with joy how he went to a Catholic priest, and begged him to instruct him and receive him into the church that God in His mercy had received him through the intercession of his Immaculate Mother and your prayers. "And now," he added, "In my turn I have the happiness of bringing souls to God." And so it was. He was employed in a hospital where there was no Catholic but himself. He was constantly and zealously employed in exhorting, instructing, and encouraging the sick to receive the Sacrament of Baptism, and procuring a priest for them. Thus, he had the happiness of sending many souls to God.

SPECIAL CARE TENT

They would rather apply to the sisters in cases where they could do so than to the doctor, so that we had to encourage them to have confidence in the doctors. We were accustomed to visit every evening a tent that was a few yards distance from the hospital where the gangrenous and the badly wounded cases were put. One evening I found a poor man (whose hand from the wrist had been amputated) suffering very much. The arm being somewhat inflamed, he complained that the doctor had that morning ordered a hot poultice and that he did not get it. We called the nurse and wound dresser to inquire why the doctor's orders had not been attended to. They told us there were none in the hospital, that the steward had gone to town that morning before they knew it. There was no other opportunity of sending to town that day. I immediately sent across the yard to the bakery and got some hops and had the poultice put on. The poor man was surprised. "The sisters" he said, "found ways and means of relieving everyone and those who made profession of the business did not even know where to look for them."

LADIES OF THE UNION AID SOCIETY

The demons tried to raise many obstacles but they all turned to his own confusion. The Ladies of the Union Aid Society who visited the hospital twice a week became jealous of the good that the sisters were doing. They feared, they said, that everyone would become a Catholic. They would like to take the sisters place there, if they could, and have everything their own way. They even tried to make the patients call them sisters, telling them that they were charitable ladies who went about doing good, but they could not succeed. The poor patients knew how to distinguish between real merit and big talk. Then they would go and consult with the most pious of their creed that they could find, to take measures to prevent so many conversions to the Catholic Faith. They even proposed and agreed upon holding their religious meetings in Ward A, but I put a medal in the door case and they did not advance a step further. They could not see or understand, they said, how the sisters could have so much influence over the patients. They showed the sisters, however, the greatest respect. They would often say, "How happy the sisters look, and they make all around them happy too. I wish my presence could be a sunshine somewhere." The poor patients thought there was nobody like the sisters. They would often say, "Indeed it was not the doctor that raised me, it was sister." When returning to their regiment, they would say, "Sister, we may never see the sisters again, but be assured you will be very gratefully remembered." Others would say, "Sister, I wish we could do something for you, but you don't seem to want anything. It is not in the power of any poor soldier to make you anything like recompense. All that we can do for you is to fight for you and that we will do till our last breath."

JEFFERSON BARRACKS HOSPITAL

In visiting Jefferson Barracks Hospital, we were also witnesses of many beautiful conversions. One day among others, we found a young man about seventeen, who was very sick. We spoke to him of God and of his immortal soul, but he seemed to know very little about either. After some instructions, he became so anxious for baptism that he begged us not to leave him until we would make him a child of God. We saw that he had not long to live and that it was impossible to get a priest then, it being nine miles from the city. Sister baptized him. The remainder of the day and during the night he prayed aloud and frequently called for the ladies with the white bonnets. To try to pacify him one of our lady nurses, endeavoring to represent the sisters, put something white on her head and went to him. At first he was deceived, but he soon discovered his mistake. He sent her away telling her that she was not the one he wanted. He did not die that night. When we went back next day, he told us how they tried to deceive him, and to make him believe they were sisters, when they were not even Catholics adding, "How glad I am, sister, to see you once more and to hear words of consolation from your lips." He would beg us to remain with him as long as we could and to talk to him of God. We were not witnesses of his death but all who were in the ward convinced us that it was happy and edifying.

In the next ward we found another whom when we first saw him, we thought he was already dead. We ventured, however, to speak to him but what was our surprise when he answered us with a clear, strong voice and begged us to baptize him. We questioned him and finding his dispositions very good, we did not delay to open for him the gates of heaven.

Another was dying in the greatest agony for several days but could not die (because he was not baptized), but as soon as he was baptized and prepared for death, he died calmly and beautifully.

These incidents will give an idea of the good feelings and dispositions of the patients towards the sisters. When we first went to the hospital, the authorities enforced it and gave themselves the example in everything. When the Medical Director would visit the hospital he would stand in the middle of the ward and state them aloud to whom they owed their comfort. The good order, cleanliness and regularity that reigned there, he would tell them, were owing to the sisters. And this respect with which they were all inspired in the beginning never diminished, but went on increasing while the hospital lasted. Without it so much good could not have been effected.

Pennsylvania
Gettysburg
SAINT FRANCIS XAVIER CHURCH HOSPITAL
COURT HOUSE HOSPITAL
METHODIST CHURCH HOSPITAL
PENNSYLVANIA COLLEGE HOSPITAL

O'Keefe Account. During the 30th [of June] the armies were making preparations for the great fighting![1] About noon on the first of July we [in Emmitsburg] heard very distinctly, the cannonading, *Boom, Boom,* so terrific. This kept on until the afternoon of the 4th, when the Confederates were defeated and retreated away as fast as they could that night. They had crossed the Potomac before the Federals reached —too late to take prisoners.

On Sunday morning the 5th of July, some poor struggling Confederates came down [to the sisters at Emmitsburg]. How they cleared themselves was a wonder for if the poor fellows were caught they would be prisoners. They got a good warm breakfast here after which they set out for what place they did not say. They told us that the battle ended late the evening before on the 4th. Father Burlando and Mother [Ann Simeon Norris] decided that some sisters had better go up to Gettysburg, so the omnibus was gotten ready and baskets of provisions for the wounded, bandages and other necessaries. Father Burlando got the carriage, taking two sisters with him, fourteen were in the bus and off they started. On reaching within two miles of Gettysburg, the road was blockaded by some trees that had been cut down and put across the road. On the side were a gang of pickets who ran towards the fence with uplifted muskets, but no sooner did they see the bus with the sisters and Father in front then they put down the muskets. Father tied a white handkerchief on the end of his cane and walked up to the pickets. This white flag represented a Flag of Truce. The men talked a few minutes to Father and in a few minutes the blockade was removed, then our driver was beckoned to drive on. As we passed, the pickets lifted their caps and bowed showing their pleasure on seeing the sisters going up to attend the sufferers. But on reaching the battle grounds, awful! To see the men lying dead on the road—some by the side of their horses. O, it was beyond

---

[1] Sister Marie Louise Caulfield, Sister Matilda Coskery, and Sister Camilla O'Keefe wrote accounts of the Daughters of Charity at Gettysburg. Each highlights different details about their service at Gettysburg. This portion of the account was written by Sister Camilla O'Keefe.

Sisters taking baskets of provisions to Gettysburg, Pennsylvania.

description! Hundreds of both armies lying dead almost on the track [so] that the driver had to be careful not to pass over the bodies. O! This picture of human beings slaughtered down by their fellow men in a cruel civil war was perfectly awful.

The battlefield [was] a very extensive space. On either side of the road, the east was [General George] Mead's stand, the West [General James] Longstreet's. On both sides were men digging pits and putting the bodies down by the dozens. One newly made pit contained fifty bodies of Confederates. By a large tree in another spot might be pointed out where the body of such a Genl. lay until removed to another location. In this frightful condition we found the battle grounds of that fearful Battle of Gettysburg.

After some time creeping along we arrived in the town of Gettysburg. Here all was in fearful excitement. The Federal officers [were] sorry enough that Longstreet and his army should have escaped being their prisoners. All those officers who had been here at St. Joseph's were very glad to see Father Burlando and the sisters. We kept on till reaching McClennen's [sic, McClellan's] Hotel.[2] The parlors of the Hotel were given immediately to the sisters for their use. This was about 1 o'clock p.m., so long did it take to reach them, having to go so very slowly, specially passing by the battle grounds where the hundreds of men lay dead. The sisters wanted

---

[2] This is The Gettysburg Hotel located on the town square, which was owned by William McClellan.

to go to work at once. Father, accompanied by some of the officers took us to the different places where the wounded had been just removed. One place was the Court House, then the different churches, the Catholic had some of the very worst amputated limbs there in the sanctuary, even the Blessed Sacrament having been removed to the Priests' house. In all the public school houses and every available building there [in Gettysburg] lay the wounded. Now was the moment to go to work and the sisters did truly work in bandaging the poor wounded, some fixing drinks, etc. After visiting the different temporary hospitals where lay the wounded, we returned with our dear Father [Burlando] to the Hotel. Father then left us for home, taking back with him two of the sisters and leaving twelve there. The sisters then took possession of the parlors of the hotel as their Military [nursing] Quarters.

We took some refreshment and went again around to see the wounded whom we now considered our patients of the battle. Impossible to describe the condition of those poor wounded men. The weather was warm and very damp for some days after the battle. Generally the case where there is so much <u>powder</u> used, [that] they were <u>covered</u> with <u>vermin</u> [and] actually that we could hardly bear this part of the <u>filth</u>. We didn't see a woman in the whole place that evening. They either escaped away in the country or hid in the cellars. The following day they appeared in their homes frightened and looking like ghosts—so very terrified the poor women were during the fearful battle. No wonder! The sisters lay on the floor that night, [and] did not sleep much. On the following day Mother Ann Simeon [Norris] sent us beds and covering—also cooked hams, coffee, tea and whatever she thought the sisters actually needed. Sister Euphemia [Blenkinsop], assistant had gone south to attend to the sisters in the Confederate Military Hospitals which was a great comfort to the poor sisters in the South.

On the second day a reinforcement of sisters came to our aid from Baltimore. Father Burlando kept looking out for his children in Gettysburg, going up occasionally to see the sisters and sending more help when he could, for in fact it was difficult to get any more. So many there engaged in the West Philadelphia Hospital, in Washington, and at Point Lookout. Only very few remained at St. Joseph's, even the Procuratrix, Sister Baptista [Dowds], was down at Point Lookout with nearly twenty sisters and where the services of the sisters were much needed and appreciated too by the government. Think of 16 hundred [1600] wounded brought in one day, Dec. 16th, after the battle of Fredericksburg, Virginia, when the Federals were defeated to pieces. Oh, that was a scene of terror. But I must come back to the Gettysburg. For three miles the outside of the town was converted into a Hospital by [using] tents and the farm houses. Ambulances were provided for the sisters to take clothing, etc. out to the wounded many hundreds of whom lay on the ground on their blankets.

Straw would be given from the barns, which the poor boys were glad to get, rather than lie on the ground. We noticed as we were going through the woods a red flag out with a board marked, "1700 wounded down this way." The driver drove on till the sisters reached a wooded area where the wounded were. Some were in a heart rendering state. Besides the clothing and jellies to make drinks, we also took a lot of <u>combs</u> which were needed the worst way. O, yes for some were in a frightful condition. The sisters too brought plenty of vermin along in their clothes! I shudder on thinking of this part of the sisters' sufferings; during the whole of the time that they were in the Military Hospitals, especially on the fields' tents in Gettysburg, the weather was very warm. We noticed one large man whose leg had to be taken off. Another part of his body was in such a condition that the big maggots were crawling on the ground on which they crept from the body. Many others almost as bad, but the whole of them were crawling with <u>lice</u> so that the sisters did a great deal for those poor fellows by getting <u>combs</u> to get their heads clear of the troublesome <u>animals</u>. This was no easy task. Three of the sisters remained in one of those field hospitals three miles out of town during the three weeks that the wounded were there until the wounded

Pennsylvania Hall at Gettysburg College.

soldiers became able to be removed to the regular hospitals in Philadelphia, Washington, or New York. When feasible they were transferred to these facilities. There were 60 of the Confederates that were baptized. This was owing a good deal, no doubt, to the influence of Dr. [A.B.] Stonelake, a United States officer, who became a convert at Point Lookout and had been baptized by Father Basil Pacciarini, a Jesuit. So this very doctor happened to step up to the [McClellan] Hotel when the sisters were putting lots of things into the ambulance to take out to any of the field hospitals that they might find. The doctor asked for some of the sisters who had been at Point Lookout. He was told, yes, such a sister, naming her was in the room. He stepped in and who would be there to meet him but Father Burlando and the sister that the doctor inquired for. We were more than glad to [see] our friend. The doctor had his order from the provost to go out to some of the tents and farm houses where some <u>prisoners</u> were in a bad condition. So the doctor, with the sisters, set off and found a number of wounded prisoners in great neglect.

The good doctor not only performed the duty of a physician, but after he had fixed up the limbs, [he] set to work like a carpenter. From the farm house he obtained a <u>saw,</u> an axe and nails, boards too. In a short time he had the men, who lay on the ground, raised upon a kind of frame so that the poor fellows thought they had beds now. The doctor remained the whole time. Those wounded prisoners were many from Georgia and Alabama. They knew no man of religion [from] a Turk, no baptism, nor did some of them believe in heaven, or hell —only to live just as long as they could and enjoy life as it came. But God in His mercy raised up the Dr. who came in their way and became converted himself. He talked & reasoned with them, giving his own experience that he would [not] exchange for all the riches of earth. Kindness bestowed on them in their sufferings had no little effect, some would say, "The sisters were Catholics, surely they must be right any way."

The Jesuit Father visited around those localities when he could. The Priests from the College also.[3] By the mercy of God, no less than sixty embraced the Faith before leaving. Some died with good dispositions. The greater number of those men were highly educated, some of them officers in the Confederate army, but had no knowledge of God. When told some articles of our faith they would make an exclamation of surprise saying, "We never heard that, never." As for the necessity of baptism they never dreamed

---

[3] Probably Mount St. Mary's College and Seminary, which is about ten miles south of Gettysburg.

of such a thing, scarcely any of them had received baptism in any form. I might say not a single one of them (of the Georgians, nor the Alabamians). But to witness the change in those men was evidently the mercy of God over His redeemed Creatures. So often they were heard to say, "Why we never heard of such things." Baptism. Three persons in God and so on. Of all the sacred truths of our Holy Faith, no hereafter [heaven] did those ignorant creatures of God believe in.

But thanks to our merciful God they believed in the doctrine of the Holy Catholic Church before leaving their poor quarters at Gettysburg. Those who died went to our Lord believing firmly all the sacred truths that they had been taught and with baptism. When removed to some other Military Hospital, they would say to the sisters when biding good bye, "We are going to prison now, but it would be no prison if we had you along to administer to our wants of soul and body." The poor fellows were actually in tears when setting out under heavy guard.

Although the sisters suffered many privations, still the fact of seeing so many of those men, baptized and embracing the faith more than paid for all that they had to bear. The officers of the Federal Army treated the sisters with the greatest confidence, [and] would give them all the privileges possible which they positively refused to ladies who came offering their services to nurse the wounded. They refused them saying the Sisters of Charity [sic][4] were caring for them. We found out that the Union officers were under the impression that the ladies from Baltimore and elsewhere were all Rebels so they would not accept of their services.

It used [to] amuse the sisters when they would go to the Commissaries for clothing and other necessaries [and] the persons in charge would say, "Sisters, I suppose you want them for the Catholic Church Hospital." "No," replied the sisters, "we want them for the Methodist Church Hospital." The officer would look with a kind of smile as well as surprise. Another time that a sister called at one of those stores to get some clothing for the prisoners in the Lutheran Hospital, [and] a similar question was put to her to which sister replied, "We want some articles of clothing for the prisoners in the Lutheran Seminary Hospital." The gentleman replied, "Yes, sister you shall have what you want for the prisoners as well as for our own. Your ladies (the sister) come with honest faces and you shall always get whatever you need for the suffering men whether Rebels or our own." He continued speaking very kindly and finished by saying, "I sincerely hope we shall all worship at the same altar one day."

---

[4] Daughters of Charity.

A sister protecting a soldier.

We noted a remark made by an elderly gentleman, who came into Gettysburg immediately after the battle to look for his son who was in the army and might be found either killed or living. The old gentleman, [along] with others, was seated on a bench outside of the hotel. Upon seeing some of the sisters stepping out with bundles of clothing, taking to the wounded to some of the hospitals, the old man exclaimed, "What! Good God! Can those sisters be the persons whose religion we always <u>run</u> down!!" "Yes," replied Mr. McClennan [sic, McClellan], the Hotel Proprietor, "they are the very persons that are often run down by those who know nothing of their charity." Mr. McClennan [sic, McClellan] told us this and that the old gentleman was quite taken back and could hardly believe what he had seen with his own eyes. Mr. McClennan [sic, McClellan] said that he had heard similar remarks from parties seeing the sisters going around nursing and caring [for] the wounded, and that they would almost <u>swear</u> that they would never again believe anything wrong of persons doing what those sisters have been doing around the battle grounds of Gettysburg.

Caulfield/Coskery Account. On 1 July 1863, the two armies met near Gettysburg, a large town in Pennsylvania about ten miles north of Emmitsburg.[5] They fought until the evening of the 3rd [of July], advancing by their movements more and more towards our peaceful vale, so that our buildings and very earth trembled from their cannons. That night the rain fell heavily and continued to do so all the next day, Saturday.

On Sunday morning, immediately after Mass, Father Burlando with twelve sisters started for the battlefield, taking refreshments, bandages, sponges, clothing, etc., intending to do the best we could for the suffering men and return home in the evening.

The roads, previous to the rain, had been very muddy and the two armies had passed over them. Now from the very heavy rains they were almost impassable.

The subdued South having retired, their thousands of dead and wounded were left on the field. The scouts of the North were stationed here and there watching their return. One of the bands seeing our ambulances was ready to fire on us, thinking they were those of the enemy.

Later we reached a zig-zag fence forming a double blockade across the road. We wondered whether we dare go around it by turning into the fields, for in the distance we saw soldiers, half hidden in the road, watching us.

Father Burlando, putting a white handkerchief on a stick and holding it high, walked towards them, while we also alighted and walked about that they might see the cornettes. They viewed Father sharply, for they had resolved to refuse a flag of truce if it were offered, but the cornettes assured them. They met Father and hearing his mission, sent an escort with him to open a passage for us through the fields.

We soon came in sight of war's ravages—thousands of guns, swords, etc., lay around—further on we saw many soldiers on horseback as silent almost as the dead that lay there, the living having been removed from this part. The rains had filled the roads with water, and here it was red with blood. Our carriage wheels rolling through blood! Our horses could hardly

---

[5] This account probably was written by Sister Marie Louise Caulfield but includes information from Sister Matilda Coskery. A large portion of the Union Army had spent 26-29 June 1863 encamped around St. Joseph's Central House with the possibility of military conflict on the property of the Daughters of Charity at Emmitsburg. See Virginia Walcott Beauchamp, Ph.D., "The Sisters and the Soldiers," *Maryland Historical Magazine* (Summer 1986).

be made to proceed on account of the horrid objects lying about them—dead men and horses here and there. Men digging graves and others bringing the bodies to them! There was a little group sitting over a fire, trying to cook their meat, in the midst of all these scenes.

Here again, Father Burlando told [about] his errand. The [military] officers seemed well pleased, [and] told us to go into the town and we would find sufficient employment for our zealous charity. Every large building in the town was being filled as fast as the wounded could be brought in, and in and around the town were one hundred thirteen hospitals in operation besides those in private houses.

On reaching Gettysburg, we were shown to a hospital where we distributed our little stores and did what we could to relieve and console the sick. Our little band of sisters was soon disposed of only two being sent to each hospital, as far as the number allowed. That evening two sisters returned to Saint Joseph's [Emmitsburg] with Father Burlando, who sent more sisters next day to aid us, or rather to take [to] more hospitals.

This section of the country knew nothing of the holiness of Catholicity, but believed much that was untrue of it; consequently, we expected to encounter some pain in our undertaking. To our surprise, all who met us lauded our charity; bitterness had lost its edge, and modesty might blush at the welcomes and heartfelt greetings that met us everywhere.

On arriving at one of the hospitals, the surgeon in charge took us to the ladies who had been attending there, and said to them, "Ladies, and you men nurses also, here are the Sisters of Charity [sic] come to save our men. They will give all the directions here. You are only required to observe them." They bowed their assent.

The soldiers seemed to think that the presence of the sisters smoothed the barb of their anguish. One day a sister was giving drink with a tea spoon to a poor dying man. It being slow work a gentleman entered and stood near her without her seeing him. He was from a distance and was searching for the very soldier she was serving, having heard that he had fallen in an engagement. Sister, standing for a moment in silence, he exclaimed in a loud voice, "May God bless the Sisters of Charity!" He repeated it emphatically, adding, "I am a Protestant, but may God bless the Sisters of Charity."

This was at the Catholic church [Saint Francis Xavier], which was now filled with wounded, mutilated men, The Stations hung around the walls, and a very large painting of Saint Francis Xavier, holding in his hand a crucifix to show to the benighted pagans the sign of their Redemption.

This was a book read by our poor men, for we had in that church but one Catholic, and our glorious Saint was for the time, resuming his Apostolic Mission among them.

The first man put in the sanctuary was soon baptized, and with truly pious sentiments. His pain was excruciating and when sympathy was offered him, he said, "O, what are these I suffer compared with those my Redeemer endured for my salvation!" Thus disposed, he died.

They were so uncomfortable, having but just been from the field, that to lessen some of their sufferings, seemed to call for our first attention. At least, in their eyes it was so, that we could only say a passing word to them of their souls, except to those nearest death and in greatest danger.

They lay on the pew seats, under the pews, in every aisle, with scarcely room to pass between them — in the sanctuary and in the gallery. Their own blood, the water used for bathing their wounds, and all kinds of filth and stench, added to their misery. Already gangrenous wounds had begun to infect the air, but no complaint came from these poor men!

So many dying from lockjaw made them require much time for receiving drinks, nourishment, etc. Many received their first dressings from our sisters, the surgeons being few in number. When the wounded would see the sister enter in the morning they would say, "O, please come and dress my wound!" Another would cry out, "O, come to me next!" etc.

Many, many wounds had piles of maggots in and about them, which must be removed before the poor limb or wound could be soothed. To all these miseries, were the privations of home, friends and home comforts, which in such times come so vividly before the mind.

Under a pew lay a tall Scotchman, his head only visible. He had lockjaw and had only a short time to live. Sister spoke to him of death. He had never been baptized, but desired it earnestly and to all her questions, he replied so loud and fervently that quite a crowd gathered around him. He was too low to be removed, and there he lay. The water was poured on his poor head which he pushed out from under the pew as far as he could. He soon expired.

How powerfully grace acted upon these poor men, for previous to baptism, all their thoughts were of their sufferings and their desire to reach home, but as soon as the regenerating water had healed their spiritual wound, they seemed only occupied on the well being of their souls. Tubs of soothing water were used for bathing those of the body, yet could not arrest disease or death. Not so with the immortal soul.

A young Cavalry soldier having seen the priest baptize a comrade had asked for and received baptism. After slumbering several hours, he partially awoke, and seeing a sister he asked, "Will Jack die?" meaning his horse. Sister, thinking him delirious, said, "O, no!" By this time he was fully himself and said, "Will I die?" "I think so," said sister. "Die!" he exclaimed, "O, no! Death! Death! O, no!"

Sister did all she could to compose him, but he repeated his fears of judgment, and his countenance becoming more and more despondent, he added, "I have not Religion." Sister said, "My poor brother did you not desire baptism yesterday and receive it?" "Yes," he answered, "but I have not Religion!" Sister said again, "Did you not desire to become the child of God, the heir of heaven, etc., etc.?" "O, yes, but I should feel Religion." Then sister spoke of the love God had for us, making at the same time aspirations of love of God. He listened, his whole face showing signs of joy and encouragement, till at last it glowed with pleasure as he looked up at sister, saying, "I do believe I have Religion!" He remained calm until death.

Another youth, not so fortunate, had been urged to consent to baptism, but in vain. The surgeon seeing the earnestness of the sister, said to her, "Sister, baptize him whether he wants it or not." Later, the father of the lad arrived and sister spoke to him, saying, his son did not seem concerned as to baptism. "O, no!" replied the father. "My son is a good boy. He volunteered in his country's cause, fought her battles, and dies for her. That will do—all is right." Sister then said, "But surely, you have been baptized?" "Yes," he replied, "But my son does not need it." When the "good boy" died, he took him home to be buried.

To the dying Protestants who had been baptized, we suggested sorrow for having broken the Law of God, the acts of Faith, Hope, Love, etc., and had the consolation of seeing them die piously.

Four sisters attended for several days a large college [Gettysburg College], now used as a prison. About six hundred men lay there.[6] The sisters only dressed their wounds, for surgeons were scarce in every place. Every morning on their return to the prison, there were eight or ten dead bodies at the entrance, awaiting internment. We kept no account of baptisms here, but they would have been very numerous if more sisters could have been there, for rarely did anyone in danger reject baptism, when we could attend to it, but to hear them calling "O, come to me when you are done with his wound!" obliged us to do violence to every other duty.

---

[6] At least four Daughters of Charity worked in Penn Hall of Pennsylvania College (now Gettysburg College) treating Confederate prisoners of war. The college was founded in 1832.

Two youths lay outstretched under a blanket, and a little ditch two inches deep was around the earth they lay on, to prevent the rain from running under them. A sister found that one was in danger. She asked if they had ever been baptized. They said, "No!" After talking to them of it, the one in danger said he could not be baptized, never having been a religious boy, etc., etc. Sister explained it to him, and then with much fear and seemingly great contrition, he asked for baptism. At the instant of receiving it, he threw his hands and arms towards heaven and exclaimed, "Thank God!" while the big tears filled his eyes. Indeed, his grace was almost visible. We saw him no more.

A sister once hearing a great noise among the patients looked to see the cause, and saw a group of men with pointed guns and one poor man standing at their mercy, while no one was trying to prevent the strife. Sister went to them, put her hand on the man they aimed at, pushed him back to the door of the surgeon, holding out her other arm to prevent the others from pursuing him. There was now a dead silence. She put the man safely inside the doctor's room and the others retired, quietly putting away their guns.

Silence continued for some time and sister resumed her duties in the mess room. Presently the doctor came to her, stood a moment, then said, "Sister, you have surprised me! I shall never, never forget what I have witnessed. I saw their anger and heard all the excitement, but feared that my presence would increase it. I knew not what to do, when you came and made all right. Indeed this will never die in my memory! Indeed, you have surprised me!"

"Well," said sister, "What did I [do] more than any other would have done? You know they were ashamed to resist a female." "A female?" said the doctor, "All women of Gettysburg could not have effected what you have! No, no one but a Sister of Charity could have done this. Truly it would have been well if a Company of Sisters of Charity [sic] could have been in the War, for then it might not have continued for four years![7] Yes, the sisters can do what they please. I shall never forget it."

A poor old soldier repulsed sister every time she showed kindness towards him. At last her perseverance caused him to show some civility towards her, and hearing that he was in danger, she spoke to him of baptism. He immediately became displeased and said he was too old to be plagued in that manner. Two weeks passed and on every occasion that offered, sister said a word about baptism, but with the same result.

---

[7] Daughters of Charity.

The last evening of his life, when she was about to leave him for the night, having her chaplet [rosary] in her hand, she saw the medal of our Immaculate Mother which she took off the chaplet and slipped it quietly under his pillow without his knowledge. She said to our Blessed Mother, "I can do no more for this man. I leave him to you."

The next morning when she saw him, he asked her for a drink, then said, "Sister, I want no breakfast today, but I wish to be baptized." "Well," said sister, "Be very sorry for your sins." "O," said he, "I have cried over them all the night, and also for my obstinacy towards your kindness. Will you forgive me?" Sister composed him and [had] only given him baptism when he expired.

Another, a young man, made objections to baptism, as being crippled, he could not be immersed. This difficulty being removed he said, "Sister, it is very strange. Nobody says baptism is necessary but you sisters." At that moment a Protestant minister stood there and hearing him, said, "O, yes, young man, I say baptism is necessary, and I am a minister and if you desire it, I will baptize you." "Well," replied the soldier, "if you do it as sister would, you may, but, sister you must stay and see if he does it as you would." "Well," said the minister, "I do so and so. Is that right?" "Yes," said sister, so the minister performed the ceremony and when it was over the sick man asked sister if it had been done right.

Sister satisfied him. He told her to stay with him when dying, praying fervently until the last breath, and trying to speak louder. Almost his last words were, "God bless the Sisters of Charity." This brought a crowd around him. As his bed was on the floor, sister was kneeling by him and she continued to pray by him to the last. Then she closed his mouth, and tied a towel about his head, etc. Those who stood by, said, "Was that her relative?" "No," was the reply, "but she is a Sister of Charity [sic] meaning, this is their way." "Well," said a gentleman, "I have often heard of Sisters of Charity. I can now testify to them having the right name."

A sister giving a medal of our Blessed Mother to a Catholic soldier, another said to her later, "Sister, you gave something to that man awhile ago, and he must be easier, for he has not groaned since. Please give me such as you gave him." She did so telling him of it, and showing him the prayer he was to say.[8] She discovered that he endeavored to suppress his moans, but his limb was very painful.

---

[8] The Miraculous Medal, properly titled the Medal of the Immaculate Conception, was received in a vision by Saint Catherine Labouré, a seminary sister (novice) with the Daughters of Charity, in the chapel at 140 rue du Bac in Paris in 1830.

Satterlee Hospital in Philadelphia, Pennsylvania.

Later he said, "I do not long to live, [but] to help my parents. The doctor says I cannot be saved but by amputation. This I cannot bear." Sister spoke to the doctor, who said, "Yes, this is one chance of life, and even now it may be too late, for he [the patient] would not consent."

Sister went again to the poor youth, and begged him to have courage. "Well," he answered, "Baptize me first, and then promise me that the doctors will not take the medal off my neck." Sister fearing his death under the operation, baptized him, and told him that he should keep his medal.

He refused the usual sleeping potion, kept the medal where he could see it, and during his great pain, only uttered twice, "O, my Mother, my Mother!" The poor fellow got well, and while convalescing, sister sent a Catholic to teach him the Catholic doctrine. Later, when moving around, he would say to his companions, "That is the sister that saved my soul and body."

Upon one occasion, when the wounded men were to be moved to another building, a sister, one attendant and a surgeon were the last to leave. Passing through a back passage, they heard a groan. They followed the sound and found a dying man who had in feeble tone barely made himself heard. As soon as he saw sister he asked, "Are you the one who is to baptize me?" The doctor asked him why he had not been removed with the others. "Oh!" he said, "I was afraid I would die on the road and I asked to remain here;

but," he repeated, "There was a Lady here last night who said she would send someone to baptize me. Will you baptize me?" After some preparation, he was baptized and soon after he died.

The Surgeon once remarked to the sisters, "You sisters must be punctual to your repasts. I see that you are often here until 4:00 p.m. without your dinner, working for others with a two-fold strength. (Where it comes from I know not), forgetting no one but yourselves. You should, however, try to preserve your health."

We notice these things because they come from Protestant lips. A Protestant General remarked to a sister that, "The Sisters of Charity [sic][9] have done more for religion during the War than has ever been done in this country before," and, he added, "the Presbyterian ministers admit this, and you know they are not very profuse in your praise."

A young man going to the provost for a pass that the sisters might enter the prisons, was answered, "Yes, the Sisters of Charity [sic] have my confidence. They may go where they please." Many of the convalescing soldiers, many of whom were officers, read our Catholic books, seemingly with such profit as might result happily.

In one of the sanitary stores a sister asked the proprietor if she could give of these supplies to the various calls for relief from the neighboring farms, encampments, etc. "Madam," he replied, "We would entrust to the Sisters of Charity our entire stock of provisions and feel that thus it would be well distributed. Give to whom you please, provided they suffer from the late engagement."

A Protestant General, whose wound seemed dangerous, was asked by the sister if he had ever been baptized. "O, yes!" he replied, "I have been carefully raised by Episcopalian parents." A little further conversation passed, when presently finding himself on doubtful ground as to argument, he tried to save his credit by saying, "Ah, well! The Episcopalians come nearest to the Catholics in creed, etc." "And," replied the sister very coolly but triumphantly, "You prize it for its nearness? Why not go to it?" Before she could fairly finish her remark, the poor General cried out [his desire to take back his words], "I unsay, I unsay, what I have said."

Several officers had been in the room and had been quite attentive to the conversation. They really enjoyed the embarrassment of the general,

---

[9] Daughters of Charity.

who was very pleasant, and took later from the sister, [George] Hay's *Christian Instructed from the Written Word*.[10]

Before his removal, he read it half through, and would say he was agreeably informed. He took it with him, for he recovered.

One day a sister was returning to her hospital laden with bundles for her sick, but finding a long line of cavalry obstructing her path, she know not what to do for she was too weary to stand and had no time to lose. Then looking up at the nearer horsemen, she asked, "Will you allow me to pass?" These drew up their bridles and opened a passage for her.

A sister from the Catholic Church Hospital had ordered supplies from a sanitary store, and soon after a sister from the Methodist Church Hospital called at the same store. When she was about to leave, the merchant said, "Where are these to be sent? I believe you belong to the Catholic Church?" "No, sir," said the sister, "I belong to the Methodist Church." This gave us some recreation.

A gentleman seeing the sisters said to those near him, "Can it be that these are the persons that I have almost hated, and now see serving our poor men with so much care,—with motherly kindness?"

Going over a field encampment we found the brother of one of our sisters, who was in a hospital in the town.[11] He had been wounded in the chest and in the ankle. The kind officer allowed him to be removed to the hospital where his sister was stationed. They had not seen each other for nine years.

In one of the rooms in which the sisters lodged, two pictures hung— one, Martin Luther, the other, Calvin! So, you see, we were not without protectors.

After the most seriously wounded had been removed by their friends or had died, the officers commenced moving the men from the town hospitals to a wood of tents, called the General Hospital.

A sister passing in the street about this time, a Protestant chaplain ran several squares to overtake her and then said, "I see Sisters of Charity

---

[10] Hay, George. *The Devout Christian Instructed in the Faith of Christ, from the Written Word* (Philadelphia: Eugene Cummiskey, 1831).

[11] This soldier was probably the brother of the Klimkiewicz sisters. Sister Mary Virginia was on duty at Gettysburg when her brother was discovered and brought to her post. Their sister, Sister Serena, also served at Gettysburg. See "Polish Sisters in the Civil War", by Sister M. Liguori, H.F.N., from "Polish American Studies," Vol. VII, No. 1-2, January-June, 1950.

A sister nurse's gentle touch of compassionate care.

[sic][12] everywhere but in our General Hospital. Why are not they there?" Sister told him that when the wounded men had been removed, none of the surgeons or officers had asked the sisters to go there, or they would have gone willingly. "Well," he said, "I will go immediately to the provost and get him to have you sent there. I feel sure that he will wish you to go."

But we heard no more from them, and as each hospital was closed where the sisters had been, they returned to their peaceful home, joyfully, while at the same time they felt sad at the thought of the sufferers they had left behind, for when they were preparing for removal, they would say, "O, if the sisters were to go with us, we could endure the rest, etc., etc."

Memory will always find a page to read of these sad, sad days, but words or pens will never tell the tale such as it was.

We know, dear Mother [Ann Simeon Norris], that you will be pleased to hear us declare, that an extra strength of body and powers of endurance were given to us from above, and while our dear Saint Joseph's [Central House] was trying to alleviate all it could of our sufferings, so, also, was heaven busy in our behalf, and we often looked at each other, wondering that we were able to resume each morning, the heartrending duties of yesterday, as though each day was the first of our labors.

---

[12] Daughters of Charity.

If the body, alone, had been engaged, it would not have disturbed us so much, but to have every faculty and energy of mind and heart constantly tried to their utmost, for the healing of their various wounds, corporal and spiritual, was for the time a painful crucible.

All the country[side] was hospital, save space for cemetery.

PHILADELPHIA
THE SATTERLEE U.S. GENERAL HOSPITAL

On the twenty-eighth of May 1862, a requisition was made by Surgeon General Hammond for twenty-five Sisters of Charity [sic][13] to nurse the sick and wounded soldiers in the West Philadelphia [General] Hospital, afterwards known as [Satterlee Heights Hospital or] the Satterlee.[14]

Wishing to have us on the spot to make preparations, Doctor [Isaac I.] Hayes requested us to be there on the 9th of June. About 10 o'clock, twenty-two sisters arrived on the grounds. The place was so large that we could not find the entrance. The workmen looked at us in amazement, thinking perhaps that we belonged to some Flying Artillery [due to the cornettes worn by the sisters]. At twelve o'clock we repaired to the kitchen for dinner. By the time dinner was finished, we found some sick were brought. There were one hundred fifty. We all went to work to prepare some nourishment for the poor fellows. They looked at us with astonishment, not knowing what kind of people we might be. Amongst them was a French soldier named Pierre who recognized the Daughters of Charity. When the patients found the sisters waiting on them so kindly, they offered their assistance.

In a short time our number [of patients] was increased to nearly nine hundred. Many were ill with typhoid fever, swamp fever, chronic dysentery, etc., etc. On the 16th of August, over fifteen hundred sick and wounded soldiers were brought to the hospital, most of them from the Battle of Bull Run. Many had died on the way from exhaustion. Others were in a dying state, so that the chaplain, Father [Peter P.] McGrane, was sent to administer the last sacraments.[15] We took care to furnish them some good beef essence, wines or other little delicacies that might revive them or which they might fancy.

---

[13] Daughters of Charity.

[14] Sister Mary Gonzaga Grace was sister servant at Satterlee Hospital and wrote the principal account of the sisters experiences there. Sister Marie Mulhern also wrote another brief account. The present day Clark Park is partly on the site of Satterlee, the Civil War's largest hospital.

[15] At this time Rev. Peter P. McGrane, a former Redemptorist, was assigned to Saint Patrick's Church, 20th and Locust Avenue in Philadelphia.

The wards being now crowded, tents were put up to accommodate over one thousand. We had at that time not less than four thousand, five hundred in the hospital.

When we first went to Satterlee, our quarters were very limited. We had one small room about seven feet square which served as a chapel, another somewhat larger answered the purpose of dormitory by night and community room by day. When we had Mass, only a few sisters had room to remain inside, and at time for Holy Communion they were obliged to come out after receiving, to let those who were in the entry come in. It was beautiful to see our dear sick kneeling around the door, and even up the stair steps, the maimed, the lame, and even the blind, drawing near our dear Lord in His Holy Tabernacle.

Doctor Hayes, who was all kindness to us, soon built four more rooms, one of them expressly for a chapel, which he supplied with seats, and told me to order the carpenter to do anything we wished to make it convenient. This was called the "Sisters' Chapel," for the Protestant chaplain had his preaching in the corridor or wherever he could collect an audience. Liberty was granted to the soldiers to come to our chapel whenever they wished. Many pious ones spent much of their leisure time in making the Stations [of the Cross], which some of their comrades had bought and placed there at their own expense.[16]

Our new refectory was so arranged that between it and the chapel we had temporary doors which when removed, made our chapel over one hundred feet long. These two rooms were crowded every Sunday and festival and it often happened that many of our invalids to secure a seat came before meditation was finished. Protestants were also attracted by the short but beautiful exhortations of Father McGrane who gave us Mass three times a week. At first we were obliged to borrow all that was necessary for Divine Service, but our soldiers after receiving their pay, made a collection among themselves, requesting Sister N. to purchase ornaments for the chapel. They did the same at different times until we had a good supply of everything. They even purchased new settees and sanctuary carpet, saying, "When the hospital is closed, the sisters must take everything we bought for the orphans."

In April 1863, Rt. Reverend Bishop [James Patrick] Wood did us the honor to administer confirmation in our chapel to thirty-one of our poor soldiers, most of whom were converts, and two upwards of forty years of age.

---

[16] The Stations of the Cross are a way of meditating on the suffering and death of Jesus Christ.

In February 1864, forty-four received this sacrament and one being unable to leave his bed, the Bishop had the kindness to go to the ward in his robes to confirm him. All behaved with the utmost respect during the ceremony. When Mass was finished, Bishop Wood distributed prayer books, rosaries, and medals which he had previously blessed and then told the Catholics to approach the railings. To his astonishment, as well as great satisfaction, all in the chapel came. He addressed a little exhortation and then dismissed them. Mass was at 6 o'clock and many of the patients were in the chapel at four thirty in order to secure seats. This was generally the case on great festivals, although some being crippled had to be carried in the arms of their comrades.

At three o'clock on Sundays and festivals, we had vespers and the rosary. The patients felt quite privileged to join in. In Lent we had the "Way of the Cross" and also during May the Devotions of the Month of Mary, both at seven in the evening. The chapel was always crowded at those times. Many took great pleasure in bringing candles and flowers for the altar of our dear Mother. When the month of May was ended, they expressed regret at not having some devotions in the evening when the sisters had theirs.

Our pious soldiers took great delight in decorating the chapel at Christmas, with green boughs, festoons, rosettes, etc. They sat up a great part of the preceding nights preparing them. Indeed it always gave them great pleasure to help the sisters in any kind of work, even preventing them whenever they found them at laborious duties.

In May 1864, the Jubilee [year] was celebrated at Satterlee Hospital. Our poor sufferers were so happy to have it in their power to obtain this great indulgence. Many approached the sacraments who had not received them for ten, fifteen and some twenty-five years. One had been over forty years without going to confession. He had lived on bad terms with his wife and sent for her that he might be reconciled before finishing the Jubilee.

The soldiers wore with the greatest confidence the Scapulars, Miraculous Medals, and *Agnus Deis*.[17] Many attributed their preservation to one or other of these. On one occasion, a thin, pale looking man, came to the door of the sister's room one morning for some medicine, appearing to suffer as he placed his hand on his breast, sister asked if his wound was

---

[17] The Latin Agnus Dei literally means "Lamb of God." Its usage here refers to a devotional religious artifact which was a small piece of pure wax, bearing the imprint of a lamb supporting the standard of the cross, which, encased in precious metal, or in some rich stuff, is worn devoutly about the neck, or suspended in a glass frame from the wall.

very painful. He answered, "No, but he knew it would have been mortal, were it not for a pair of scapulars his dear mother had given him before he left home," the bullet had gone through his uniform, battered his watch to pieces and lodged in his scapular, leaving only a little soreness. He now wished some instructions that he might be invested with them by the chaplain, before he returned to his regiment.

Another, a Protestant, said a Catholic friend of his had put the scapulars on his neck the morning he left home, telling him the Blessed Virgin would protect him and bring him safe through all dangers if he said a prayer to her every day. He did so, and although his comrades, fell on all sides and shells tore up the ground quite near his feet, he remained unhurt and even fearless. He said to sister, "I wish to be instructed and baptized." But as he was ordered to his regiment there was no time for him to do so. His good dispositions, however, gave us reason to hope that he was faithful to grace.

We distributed great numbers of medals and *Agnus Deis*, and the Protestants would ask for them before returning to the field, promising to wear them with respect and to say the prayer every day, because they said, the Catholic soldiers who wore them escaped so many dangers.

Sisters met angry rebuffs with kindness.

Smallpox Hospital. Cases of smallpox had occurred in the hospital from time to time, but the patients were removed as soon as possible to the Smallpox Hospital which was some miles from the city. The poor men were most distressed on account of their being sent away from the sisters, than they were for having the disease. It was heart-rending when the ambulances came, to hear the poor fellows beg to be left even if they were entirely alone, provided the sisters would be near them to have the sacraments administered in case of danger.

We offered our services several times to attend these poor sick, but were told [that] the government had ordered them away to prevent the contagion spreading. At last our surgeon in charge obtained permission to keep the smallpox patients in the camp, some distance from the hospital. The tents were made very comfortable with good large stoves to heat them and flies (double covers) over the tops. The next thing was to have a sister in readiness in case their services should be required. Everyone was generous enough to offer her services, but I [Sister Mary Gonzaga Grace] thought it more prudent to accept one who had had the disease.[18] As soon as the soldiers heard a sister had been assigned to the camp, they said, "Well, if I get the smallpox now, I don't care, because our sister will take care of me."

From November, 1864 to May, 1865 we had upwards of ninety cases. About nine or ten died. Two had the black smallpox and were baptized sometime before they died. We had, I may say, entire charge of these poor sufferers, as the physician who had charge of them seldom paid a visit and allowed us to do anything we thought proper for them. They were much benefitted (and very little marked) by drinking freely of tea made of "Sara-Cenia Purpura," or "Pitchers' Plant."[19] When the weather permitted, I visited those poor fellows almost every day. Like little children at these times, they expected some little treat of oranges, cakes, jellies, apples or such things, which we always had for them. They often said [that] it was the sisters that cured them and not the doctors, for they believed they [the doctors] were afraid of taking the disease. Our patients appeared to think the sisters were not like other human beings or they would not attend such loathsome and contagious diseases which everyone shunned.

One day I was advising an application to a man's face for poison. He would not see the doctor because, he said, he did not do him any good. I told him these remedies had cured [a] sister who was poisoned. The man

---

[18] This probably refers to Sister Josephine Edelin who stayed with the patients with contagious diseases in order to care for them.

[19] Sarracenia purpurea or Pitcher's Plant.

looked astonished and said, "A sister!" I answered "Yes," "Why," said he, "I did not know the sisters ever got anything like that." I told him, to be sure they do. "Are they not liable to take diseases as well as anyone else?" "To be sure not," he said, "For the boys often say they must be different from anyone else or other people, for they never get sick and they do for us what no person else would do. They are not afraid of fevers, smallpox or anything else." They had more confidence in the sisters' treatment than in the physicians. They, themselves, acknowledged they would have lost more of their patients had it not been for the sisters' watchful care and knowledge of medicine.

The officers as well as the soldiers showed the greatest deference and respect to the sisters. The surgeon in charge, Doctor Hayes, often remarked with pleasure that the sisters had such influence. No matter how rudely the soldiers were behaving, as soon as a sister made her appearance they were quiet and orderly. They often refused to go on night watch or detail duty for the doctor, but never refused when sister asked them to do so.

The surgeon in charge, on our first going to the hospital, gave orders that any want of respect or obedience should be immediately reported to him and the guilty one should be severely punished. Happily there was not a single instance of either. One occurrence will show the good feeling of all towards the sisters. One of the patients in ward N had been in town on pass, and of course had indulged too freely in liquor, but on his return went quietly to bed. Sister not knowing this went with his medicine and touched his bed clothes to arouse him. The poor man being stupid and sleepy thought his comrades were teasing him, and gave a blow, sending sister and the medicine across the room. Some of the convalescents seized him by the collar and would have choked him, if sister had not compelled them to desist. However, he was soon reported and sent under an escort to the guard house where stocks were being prepared for him. Nothing could be done for his relief as the surgeon in charge was absent. As soon as he returned we begged the poor man might return at once to his ward, and also be freed from all other punishments, as well as from the guard house. The surgeon said, as he could refuse nothing to the sisters, their request must be granted, but in order to make a strong impression on the soldiers, he dispatched an order to all the wards which was read at roll call to the effect that this man was released only by the earnest entreaty of the sister superior [Gonzaga Grace] and the sister of his ward, otherwise he would have been dealt with the utmost severity. When the poor man came to himself and learned what he had done, he begged a thousand pardons of sister and promised never to taste liquor again.

Prisoners. On great festivals, such as Christmas, Easter, Thanksgiving Day, etc., at our request all the prisoners in the guard house were liberated. The officers often came to us to solicit favors for them of Doctor Hayes, as they knew he would not refuse the sisters whatever they asked.

Visitors and Volunteers. Amongst the visitors at the hospital, some in the beginning were prejudiced and one day asked Doctor Hayes why he had the Sisters of Charity [sic][20] to nurse in his hospital when there were so many ladies who would be happy to do that service? He answered, "Because the Sisters of Charity were the only women in the world that he knew capable of nursing the sick properly." Another time a committee of ladies from an association waited upon him with letters of recommendation, accompanied by a large donation of clothes, fruits, preserves, etc., and offering themselves as an organized body to attend to the affairs of the hospital, and take turns to nurse the sick. The doctor thanked them saying, he had an excellent organized body to attend to the affairs of the hospital, working under his own eyes so well, that he was unwilling to change it for any other. This body was the Sisters of Charity [sic][21] who had his entire confidence, but if they wished to do some good they might take the place of some outsiders who were disposed at times to be rather troublesome. He then directed his orderly to take what they brought to sister in the donation room. The ladies left rather embarrassed at their cool reception.

Sister Nurses and Pastoral Care. From our taking charge of the hospital 9 June 1862, to our leaving 3 August 1865, ninety-one sisters had been on duty there. The changes with the exception of three or four were made by the superiors.

The war being over, the government only required our services until the convalescents could obtain their discharge. The physicians, however, begged that we remain until all the sick were removed, either to the Soldiers' Home, or well enough to return to their own homes.

The eve of our departure the executive officer said to me: "Sister, allow me to ask you a question. Has there ever been any misunderstanding or dissatisfaction between the officers and sisters since we came to this hospital?" I answered, "None at all." He said, "Well, I'll tell you why I asked. The other evening we were at a party. The conversation turned on the sisters in the hospital. I said there never had been a falling-out between any of us at Satterlee [Hospital], that we were all on the same good terms as the first day we met. Some of the City Hospital Doctors said, they did not

[20] Daughters of Charity.
[21] Daughters of Charity.

believe that forty women could live together without disputing, much less be among such a number of men."

The number of baptisms noted were fifty-seven, some of whom were mentioned in the memorandum sent. The number of communicants could not be ascertained as some approached the Holy Table almost every Sunday.

After the Battle of Gettysburg we received a large number of patients very badly wounded. In all we had nearly nine thousand. The wards were densely crowded, however, three hundred tents were erected and additional physicians and nurses were on duty, but a considerable number died from their wounds. Many converts among them died in the most edifying dispositions. Although every precaution was taken to prevent hemorrhages, numerous deaths however occurred in the tents, many dying as they had lived without any fear of the future and unbaptized. It was heart-rending to witness their sufferings and feel that you could do nothing to relieve them.

The greatest number of sisters employed in the hospital in those times when we had so many sick was forty-three.

One poor Catholic quite advanced in years, pale and furrowed, just received the last sacraments in time to breathe his last sigh. The poor man had never been to confession before and had no idea of religion, having spent the greater part of life as a sailor. Thus at the close of a long life spent in sin, this soul found that grace and mercy so justly denied the unrepentant sinner. Such are the ways of an all wise God—Praise be to His holy name forever.

On my arrival at the hospital, I was placed in ward H., which was roughly built and without any convenience whatever, to render the patients comfortable. We had but one cook to prepare the food for all the inmates of the hospital, and whoever was fortunate enough to come first was the best supplied. I remember having sent for the meals and instead of them would get an answer, "Not another ration to be cooked in the kitchen."

The Cook. One day having received the above answer, I went to the cook and asked him if there was anything to prepare for the patients' dinner. He replied, "Yes, sister, plenty, but I am really too tired to do anymore cooking and I think the boys in bed can do without until supper time." Meanwhile I sent word to the patients that they would get their dinner, but it would be a little late, and as there was a good fire, I soon prepared dinner.

While [I was] cooking, the Surgeon in charge and the steward entered the kitchen and inquired how it was that I was obliged to prepare the dinner? I told him that there was but one cook and he was not able to cook for the whole establishment. Immediately, he turned towards the steward and told him to put three more men in the kitchen to assist him, and from that day forth we had plenty of cooks.

Mr. Wing. The hospital was kept filled with patients and we had many edifying conversions. One poor patient (Mr. Wing) had been in my ward about two months suffering from consumption. When he first came he seemed to have been very prejudiced and was short in his answers to the sisters, but as he was very low, I was obliged to go to him frequently. After a week had lapsed, he became as docile and childlike as the others, placing every confidence in the sisters as far as his corporal wants were concerned. For a month or so he seemed to improve, during which time I had entered into conversation with him concerning his family, etc., and in the course of it, having asked him, in what church had he been baptized. He answered in a rather quick manner, "I was never baptized nor do I ever intend to be." Concluding that he did not relish spiritual matters, I changed the subject and did not refer to it again in a hurry, as his state was not alarming. He felt quite at his ease, spoke often of his family, etc. Four months had elapsed, during which time he had witnessed many edifying deaths. Many who had neglected their duty for years, approached the sacraments and became reconciled with our Lord, after which they would proclaim aloud His Mercies to their companions, for the favors he had bestowed on them in bringing them to a place where they could receive the consolations of their Holy Faith.

One poor man having been from Ireland but a short time, would cry out to each patient as he passed by his bed: "For God's sake go and bring me the priest, for I have not been to my duties since I left Ireland, and I want to go to confession and prepare myself to appear in the presence of God." Well! In less than ten minutes I had about twelve patients, all Protestants, who begged to be allowed to go for the priest for that poor man who they feared would die without being gratified. I was obliged to go to him two or three times to calm him and assure him that the priest would come soon. Finally the priest came and administered to him all the last sacraments, after which he became quite composed and died that same night, while repeating some prayer in his native tongue.

But I must return to poor Mr. Wing, who had been feeling much worse. On one occasion he said to me, "Sister, how can you give so much medicine, wait on patients suffering from disease and so many different fevers, without getting sick yourself? I cannot understand what could have induced you ladies to embrace such a life." My time being then very precious on account of the number of very ill patients, I gave him only a brief explanation of the motives which actuated us and the reward that we expected for our labor. He then said, "But sister, do you think that all that is necessary to go to heaven?" Having answered his question, I embraced this opportunity to speak to him again on the necessity of being baptized, to which he now listened most attentively and said that he would like to know something of the Catholic religion. He continued to grow weaker every day, and I gave every spare moment I had to instructing him. Finally he begged me to send for a Catholic priest to baptize him, as he said, "I believe the Catholic church to be the only true one, and in it I wish to die." I sent for the priest, who having been absent at the time did not come. However, the patient began to grow weaker, and as it was my turn to sit up that night, I went to him about twelve o'clock. He then told me that he was much worse, and that he could not die as he had lived, begging me at the same time to give him private baptism. I hesitated for some time when on a sudden his agony commenced. He then made a short profession of faith, and I baptized him. He was speechless for some moments, but perfectly conscious. After his baptism he rallied a little and continued praying, asking us to pray for him, which we did. Towards morning we called again and found him a little better. On inquiring how he felt, he replied, "I feel happy, I can now raise my heart and eyes to God with confidence as to a good and merciful Father. My only desire on earth now is that I may be restored to health and return to my wife and children, that I may have them also baptized. It is so hard for me to leave this world and leave them without the knowledge of God." I reminded him that his prayers for them in heaven would be more efficacious, and that our Lord loved them much more than he did. He then replied, "My God, thy will be done. To Your merciful care and divine Providence I confide them." The next morning the priest came, heard his Confession and gave him Holy Communion. His happiness was then complete and he expired an hour afterwards, praising God for His goodness towards him.

Isaiah Wells. Another patient, (Isaiah Wells) had been suffering sometime from pneumonia. This poor boy was unbaptized and knew nothing of any religion. However, he said [that] his parents called themselves Methodists, yet he did not remember having ever seen them go to church but thought they were very good, and would likely go to heaven the way they were going. I asked him if they were baptized. He said he thought not, and was certain that he had not been. I explained how necessary baptism was for salvation, but as he was very weak, much could not be said to him at a time. Shortly after he asked me to give him an explanation of my belief, which I did. He then said, "Ah! I only wish that my parents heard that, and I am sure they too would be baptized." Then replied, "Yes, sister, I want to be baptized. Will you be kind enough to telegraph my father and ask him to come on immediately, as I wish him to be present at my baptism." In the meantime while waiting for the Father to arrive, when I had a moment I explained to him the principal mysteries of our holy Faith. He continued to grow weaker every day, and as his father had not arrived at the appointed time, I did not fail to tell him of his critical state, asking him at the same time if he had not better be baptized at once, to which he answered, "Oh! sister I only wish that I had been baptized two weeks ago when you first spoke to me of it, that those few days of my life might have been spent in thanksgiving to God for making me His child and an heir of heaven." I then suggested to send for Father at once, but he said, "Since I have waited this long I feel sure that my father will be here tomorrow morning, but should I happen to get worse, I depend on you not to let me die without baptism." I was up that night. The hospital having been filled with sick wounded, it took quite a long time to go around to each different ward. On arriving at my own, I asked the attendant how Isaiah was. He replied, "He is much better. He has been quiet since you last left him and is now, I think, taking a nice sleep." Hearing this I sent the nurse to wait on some of the other sick, and I hurried to Isaiah's bed and found him in his agony, but perfectly conscious. Having intimated to him that his last moments had approached, and our Lord was about to take him to Himself, I asked if I would baptize him, to which he bowed his head in assent and joined his hands making an effort to pray. I then baptized him, after which I made for him some aspirations for the dying. In about three minutes he expired.

Those whose minds were full of prejudice against Catholicity on entering the hospital, if not converted, their prejudice at least was removed. One instance of this I will relate here. Some Protestants who had been in the hospital but a day or so, finding so much of the Catholic spirit prevailing in the wards, and hearing their companions speaking of the instructions, they commenced to ridicule the Catholic religion and give their ideas concerning confessions, etc. There were no Catholics in the ward at the time, but one, who seemed to have had a great deal of faith, but uninstructed and uneducated, consequently unable to answer their questions. However, he satisfied himself with a reply something like the following, "Oh! God help yees, ye ignorant set, shure I would not think it worth my while to tell yees anything." One having asked him if it wasn't true that he could get all his sins forgiven for a dollar, he replied, "I know you couldn't anyhow, fine ways ye are ridiculing the sisters of religion." The other said, "No, I didn't mean to say anything against the sisters. I knew they were all right."

"Well," answered the other "Whatever yees say against the Catholic religion is against them." This ended, they commenced to ask questions concerning praying to the Blessed Virgin and the Saints, etc., etc., none of which the poor man was able to answer. However, they continued, spoke of our manner of praying and denied the Immaculate Conception of our Blessed Mother, when one of the Protestants seeing the poor man's embarrassment, and knowing the contrary, having been at the hospital for a long time, had read a great deal and attended many instructions in the chapel, stood up and defended the cause of our Immaculate Mother most eloquently. The others were perfectly astonished at his sayings, and said they were not aware that he was a Catholic. He replied [that], he was not a Catholic, but he liked justice and truth, and told them the names of the books from which he had derived his knowledge, inviting them at the same time to read for themselves. One of the party who was well acquainted with his family, said to him, "Oh Wright! What would your poor mother say if she had heard you, for anybody could tell that you were Catholic at heart," but the boy replied, "I wish I was a good one." The poor youth being fit for duty and his name having been put on roll, he went to his regiment the next day. Before leaving he came to me and asked me to give him a medal of the Blessed Virgin and remembering his great prejudice when he came to the hospital, I wanted to know why he had desired a medal of the Blessed Virgin. He replied, "I have every confidence in her, for I know that she is all-powerful with her Divine Son, otherwise I would not have asked for it." I gave him one, telling him at the same time, that as long as he would place confidence in her, she would never abandon him. He said that he would wear it as long as he lived, and if he should happen to lose it he would try his best to procure another. I then told him, in case he desired to be baptized and become a Catholic, he might apply to any priest and he would instruct him. He said that it had been his intention to be baptized, but having been summoned off so quickly, he did not have time. After his departure from the hospital, he was engaged in several battles, and whenever opportunity offered, he would send word to me that he had escaped unhurt from the [cannon] balls, and on one occasion he said that the balls had passed through his clothes, without even scratching him. The last time I heard from him, he had served out his time in the Army and was at home with his parents, without having received a single wound. I hope that the poor boy may embrace [Catholicism] and die in the true Faith.

A Youth. Another boy quite young, while helping me one day, said how near dying he was in camp, after he had been wounded. I asked him how he felt and if he wasn't afraid to die. He said, "Oh no, I wasn't afraid."

I then said [that] I suppose you were a very good boy. "Well," he said, "I don't know that I ever did anything very bad." Then I asked, "In what church were you baptized?" "Oh," said he, "I was never baptized at all." I then told him how necessary baptism was, and as he was a good simple youth he listened very attentively and believed all that I had said. When I had finished, he said, "Indeed you ought to tell that to all the boys, for I don't believe that there are half a dozen in the whole ward baptized." After that I gave him books of instruction to read, and referred [him] to the chaplain for baptism.

A Spouse. Another night as I was going through the hospital, I saw in one of the wards a lady who was seated at the bedside of a very sick man. When she heard my footsteps she arose and advanced to meet me, but on her approach, apologized saying that she thought I was the sister of the ward. I asked who belonging to her was sick. She answered, "My husband who I think will not survive through the night." She then asked if I would not go and see him.

After informing her that such was the object of my visit, I stopped to sympathize with her for awhile, and then begged her to go into the medicine room attached to the ward, where there was a bed prepared for her, that she might take a little rest, and I would see that her husband was well cared for. I then inquired if her husband was aware that he was so low, and if he had made any preparations for death. She said, "Oh, dear sister I have not had the courage to speak to my husband of death, or to prepare to meet the Savior." I inquired if he had been baptized? She answered, no, that all his family were Methodists and Baptists and he was the only exception. I, of course, made every allowance for her feelings in not having been able to speak to him of his last end, and said, "Have you any objection to my mentioning the subject to him?" To which she replied, "Oh dear sister, I would be most grateful to you for I know that he is not prepared to meet the Savior." I then left her to go to the patient, whom I found very weak. Having given him some little nourishment which the sister of the ward had left prepared, I told him that I was sorry to find him so low, and asked him how long he had been sick. He told me that he had been in the hospital a considerable time. I spoke to him of the goodness of God in sparing him so long to prepare for Eternity, and supposed that he had profited well of the time. Hearing this he raised his drooping head and looking straight at me said: "This time has passed as the rest of my life." He seemed to have been very intelligent and to have had received a good education. He then asked, "Sister, do you think that I will not get well?" I replied, "I do not wish to disquiet, neither to deceive you, by giving you false hopes of recovery, for I think your case a very critical one at present." He then cried out, "Oh sister, if I could only see a Catholic priest, but it is too late!" Not having suggested this in any way to him I was perfectly astonished and said: "Why I did not know you were a Catholic." He replied that he had not been a Catholic, but now believed the Catholic church to be the true one, and in it desired to be baptized, but repeated again, "I am too late, too late!" Having encouraged him a little, I said that I would send for the priest right away, and he said, "May God bless you, sister. It was our Lord that sent you to me this night, but what will my wife say? She will never give her consent to my becoming a Catholic." I then told him that it was his wife who had asked me to speak to him and therefore did believe she would not have the least objection to his acting according to the dictates of his own conscience. He then asked if I would mention it to her, which I consented to do, thinking that she would be delighted to see her husband in such beautiful dispositions. I went to the room and told her all that had taken place, but she repeated as soon as I had finished, "A Catholic! Never shall I permit him to die a Catholic and disgrace my family." She could not understand how he had ever thought of such a thing, and that I certainly must have misunderstood him. Saying this she left the room, went to him and said, "My dear, what do you mean? Did you say that you wished to see a Catholic priest?" "Ah, yes! Mary I do wish to have a Catholic priest baptize me. The Catholic church, Mary, is the only true one. In it I wish to die." Here she interrupted him saying, "You are perfectly crazy, James, you are full of brandy." He declared to her that he had not tasted brandy, as it did not agree with him, the doctor discontinued it the day before. He continued: "Mary, for God sake allow me to follow the dictates of my own conscience. Should I die as I am, I will never be saved." But, she replied, "I shall never consent to your being baptized in the Catholic Church. What! do you want to disgrace me." He replied, "Ah, Mary have I ever refused you anything, or have you ever had a wish that I did not endeavor to gratify? Don't then for God's sake, don't oppose that which I deem necessary for salvation." She replied, "Do you know what you are talking about? Don't you know that it is too late for you to think of baptism?" Here the poor man turning to sister said, "Do you think that I am too late?" After assuring him of the mercies of God, that it is never too late to repent, and that God is ever ready to receive us even at the eleventh hour, provided we come to Him with a contrite and humble heart, the poor man joined his hands and made aloud an "Act of Contrition" for his past life. Here she interrupted him again and reminded him that the Scriptures said, "Do penance and be baptized," "Now what penance are you able to do?

Nothing," she answered herself, "Nothing, so you must die as you are." To all of these questions I answered for him, seeing that the poor man was too weak to talk. "You are willing to offer your life in expiation for your past sins?" Here he raised his eyes and hands towards heaven and said, "Yes, My God I offer You my body and soul. Do with me as you please. Ah! My God, how could I have spent my life in forgetfulness of You, never again will I forsake you for creatures. Should I get well, the rest of my life shall be spent in Thy service, but should it rather please You to accept the desire which I now feel of serving You on earth, then take me if You please. Here I am ready to suffer, or die, just as it pleases you." At this he looked pitifully at her and said, "Ah! Mary, it is foolish indeed to have lived for the world. Soon my poor soul will be summoned before its Maker, then let me entreat you once more to grant my last and only request." She replied, "Don't ask me that again, for I never shall grant it." Here I said that the poor man had already talked too much and we must leave him to take some repose, telling the wife at the same time that she, too, was very tired and must like [to lie] down and take a little rest. I then gave instructions to the nurse to wait on him, in case I would not be back again that night as I had several very sick persons to attend to.

This was joyful news for the poor wife, but the poor patient seemed to be in perfect agony at our leaving him. On this the sister who accompanied me, went to speak to the lady to divert her attention, while I told the poor man that I would return in about a half hour. We then left the ward, and our doing so dispersed the lady's fears, and she went off to enjoy a good sound sleep, but before retiring directed the nurses to knock at the door of her room in case her husband was dying. We returned to the ward in about an hour's time, but it was too late to send to the city for a priest. After giving him the necessary instructions I told him that it was not necessary to have the consent of his wife to be baptized. He then said, "Sister, baptize me for our Lord's sake. I feel that I cannot survive until morning." Seeing him in a dying condition, I baptized him conditionally at about three o'clock in the morning, and he breathed out his last sigh most fervently in the evening of that same day.

Andrew Hopkins. Another patient, Andrew Hopkins, whose baptism we had the happiness of witnessing in our chapel, had been very sick and suffering very severely for two months. As soon as he was able to go about, he was sent to assist me in carrying the extra diet from the kitchen and in the performance of sundry little offices. Andrew would daily ask some questions regarding religion, to which he generally received brief replies as his and my time were so occupied. However, he would generally conclude by something like the following, "I wish that I was a Christian, but I think God must have never intended me to become one. I have tried so often already, but there is so much to be done to be a good one, that I think I could never go through the half of it. I never was baptized, and have always been knocked about the world, up to the time of my entering the Army." He lost his parents while yet very young and since then had no one to take an interest in him, still he showed signs of a good disposition, and was attracted to the practice of virtue more than many who have had the advantages of a good education. I gave him the *Catholic Christian Instructed* to read, telling him that he would find therein the way to know how to love and serve God, and become a good Christian.[22] After perusing it, he immediately applied to Father McGrane for baptism. After a long conversation, the priest admired very much his disposition and told him to come to him that same evening after vespers, at which time he gave him an instruction and immediately after baptized him, fearing that he would be sent to his regiment, and it seemed providential for on the next day he received orders to be in readiness the day following. He regretted very much having had to leave without being better instructed, that he might be able as he said himself to instruct others, should he happen with any like himself. He said he could not complain. Our Lord had done so much for him, and with what different feelings he could now enter the battlefield, as he felt that he was a child of God, and had a right to his place in heaven. He went cheerfully to perform any duty, offering all to our Lord in thanksgiving for his great favor. I gave him a medal and told him at the same time to place himself under the protection of our Blessed Mother, and that she would obtain all for him, and in case his regiment would stop at any place for a considerable time, he might apply to the nearest priest and ask to be instructed for his First Communion. With this hope he was quite delighted, and left the next day for his regiment.

In the bustle of hospital life, poor Andrew had been forgotten, when a letter arrived from Reverend Mr. [Thomas R.] Butler, showing us that he did not neglect to profit by every means of being instructed in the religion which he had happily embraced.

---

[22] This may refer to the following work by Rev. Richard Challoner, *The Catholic Christian Instructed in the Sacraments, Sacrifice, Ceremonies and Observances of the Church by way of Question and Answers* (London: Keating, Brown & Co., 1819). First published in 1737, probably by Thomas Meighan, this became a standard text for instruction for nearly a century.

August 8th

Mr. Peterson (Ward T). A very sad death occurred a few days since in ward "T". The name of the person was Peterson. He was a veteran of many battles and had his arm torn out from the shoulders by a ball. The wound looked favorable during the first six days, but on the seventh commenced sloughing. Afterwards the artery gave way and he had two severe hemorrhages. It was then decided by a consultation of physicians that an incision should be made higher up in order to secure the artery in a healthy part. All again appeared bright for the poor sufferer and he was very grateful. Stimulants and tonics were frequently given to sustain life, and sister was constantly watching the least change or movement. But alas, while washing his wound the artery again burst forth, besmearing the wall, bed and face of the poor patient. What was now to be done? Another incision could not be made without the loss of life. As a last resort it was decided the artery must be compressed tightly by the fingers until a clot of blood would be formed. This duty was assigned to the cadets, fourteen in number, who were to take turns day and night, thirty minutes at a time. The least change (from the proper place) of the fingers would cause the blood to reflow (and as the sufferer himself remarked) the next time that the artery would bleed he would surely die. He remained on his back the whole time perfectly conscious of his danger, and yet no prayer escaped him, nor desire for baptism and no apparent thought but the anxious desire to recover, which his pale and sunken features so vividly expressed. It was [very sad] to see him die in this way, and Sister Elizabeth did all she could to excite him to contrition and to make the sacrifice of his life to God, who is the good Father of all, and to place all confidence in Him.[23] He continued in this state from eight o'clock in the morning until six of the next day, when the moment arrived for a cadet to change his painful position. But the removing of the fingers as was apprehended caused the blood to gush forth anew and all that could be done was hastily to stuff a handkerchief into the open wound. At this moment sister again inquired if he did not desire baptism and thereby become a [child of] God. He replied that he did and assented to her doing so. A moment after and he was no more. He never professed any religion, and knew very little of the goodness of God, therefore, we trust that He accepted this, his weak desire for baptism in his last moments.

August 16th

Harry Curren (Ward Y). A patient in ward "Y," named Henry Curren, was baptized last night (the Feast of the Assumption of our Blessed Lady).

---

[23] This may refer to Sister Elizabeth Griffin (1832-1899) who worked at Satterlee Hospital.

He had suffered much, particularly during the last two days, and could not take any nourishment. However, sister did not think him in immediate danger and spoke to him in the evening about his salvation and inquired if he did not desire to see a clergyman. He replied that he did not, as they could not do him any good. Sister then reminded him of the uncertainty of his recovery and that if he died without being baptized he could never go to heaven. He promised to reflect on her advice, saying at the same time that he had never attended church or professed any religion, and that his parents were Methodists but did not live up to it. Sister made a few remarks and then bid him good night. About half-past eight a message came from the ward for sister to hasten back as quickly as possible, that Henry was dying and desired to see her. Sister Julia went with Sister Angeline immediately, and when they arrived at his bedside, he said to them in the most supplicating tones, "O pray for me sister, I feel that I am dying!"[24] Sister desired him to place all confidence in our good God, that He was a good Father to the repentant sinner, and that He never rejected anyone, even in the last hour, if they returned to Him with their whole heart. Sister inquired if he wished to be baptized, and he replied, "O yes! Baptize me in the religion to which you belong." He then repeated with her the "Our Father, Hail Mary, [and] Acts of Faith, Hope, Charity and Contrition" most fervently, then professed his belief in the principal mysteries of our Holy Religion, after which sister baptized him. He inquired for the sister's name and begged that she would pray for him. He then said, "O Lord have mercy on my poor soul," and repeated again with Sister Angeline, "Jesus, Mary and Joseph, etc.," then falling back gently on his pillow breathed his last sigh, about ten minutes after receiving baptism.

Was not this a consoling death! Praise be to God!

Feast of the Exaltation of the Holy Cross.

This morning we had the consolation of witnessing the baptism of a German named Paul Hegan, aged 27 years. He came to the hospital on the 5th of July, and was severely wounded in the arm. However, it healed rapidly and in a few weeks he was able to visit the Protestant chapel. About two weeks after he asked a little Catholic boy who slept next to him in the ward, to go with him to meeting on Sunday afternoon. The boy replied that he could not go but would he not come with him to sisters' chapel. At first he refused but afterwards consented. They were greatly attached to each other and belonged to the same regiment, which was the cause, I suppose, of his yielding so readily. Our devotions on Sunday afternoons

---

[24] Possibly Sister Angela Mahoney, (b.1840), and Sister Julia Fitzgerald (1840-1920).

were, as you are aware, the rosary and vespers [in Latin], which of course he could not understand, as he could not speak a word of English. Our Blessed Mother must surely have interceded in his behalf, for he left the chapel determined to go again, and asked his little friend, when there would be meeting. He told him on Tuesday, and Paul was one of the first in the chapel that morning, making the sign of the cross and taking holy water like the others. He remained kneeling in a very humble posture during the whole time of service. He told his little friend (whose name was Fred) that he would like very much to see a German priest, and that he intended going to the sister's chapel in future, which he continued doing while he remained in the hospital. Little Fred who acted as interpreter for him, came quite delighted with the good news to sister and desired to know when the German priest would come. Sister said, "I expect the German priest here on Thursday to hear German confessions and that he would then have a good opportunity to see him if he wished." Paul repaired to the chapel at two o'clock Thursday and remained waiting until nearly five, but no priest came, having been unavoidably detained. The next morning, however, he said Mass for us and heard confessions. Paul remained in the chapel but did not go to the priest, as the thought occurred to him that he must begin his confession at once, and not knowing what to do, he thought better to defer it until he was a little more instructed. Sister gave him a medal of our Blessed Mother and a German prayer book.

The following Thursday, he had a long conversation with the priest, who said he found him in most excellent dispositions and promised to send him a catechism which would instruct him on baptism. On the following Monday, September 14, he was baptized. Afterwards he requested us to give him some books that would enable him to prepare for his First Communion. He remained only a few days longer, during which time he had the happiness of making his First Communion. He received orders to return to his regiment, only ten minutes before leaving the hospital.

Michael Davis (Ward N). Three more soldiers made their First Communion within the past week. One of them, a young man named Michael Davis in ward N, was born in Ireland and lost his mother while very young. He came to this country with his father, shortly after his mother's death, and the father squandered all that he possessed. Michael, soon after his arrival was employed by a sea captain, and from that time he was in the company of those who professed no religion.

Having entered the Army two years ago, he was brought here from the battle of Gettysburg with a severe wound in his hand. He told sister at once of the careless life he had led, and promised her that he would now begin to prepare for a general confession. Sister gave him a Catechism, a Prayer book and a Medal, desiring him to put himself under the protection of the Blessed Virgin.

In order to probe his wound, he was put under the influence of alcohol. While in that state, he imagined that he was sentenced to hell and that those who were standing around him were demons waiting to receive his soul. He cried aloud most pitifully, "Don't kill me yet! I am not ready to die!" He said afterwards that he could never forget the horrible feelings he had experienced and that if it had been all real, he could not have been more frightened.

He was now more anxious than ever to prepare for his First Communion. When sister asked him why he did not avail himself of a pass to the city in the afternoon like the others, he replied, that he was afraid of yielding to temptation like so many of his companions. On another occasion, when he was urged to go to the reading room, where there was a grand concert to be given, he avoided answering them, and watching his opportunity, he asked sister if there would be anything wrong in his going, fearing, as he said, that it might be a snare to draw him to their meeting.

His companions often made him the subject of ridicule and would attack his religion indirectly. Then, again, they would pretend that he was influenced by the regard which he felt for the sisters. To all their taunts he made no reply. He made his First Communion on the 19th of September and from that day forward, until he left the hospital, he continued as edifying and fervent as he had commenced, and he promised on leaving, that he would always try to be faithful to the practice of our Holy Religion.

September 26th

Robert McGill (Ward "C"). Robert McGill, a patient in ward "C" was baptized this morning. He had been sick a long time of typhoid fever. Previous to his baptism, he was much prejudiced against the Catholic religion, although his wife was a practicing Catholic.[25] She was constant in her attentions to him but avoided speaking to him on the subject of religion, fearing to irritate him instead of benefitting him. She begged the sister to mention it to him, saying that he understood the Catholic religion very well, but pride and regard for his family deterred him from embracing it.

Doctor [Nathaniel] West, the Protestant chaplain, had been with him the day before, exhorting him to place all his hopes for salvation in the Lord, and promised to return again. His poor wife was in great distress. She

---

[25] One who practices Roman Catholicism in daily life, e.g. a practicing Catholic.

could not make up her mind to see him die a Protestant, and she continued praying fervently to our Blessed Mother to obtain his conversion.

The same evening the doctor pronounced him incurable and said he could not live through the night. Consequently, the sister remained with him until twelve o'clock. When all had become quiet in the ward, the sister inquired if he was perfectly satisfied to die as he had lived, or did he not rather desire to be baptized in the True Church, of which his wife was a member. He replied, "I do, and wish to see a priest at once."

We sent immediately for the priest but he did not arrive until morning. At the sick man's request, sister baptized him conditionally, after a brief explanation of the sacrament. I regretted very much the absence of his wife. Towards morning, he revived a little and was very anxious for the priest. As soon as the priest arrived, he performed the ceremonies of baptism. He afterwards heard his confession, administered Holy Communion, and anointed him, then said some prayers and aspirations, which the patient repeated very fervently. On leaving, the priest bade him farewell, expressing his hope to meet him in a better world, urging him at the same time to keep himself calm and recollected and left him in the very best dispositions.

A few hours after the priest had left, the minister came, saying as usual, "Well, my friend, how are you this morning?" To which the sick man replied, "I do not want to see you now, Sir, I was baptized in the Catholic church last night." This he said in the presence of his wife. The minister soon left and addressing sister, repeated what had been said, inquiring if such were the case, if so, it was very strange.

Sister replied that all enjoy liberty of conscience here as well as elsewhere and that her patient wished to become a Catholic, believing that in that church, alone, he could be saved. The minister appeared nettled and went off saying, he wished her patient God-speed. The poor wife returned home as her husband was apparently much better that evening and she promised to come in the morning.

After seeing everything provided for him for the night, sister called George Stewart, a convert, who belonged to the same ward, to remain with him during the night. About ten o'clock a change took place for the worse, and before one o'clock, he breathed his last sigh. The next day the poor wife arrived and was inconsolable, to think, she said, that neither sister nor herself was with him when he died. However, in a short time she became more reconciled, after reflecting that if he had died at home as she at first desired, he would have been surrounded by his friends and in all probability would have died a Protestant.

October 25th

Charles Durkin (Ward W). Two of the patients made their First Communion this morning. One patient, named Charles Durkin has been in Ward W since the 17th of July. The other, Henry Conkle, I will speak of another time.

Charlie was brought here severely wounded in the thigh and appeared to suffer intensely. When any of the sisters performed the least service for him, he would express his gratitude and say that if he should get well, he would turn over a new leaf and become a better man. He was taken very ill, and the doctor entertained very little hope of his recovery. He appeared to be conscious of his danger; having spoken to sister of his great desire to live that he might reform and join some church. Sister inquired if he had been baptized. He replied in the negative. She then asked if he knew the necessity of baptism without which there is no salvation, quoting at the same time some of the Sacred Scripture which commands baptism.

Having acknowledged his ignorance on the subject of religion, clasping both hands together, he exclaimed, "For God's sake, sister, do not let me slip out of your hands without baptism!" Sister asked him whom he desired to see. He replied that he would like to see the chaplain who says Mass for the sisters. A few hours after, he was baptized by the Reverend Father McGrane and expressed lively sentiments of faith, gratitude, and contrition.

The doctor, still considering him a hopeless case, appointed a night watch to notify him of the least change. Before retiring, sister gave him a medal of our Blessed Mother, recounting to the man miracles that had been effected by wearing it in Her honor, and added that if he wore it with confidence, perhaps our Blessed Mother would obtain his cure. He listened attentively, then eagerly grasped the medal, promising to wear it faithfully. After making a few aspirations with him, sister left him for the night, not expecting, however, to see him alive in the morning. Thanks to our Blessed Mother, she found him much better, but in much trouble as he "had lost his piece," he said, "and feared that someone had taken it." The sister soon found it which afforded him much joy.

The doctor was much astonished on his arrival in the morning to see the improvement that had taken place. Poor Charlie meanwhile procured a string long enough to reach his wounded leg, upon which he put his precious "piece." He was now fully convinced that it was our Blessed Mother that obtained his cure. He improved rapidly and was able to walk on crutches in a few weeks. This was more remarkable as there were many others in the same wards whose wounds had undergone the same treatment, although not considered so dangerous, and they were considered to be doing very well though the patients were not able to leave their beds.

Charlie's first visit was to the chapel, and he now rises at five o'clock every morning to be in time for Mass. He listened to the instructions of the priest with the greatest attention, and counted the time until the following Sunday. After a month, his wife visited him in the hospital. He then informed her of his conversion to the Catholic Faith and told her how much happier he had been since it. His greatest anxiety was on account of the displeasure he feared his wife would show towards the sisters, however, his mind was soon relieved on receipt of a letter from her, expressing her kind feelings and sincere thanks to the sisters.

He petitioned for a furlough, in order to have his children baptized, and if possible, to convince his wife of the great advantage of being a member of the One True Church. This he readily effected, contrary to his expectations, she consented to apply at once for instructions, and to have their children baptized.

He returned quite pleased and grateful for the many favors he had received from the Almighty, through the intercession of our Blessed Mother, to whom, he believed, he owed everything. He applied himself at once to prepare for his First Communion. Sister Amelia [Davis] gave him instructions, daily, and he made his First Communion on the 25th of October in the most edifying dispositions.[26] He and his companion sobbed like children, and they appeared unable to restrain their tears.

Henry Conkle of Ward W. The history of the other patient, Henry Conkle, is no less interesting. He was very quiet and retiring in his manner and at first, avoided speaking to the sisters. One day, while sitting at the bedside of a young man, who was suffering much, he took up from the table a book, *The Hours of the Passion.* [27] The youth told him that it belonged to the sister. Having obtained permission to read it, he sought every opportunity to ask some questions about the Catholic religion and desired a book that would instruct him more fully.

---

[26] Sister Amelia Davis was the assistant to Sister Gonzaga Grace, who was the Sister Servant at Satterlee Hospital.

[27] This may refer to an early version of the following work: Cowper: *Meditations on the Supper of Our Lord and the Hours of the Passion* (Early English Text Society: Boydell & Brewer, n.d.).

Sister gave him *The Catholic Christian Instructed, Ground of the Old Religion proved from the Scripture*, and several books equally instructive. He requested sister to explain to him the devotion of the Stations, to which afterwards he had a great devotion. He commenced attending Mass and vespers from that time, and almost every day, spent an hour in the chapel, although he frequently said that he felt unworthy to be there. We often surprised him when he was bathed in tears and praying most fervently.

At last, he told sister that he was determined to be a Catholic, no matter what the consequences would be. He had never professed any religion before and had always said that he would never join any church until he could be convinced that he had found the True One, and now, he was sure he had discovered the True Church, and desired to be baptized at once.

The Reverend Father hesitated, however, fearing that he was influenced by the sisters; also, his wife being a Protestant, he dreaded the consequences, in case he was not sincere. But the poor man's fervor and perseverance gave sufficient evidence of his sincerity and the Reverend Father consented to baptize him on the Feast of Saint Teresa [of Avila].[28]

From that time he became more fervent than ever, frequently spending hours in the chapel and shedding an abundance of tears. In truth, he seemed to experience some of those emotions of love, which made Saint Augustine [or Hippo] cry out, "Too late have I known Thee, too late have I loved Thee, O, Beauty, ever ancient and ever new!"

He told sister that he could not express his happiness, since he had found God, in the one True Church, where alone he is to be found. He made his First Communion on the 25th of October, as before mentioned, and immediately after procured a furlough to visit his wife and children and inform them of his new religion.

He told his wife, in answer to her fears, that this change should not separate them but, on the contrary, it would oblige him to become a better husband. His wife had not the least knowledge, whatever, about the Catholic religion, and was not prejudiced, readily consenting to study and read for herself. Many of his friends, (all good simple country people), begged him to leave them some books of instruction, which he did. His daughter insisted on having his rosary, and all were pleased at the accounts he gave of the Catholic religion and the sisters.

---

[28] October 15.

He feels sure that his wife and children will all become Catholics, and full of these pleasing anticipations for the future he returned home, and is now preparing for confirmation, which we hope to have administered here before Christmas.

Other Patients. Two more patients belonging to Sister Angela's ward have become Catholics.[29] One of them, (the sick boy alluded to before), is remarkably fervent. He came to the hospital with a very severe wound in the face, just below the eye. Sister undertook the charge of dressing it and during these moments, she spoke to him of our Lord's sufferings, and told him to try and offer all that he then suffered in union with our Divine Savior, in atonement for the sins he might have committed in his past life.

He listened attentively for he had never been baptized and had lost both his parents. Day after day, the simple country boy would ask sister to tell him more about the sufferings of Our Lord, and what he must do to believe, so that he could join that church that taught such beautiful doctrines. He often requested sister to read to him some of the Meditations on the Passion. Sister also taught him the Catechism and his prayers. The other patient, who had received the first impressions of grace at his bed, assisted him very much, by telling him what he had learned by reading and from the priest's instructions. They used to spend hours conversing on the subject and whenever an opportunity presented itself, they would ask sister to explain anything which they could not understand.

The Feast of Saint Teresa arrived and poor No. 7, as sister called him, was still too weak to walk up to the chapel, for he had hoped to have been able to receive baptism with his friend. The disappointment was almost too much for his weak state. One could scarcely believe that he would regret the delay so deeply, but when sister reminded him that such a want of patience was very unlike the silent endurance of our Lord under His sufferings, he immediately dried his tears and endeavored to become reconciled, but not until sister promised to have him baptized on the 27th of October, Feast of Sts. Simon and Jude.

From that time, he visited the Blessed Sacrament daily, and had the greatest devotion to the Stations of the Cross which sister was obliged to explain to him. She gave him a crucifix, which he constantly kept about his person. We had the Forty Hours Devotion on Sunday, November 14th, and he was one of the first in the chapel that morning, but the effort of rising so early caused him to feel, during the remainder of the day, so fatigued that

---

[29] Possibly Sister Angela Mahoney.

he was not able to attend the instructions in the afternoon on the Institution of the Holy Eucharist.[30] However, on the following Sunday, Feast of the Presentation, he made his First Communion and is now preparing with his friend for the Sacrament of Confirmation.[31]

James Cook. James Cook, the third mentioned patient of the same ward, had been studying and reading much longer than either of the two, and desired to read several books unfavorable to Catholic Doctrine, before deciding, acknowledging, however, that he believed the Catholic religion to be the only true one. We observed that he was very devout to the Blessed Mother and he recited, daily, the *Hail Mary*, having acquired the habit by means of a small white rosary which he had found on the battlefield and which he supposed belonged to one of the dead soldiers. He admired it and took it with him, without knowing the use of it. When he came to the hospital, he showed it to sister and asked an explanation, and this was his first lesson in the Catholic Doctrine.

He admired the devotion to the Mother of our Savior, and said that he would now value his beads more than ever, applying himself at once to learn the above named prayer. After he had read many controversial works and discussed the subject with the priest, grace finally triumphed, and he was regenerated in the holy waters of baptism on the 27th of October and made his First Communion on the 25th of November. He is still here and is a model for some of the Catholics, many of whom alas, forget to practice the religion of their fathers.

Newly Baptized Patient (Ward L). Another baptism took place sometime ago, in ward "L." This patient only consented to be baptized when the sister was about to raise him up in bed as he requested, and she discovered that he was bleeding to death. His wound had often bled before and it was understood that a reopening of the wound would be instant death. The sister told him that he had but a few moments to live. He asked to be baptized as he said "He wanted to go to heaven." He then cried out in a loud voice, "O! Lord have mercy on my soul and grant that since I cannot see my parents on earth, I may see them on the other side of the Jordan,"

---

[30] For several centuries, the traditional Forty Hours Devotion has been celebrated in parishes as a time of annual renewal and prayer. It is a parish devotion of public veneration of the Most Holy Eucharist for an extended period during which a procession, special prayers, sermons, and may be held for the congregation. This devotion originated in the early part of the sixteenth century at the Church of the Holy Sepulcher in Milan, Italy. It is probably a commemoration of the forty hours that Christ's body lay in the tomb between his death and resurrection.

[31] Feast of the Presentation is February 2.

Cooks' tempers flare—Military Hospital, Winchester, VA.

and immediately expired. Such deaths although not as fervent as we would wish, leave at least some hope of their salvation.

Albert Brian (Ward O) and Jesse Robinson (Ward G). On the 17th of January, there were two baptized in the chapel: one, a patient from ward "O," named Albert Brian. The other a patient from ward "G," named Jesse Robinson, was brought here from the battlefield suffering from Camp Fever and diarrhea, which reduced him very much. After a few months treatment, he [Jesse Robinson] improved very rapidly and was able to go about for some time. He had a relapse and the doctor despaired of his recovery. Sister spoke to him of the necessity of preparing to appear before our Lord. He told her that he was a Methodist and felt no anxiety about the future. However, our Lord did not permit him to die in this state. He grew better every day, and was soon able to go home on furlough.

On his return, he told sister that he was delighted to find himself again at the hospital. He seemed thoughtful and anxious for some days. One evening as sister was about to leave the ward, he said, "For some time past, I have wanted to speak to you about religious matters, but had not the courage to do so. I would like to belong to the church you belong to, as I am convinced it is the only true one." Sister told him to reflect well on the step he was about to take. He replied that he had done so, and wished to be instructed and baptized as soon as possible.

Sister gave him some books of instruction, and a few days after, the priest baptized him. After baptism, he said: "I never felt so happy in all my life! I am now ready for any duty they choose to put me at." A short time after, he made his First Communion, and continued to go every time the sisters went. If the sisters approached four times in the week, he would also go.

The priest told sister to tell him kindly not to go to Holy Communion so often. Once a month was sufficient for a soldier. He replied simply, that he thought he could go as often as the sister, if his conscience did not reproach him with anything. So great was his love for our Lord in the Holy Communion that it was a great sacrifice for him to make. However, he continued to lead an edifying life, hearing Mass daily, not caring what his Protestant companions would say to him. He wore the medal of our Blessed Mother with great devotion. Before he had the happiness of being confirmed, he received orders to leave the hospital, and as he bade us farewell, he said, "I shall never forget all that God has done for me, and I shall ever, with the help of God and His Blessed Mother, live and die a good Christian."

During the holy season of Lent, the priest gave many beautiful instructions, reminding the soldiers that it would be the last for many of them. He asked, "Where are those who were in their midst last Lent?" "They are no more. But where are their souls? If they have been faithful, they are now with God. If you expect a glorious resurrection you must lead a life of penance and mortification." Many of them would soon return to their regiments. How favored they had been by Almighty God, who had brought them to this hospital, in preference to so many others, who had died on the battlefield without a moment's warning, and others, who were in hospitals where they had not the advantage of hearing Mass, etc. He exhorted them to profit by this opportunity, or God would call them to an account for abusing His graces. All appeared indeed very grateful to Father P. McGrane, for the interest he manifested in their regard.

March 28th

Enos J. Kitchen (Ward J). This morning the priest baptized a young man from ward "J," named Enos J. Kitchen, who was a contract nurse here, and who, previous to his coming here, was a soldier in the Confederate Army. He took the name of Joseph, when he was baptized. He made his First Communion and was confirmed, and like our former convert, mentioned above, he went to Holy Communion whenever he saw the sisters approach.

The priest noticed him and told him kindly that he must go to see him before he went to Holy Communion. He still remains in the hospital a practical Catholic.[32]

St. Joseph's Hospital

On 15 March 1862, I was sent from St. Mary's Orphan Asylum, Baltimore, Maryland, to join Sister Gonzaga's band of sisters for a Military Hospital in Buttanwood, Pennsylvania, but the surgeon in charge who had asked for our sisters was in the meantime removed to another state, and his successor not having shown any desire for the service of the sisters, we did not go there. I was then sent to <u>St. Joseph's Hospital, Philadelphia, Pa.</u> where they had received a great number of sick and soldiers, and not having a sufficient number of sisters to wait on them, nor beds to accommodate all, we were obliged to arrange temporarily, as at that time there were not many Military Hospitals built, and after the first battle they had to crowd the small hospitals that were erected with the sick and wounded.

The poor creatures were in a deplorable condition. I believe the sisters were up the greater part of the night, washing them and giving them refreshments. To look at them you would hardly take them for white men, they had gone through so much and had been so neglected, for at the commencement of the war they did not take a sufficiency of anything to the fields to supply their wants. It would seem almost incredible from their own observation that human nature could stand all that they had endured, and one who was laboring for our Lord would feel ashamed to think of her own rest or convenience, while waiting on those who had undergone so much through love for their country.

Here the soldiers were entirely free from military restraint. During my stay at this hospital which was only three months, four of the soldiers died in a very edifying manner. From there I was sent to Sister Gonzaga to join her band of sisters for Satterlee Hospital, West Philadelphia, Pennsylvania, for which the government had solicited Reverend Father Burlando for fifty sisters to attend the poor sick and wounded in that large hospital.

---

[32] Refers to one who professes the Roman Catholic faith and puts it into practice in good deeds of charity of justice, e.g., members of the Knights of Columbus.

VIRGINIA
Manassas, Gordonsville, Danville
and Lynchburg

Manassas. Left Richmond for Manassas on the 9th of January, 1862, at the solicitation of Doctor [Thomas] Williams, Medical Director of the Army of the Potomac.[1] We were five in number and found on taking possession, 500 patients, sick and wounded of both armies. Mortality was very great, as the poor sick had been very much neglected. The wards were in a most deplorable condition, and strongly resisted all efforts of the broom to which they had long been strangers, and the aid of a shovel was found necessary. At best, they were but poor protection against the inclemency of the season, and being scattered, we were often obliged to go through snow over a foot deep, to wait on the sick.

For our own accommodation we had one small room, which served for dormitory, chapel, etc., etc., which when we were fortunate enough to get a chaplain, the Holy Sacrifice was daily offered in a little corner of our humble domicile. The kitchen, to which what we called our refectory was attached, was, I do not think I exaggerate when I say a quarter of a mile from our room. Often it was found more prudent to be satisfied with two meals, than to trudge through the snow for a third, which at best, was not very inviting, for the culinary department was not under our control, but under that of Negroes, who had a decided aversion for cleanliness.

On an average, ten died every day, and of this number, I think I may safely say, four were baptized, either by Fathers Smulders or Teeling, or by our sisters.[2] It happened several times that men, who had been until then totally ignorant of our faith, and I may say even of God, sent to us in the middle of the night, when they found that they were dying, and begged for baptism, which astonished as well as consoled and edified us.

On the 15th of March we received orders from General Johnson to pack up quietly and be ready to leave on six hours' notice, as it was found necessary to retreat from that quarter. Oh, the horrors of war! We had scarcely left our post than the whole camp was one mass of flame, and the bodies of those who died that day were consumed.

---

[1] Sister Mary Angela Heath (1830-1912) wrote accounts of the Daughters of Charity at Manassas, Gordonsville, Danville, Lynchburg, and Richmond.

[2] Father Egidius (Giles) Smulders, C.Ss.R. (1815-1900), and Rev. John Teeling (?-1870) of Richmond.

Gordonsville. Our next field of labor was the Military Hospital, Gordonsville. We were but three in number and found 200 patients very sick, pneumonia and typhoid fever prevailing. Here again privations were not wanting. The sick were very poorly provided for, though the mortality was not as great as at Manassas. We had a small room which served again for all purposes. One week we lay on the floor without beds; our habits and a shawl loaned us by the doctor serving for covering. The refectory as far as distance is concerned, was more convenient, but accommodations were even less extravagant than at Manassas. The trunk of a tree was our table and the rusty tin cups and plates which were used in turn by doctors, sisters and Negroes, were very far from exciting a great relish for what they contained.

Father Smulders who was chaplain at that time received about twenty-five into the communion of the church, some of whom died shortly after. One morning as Sister Estelle [Gibbons] was visiting her patients before Mass, one called from the lower end of the ward, "Oh! Sister, sister do come and save me, let me die in the church that you sisters belong to. I believe all that you believe."

Father Smulders who was vesting for Mass, was at first unwilling to wait on him until after, but as sister insisted that no time was to be lost; he went and baptized him, and as we knelt at the "Et Verbum Caro factum. est.," he expired.

Danville. The approach of the Federals compelled us to leave Gordonsville on Easter Sunday, and we retreated "in good order" to Danville. Having been obliged to stop in Richmond sometime, we did not enter on the new field until the 2nd of May. Here we found 400 sick, much better provided for than in Manassas or Gordonsville. The sisters had a nice little house, which would have been a kind of luxury had it not been the abode of innumerable rats, of whom we stood in the greatest awe, for they seemed to be proprietors of the mansion. During the night shoes, stockings, etc., were carried off, and indeed, safe we did not feel for our fingers and toes which we often found, on waking, locked in the teeth of our bold visitors.

Most of our patients were Catholic, at least in name, for many had almost forgotten their duties as such, but it was our consolation to see them entering again upon them with the simplicity of children. The zeal of good Father Smulders led many to a knowledge of our holy religion and about 50 were baptized.

Lynchburg. In November, the Medical Director removed our hospital to Lynchburg as there were no means of heating that in Danville. Our number had increased to five as the hospital was larger and contained 1,000 patients, whom we found in a most pitiful condition.[3] The persons who were in charge had a very good will, but not the means of carrying it out, and although the fund was ample, the poor patients were half starved owing entirely to mismanagement.

As we passed through the ward the first time, accompanied by the doctor, a man from the lower end called out, "Lady, oh Lady, for God's sake give me a piece of bread." To give you an idea of the care the sick had received, it will be sufficient to say that, though the whole establishment had been cleaned for our reception some of the sisters swept up the vermin on the dust pan. The doctors soon placed everything under our control, and with a little economy, the patients were well provided for, and order began to prevail.

Father [Louis-Hippolyte] Gache a zealous and holy priest, effected much good and removed many prejudices from the minds of those whom a faulty education had made enemies—bitter enemies of our holy faith.[4] During the three years that we remained in Lynchburg, he baptized 100. Of those who resumed the practice of duties long neglected, we kept no account, but scarcely a day passed without witnessing the return of some poor prodigal.

During the year 1863, the Methodists and Baptists had a grand revival in Lynchburg, and every day members of both, ladies and gentlemen came to induce the officers and privates to attend, hoping to effect their conversion. Meeting one in whom they seemed to take a particular interest, I asked if their zeal and perseverance had not made at least some impression. He answered, no, that the modest silence of our sisters spoke far more loudly than the enthusiastics even of his own persuasion.

---

[3] For a description of General Hospital #3 where the Daughters of Charity served, see Gache, War Letters, 149; 167. General Hospital #3 which had two sites: the Old Lynchburg College building (Division #1) and Ferguson's Tobacco Factory (Division #2). The sisters also assisted in the Pest House under the direction of John J. Terrell, M.D., in 1862. The sisters remained after the battle of Lynchburg to nurse the wounded and veterans as the war progressed.

[4] Father Gache was a Jesuit priest who esteemed the Daughters of Charity for their selfless service to the sick and wounded. See Louis-Hippolyte Gache, *A Frenchman, A Chaplain, A Rebel: The War Letters of Rev. Louis-Hippolyte Gache*, trans., Cornelius M. Buckley (Chicago: Loyola University Press, 1981). Hereafter cited as Gache, War Letters.

The approach of the Federals placed our hospital in imminent danger and it was decided to move the sick and the hospital stores to Richmond. Father [Hippolyte] Gache [S.J.] accompanied us and continued his mission of zeal and charity.

HARPERS FERRY
MILITARY HOSPITAL OF BOLIVAR HEIGHTS

On 7 June 1861, a telegram from Harpers Ferry, a town in [West] Virginia, on the border line, of the Potomac River, reached our peaceful home, St. Joseph's, asking for sisters to serve the sick soldiers of the Confederate Army.[5] Nearly every sister that could be spared was already engaged in the various locations where war's ravages had begun, but our zealous superiors did their best here also, by sending them three sisters.[6]

On the 9th we left by stage for Frederick City, with a good outfit of prudence, caution, etc., from our dear Mother Ann Simeon [Norris], lest we meet trouble as we had the Northern Army and sentinels to pass. An escort had been sent for us, but the telegram had left him far behind, and we met our intended guide without knowing it, he passing on to St. Joseph's [Emmitsburg] for us. Our Lord, it seemed, wished the work to be His own.

An unexpected engagement kept villagers and farmers quietly at home, and men cautiously whispered their fears or opinions. To see people bold enough to travel just then was looked at with surprise. For this reason the sisters tried to sit back in the stage, hoping to pass unobserved, but, halting in a little town for mail, the driver, opening the stage door and handing a letter, said in a loud voice, "A gentleman in Emmitsburg desires you to put this letter in the Southern post office after you cross the line."

All eyes of the astonished people were on us, and we, too, were surprised, as we were not even aware of the driver's knowing our destination. However, nothing more was said and we passed on. The heat was excessive. One of our horses gave out. After some delay, we arrived in Frederick City. A few sentinels stood here and there, but no one noticed us, as the sisters were so often on the road. However, the knowing men of the city gathered round our carriage, saying, "Why, Ladies, where are you going?" Several asking questions at a time, we replied to those more easily answered, without their being better informed.

---

[5] Sister Matilda Coskery wrote this account of the Daughters of Charity at Harpers Ferry and their arrival at Winchester, Virginia.

[6] The following Daughters of Charity were the first to serve at Harpers Ferry: Sister Matilda Coskery, Sister Frances Karrer, (1834-1906), and Sister Lucina Maher, (1830-1875).

As hostilities had stopped the cars, we had to continue our journey in the stage. A Southern lady and gentleman trying to return south joined us. Almost sick with the heat, we journeyed on until another horse gave out. Here, again, suspense! The rocks of the Maryland heights on our right and the Potomac River on our left—here our carriage became fastened in the road and we feared we should have to walk [the rest of] our way.

At last we proceeded and about twilight we saw the Southern pickets, for the South held a portion of Maryland still. The first picket inquired where we were going and to what intent. He then passed us on to the next and so on until we came to the last who said, "We have just received such strict orders as to crossing in or out that it is not in my power to pass you on." But he sent for the captain of the guards and we were soon over the Potomac bridge, on which kegs of gun powder were already placed so that the moment of the enemy's approach, it might be destroyed.

We alighted at the Military Hotel. The whole town [Harpers Ferry], nearly, was a barrack, and soldiers and Negroes were by far the majority of human beings to be seen.

The officer who received us said, "Sisters, you are not here too soon." He took us in, saying, our apartments would be ready for us directly, but the good pastor of the place, Reverend Doctor Michael Costello, came immediately, telling the officer that there were more private arrangements made for us near the hospital and that he was ready to show them to us.[7] We followed the good priest on foot, the stage having gone away, not daring to stay on an enemy's shore. Every step for half a mile was an ascent, and never had a cornette been seen there.

Harpers Ferry, the town, is at the junction of the Potomac and Shenandoah Rivers, the Potomac separating Maryland and Virginia, while the Shenandoah runs into Central Virginia. Very high mountains bounded both rivers. Another height many, many feet above the town and between the two rivers, was the Bolivar Heights, on which our hospital stood.

The neat little church was about midway between the valley or town, and the mount of our hospital. The hospital was filled with sick, and around the town lay about 40 or 50 thousand men just arrived from the most remote southern states, and a cold, wet spell having preceded the present heat, they were sick and lay in their tents until there were vacancies or turns for them in the better sheltered houses in the town. One regiment had contracted

---

[7] The title "Reverend Doctor" indicates a clergyman with some sort of advanced degree or education.

measles on its march, and this spreading among others in such exposure, thinned their numbers before the balls and swords had begun their quicker work.

On reaching our lodgings, supper was prepared, and soon we retired to bed. The stillness and darkness of the town were frightful. No sound but our own voices or footsteps was to be heard. Not a light gleamed from the thousand windows all over the place, for fear of a discovery to the hidden enemy. The whole army there, had been sleeping or rather resting on their arms since their arrival, expecting hourly attack.

The Medical Director, he, who with the officer in charge of that section, had sent for us, came early in the morning to take us to the hospital. He, with his assistant, took us from room to room, introducing us to the sick, saying to them: "Now you will have no cause to complain of not getting medicine, drinks and nourishment in right time, for the Daughters of Charity will see to these things."

An apartment was given to us in the hospital. We noticed one man who seemed to be very low. He told us, on being asked, that he had never been baptized and hearing of its necessity, advantages, etc., he asked earnestly to receive it. We sent for the good Doctor Costello, who not only baptized him but formally christened him also. The poor man was fervent and grateful; looking at sister, who had spoken of it to him, he said to her, "May God bless you!" He died during the night. This was our first day of the hospital.

This town had been by turns in the possession of North and South, and therefore completely drained of provisions, necessary conveniences for the sick, etc., so that the poor sick and all around them had much to suffer. Notwithstanding, these difficult things were beginning to look more comfortable, when suddenly a telegram from Winchester, a town more central and much larger, came, ordering the whole Army with its accompaniments to repair there [Winchester, Virginia] immediately.

WINCHESTER

Departure from Harpers Ferry. The North Army, it was rumored, was to cross the Potomac above and below us at some distance, and thus surrounding us, cut off all supplies whatever.[8] The Army moved at once, but they who served the sick, and those that were to collect tents, finally destroy bridges, rail tracks, etc., were still delayed some. Provisions were

---

[8] Sister Matilda Coskery wrote this account of the departure of the Daughters of Charity from Harpers Ferry and their time in Winchester.

cast into the river to deprive the enemy of them. Then came new orders to wait awhile; but the poor sick had already been moved to the depot to wait there for the return of the cars from Winchester.

Before leaving the sick [in Harpers Ferry] for their removal, we instructed some who seemed not ill enough for baptism, that if they grew worse they must ask for that sacrament, and in case of impossibility, they must offer their desires to Almighty God, etc., etc. Two of these died, we heard, on their way to Winchester.

Arrangements were now being made for the several explosions and we were sent to remain with a worthy Catholic family, further from these buildings. During the night, one after another, the Grand Bridge in its turn shook heights, valley and town. The little church (Catholic), the only one that had not been applied to military purposes, was filled and surrounded by the frightened people. The poor worn-out pastor, their only consoler, and his weary breast the only safe spot for his gracious Lord to rest on.[9] He was nearly exhausted from former labors, attending the sick, hungry, sleepless and constantly on foot. We looked at the awful destruction around us, and felt ourselves encompassed with desolation. All next day we expected hourly to be called to the cars, but no such word came.

We now heard that the Ladies of Winchester had written to the Medical Director, "not to have the Daughters of Charity serve the sick, that they would wait on them." We knew also that those ladies had been enthusiastic in their favor in the comforts they from time to time had sent them.

Thinking, then, that our delay here was owing to the embarrassment the doctors might be in regarding this, we said to them: "Gentlemen, we are aware of the ardor with which the Winchester Ladies have labored for your poor men, as also of their desire to serve them alone, that is, without aid of ours. Therefore, be candid enough to allow us to return to our home, in case you feel any difficulty respecting the Ladies of Winchester. It is reasonable that they should wish to serve them themselves, and we will not be pained, but rather truly grateful for your friendly candor, etc." They said, No, that they cared nothing for the objections that had been made to them on that matter; that those Ladies could never do for the sick as the Daughters of Charity would do, and therefore, unless we insisted on returning home, they held us to our undertaking. They begged us not to leave the town, but wait

---

[9] Refers to Eucharistic altar bread used for communion in the celebration of the Sacred Liturgy.

Hurried departure from Harpers Ferry amidst darkness and danger.

for the signal for departure. Expecting all day and even until 11:00 p.m. to be sent for, and feeling rest absolutely necessary, we were getting into bed when the kind lady of the house came into our room; saying, "My poor, dear sisters, the wagon and your baggage are at the door for you." We soon left our benevolent host who wept to see us pursuing hardships. An open farm wagon with two Negro men to drive—our worthy pastor, who was determined not to leave us entirely to strangers, and our good Lord, still on his breast, was to be our Blessed Guide and Companion. Our trunks formed seats for us. The heavy spray from both rivers was thick in the air. Here and there a star appeared between broken clouds, giving barely light enough to see the sentinel at his post, who in turn advanced, asking the countersign, that the good pastor gave him. Our wagon running on a high terrace edge, on the Potomac river, made with the darkness, a gloomy prospect before us. On reaching the depot, an officer met us, and offered to find us a shelter until the car would arrive. He conducted us over two boards raised up, and by his lantern we could see water on one side of us, so that we must watch to pick our steps lest we might get off the boards. At last he opened a little hut, whose door was almost washed by the river. Here we entered, sat down resting our foreheads on our umbrellas, until between 3:00 or 4:00 o'clock [in the morning], when taking the cars, we arrived in Winchester in five hours.

Arrival in Winchester. Nearly the entire town was occupied by the soldiers, so that hotels were scarcely to be made use of. The one we went to seemed filled with the families, wives or sisters of the wealthier officers of the Southern Army, who came to be near them, for a vast Army now lay around the town. These ladies, also those of the hotel, received us even with affection, but had no room for us, save to rest an hour or two on the bed of the lady of the house. After the poor priest had rested also, he said he would take us first to the church, then go in search of lodging for us. The church, the poorest, poorest old stone building, stood in the suburbs. A crowd of ignorant men and women followed us as we walked. Taking the Blessed [Eucharistic] Host from his breast, the poor priest placed it on the altar; no tabernacle there. Then placing an altar card before it, he lit a candle.[10] The group that followed us crowded in and about the door, and when they saw us go by turn to the confessional, they went around outside and peeped through the cracks at us, right in front of our face. While making our thanksgiving, the good Father went out, shutting the door hard after him, to get away [from] those people, we thought. Well, after we were tired [of] expecting him, we went to the door and really perceived we were prisoners, for the door was locked. We returned to prayer for the Gracious Companion of our journey was with us. After some time he returned, but truly we did fear the dear priest had lost his mind, and would not return. We knew his hardships had been excessive, besides being sick, without sleep or food. But he returned and took us to a plain, worthy Catholic family. Never had a Daughter of Saint Vincent been on that ground before.

The next morning being Sunday, we walked to church. Just at the gate we had to halt to let a company of soldiers enter, we making the rear. About twenty or thirty Catholics made up the congregation, but on this day the soldiers and sisters made quite an assembly. They had a band of Sunday school children, of about twelve in number; these their teachers brought to see us in the evening. We distributed medals, pictures, chaplets, etc., among them, making them very happy, as all those little matters were almost new to them.

We were waiting patiently for the doctors to take us to our duty, as Reverend Doctor Michael Costello had called on them from time to time, telling them we were anxious to be among the sick. They came for us after a few days, for the rest was really necessary for us, if rest it was, for here and there the sisters were asked to go to such and such a house, to see some poor

---

[10] The prayers of the Mass were printed on altar cards for the convenience of the celebrant of the Sacred Liturgy.

sick person. They were taken to see a Lutheran woman, whose husband was a Catholic. She was ill, doubted of her eternal safety because she believed more in the Catholic religion, but having sworn never to leave her own she could not, as she thought, hope for salvation if she broke her vow. She took the medal of our Immaculate Mother, however, from the sister and a visit or two finished the work of divine grace in her soul, and she died with every desirable sentiment.

The Medical Director asked us if we must remain in one hospital, or would each sister take charge of a separate one? We told him our number was too small to divide, we would remain at this one; this was his own—heads of families remained in town, while grown up daughters and children were sent to country seats, the mothers of these staying at their houses in town and receiving and serving as many sick soldiers as they could. We received much kindness from these ladies, for they knew the common rations of the soldiers were quantity and quality, very, very wretched. Indeed our greatest distress as to the duty was, that we had not for the poor men what their suffering condition called for.

The Medical Director told us one day that he had gone to different families, and speaking of the Daughters of Charity in their hospital, all expressed their approbation and satisfaction, but one old maid (a prayer meeting devotee) who expressed her objection. The doctor was very happy to tell us this. At one time we heard loud threats and angry jargon in our kitchen; two sisters hastened there and found two colored men, a cook and a nurse fighting; the sisters forced them apart by stepping between them, and mildly requesting each man to calm himself. This was soon done.

Our house, every spot, was filled with sick and there was occasionally a death, but not very frequent, for as yet we had no wounded men. No Catholics, or very few were here, as that part of the South know but little of our holy religion, but nearly everyone that died in their senses accepted the spiritual assistance offered to them.

The labors began to show on our poor sisters, being but three in number, when the doctor said there would be no way of sending for more, but by one of us to go home, since only the Daughters of Charity could travel now. She went partly by car, then stage, and a dangerous crossing the Potomac in a flat canoe, then on foot as fast as she could walk, and often running for a mile to reach the next car before it would leave, and here the cornette gained admission for her.[11] The evening of the next day she

---

[11] Probably Sister Matilda Coskery herself.

reached St. Joseph's [Emmitsburg], where she was received as if from the grave, for our anxious superiors had heard nothing from or of us, except as public news told of the movements of the two armies. Our dear Sister Euphemia [Blenkinsop], now our Mother [for missions in the Confederacy], then left with three companions for Winchester, to relieve the sisters there. At the same time they telegraphed to dear Sister Valentine [Latouraudais], at St. Louis, to come immediately and replace our dear Sister Euphemia [Blenkinsop] in Winchester, as she was destined to proceed more southward, for in Richmond, Virginia, our sisters were almost overcome with duty, the severest battles having been fought in that section.[12]

Our dear sisters, now six in number, continued their labor in Winchester until very few remained in the hospitals, happy in seeing our holy religion casting sacred influence among the people, who until now, only knew how to condemn and despise it. The healthy and convalescing army had been leaving the place for some days towards Richmond. Our sisters there had been urging those in Winchester to come to their aid [in Richmond]; the sisters informed the doctors [at Winchester] that they wished to comply, as there were so few now to nurse. "Oh! No sisters," said the doctor, "We cannot let you go while the hospital is open; see all our men well first." However, new appeals from Richmond brought new "petitions to be gone" by our sisters [to leave] here [Winchester], until the doctors consented, they having about ten or twelve sick then. Our kind friends there grieved to see the cornettes leave their town [or Winchester].

NORFOLK AND PORTSMOUTH
ST. VINCENT'S HOSPITAL
PORTSMOUTH MARINE HOSPITAL

St. Vincent's Hospital. Our Missions in Norfolk had for many years been in peaceful operation until 1861. The war between the North and the South was beginning to be felt by us also.[13] April 28 brought its first violence, a bombardment of the two cities which were divided by a narrow neck of the sea or bay.

---

[12] Since November 1861 Sister Euphemia Blenkinsop was the official representative of the superiors of the Daughters of Charity at Emmitsburg for the sisters on missions throughout the Confederacy.

[13] The Daughters of Charity had opened Saint Vincent's Hospital (1857) and Saint Mary's Asylum (1848) in Norfolk.

The Navy Yard of Portsmouth in flames.

The establishments of the sisters were one hospital, an orphan asylum and a day school.[14] The first thing to be done on hearing the terrible news was to place ourselves confidingly in the arms of Divine Providence; then placing a light before several statues of our Immaculate Mother, thus claiming her powerful assistance, we felt prepared for the issue.

Soon we beheld what the tolling bells had announced, the destructive fire! The Navy Yard of Portsmouth was in flames! Large magazines of powder exploding shook the two cities to a fearful trembling. This occurred on Sunday morning. A heavy train of powder had been secretly laid, intending an entire overthrowing of the place but, an Infinite Power said here, as formerly: "Thus far, thou shalt go, but no farther," and they were spared.

The Confederate troops were filling Norfolk, and our hospital [Saint Vincent's] was crowded with sick. Many died, but baptisms and conversions were numerous. Those who recovered and left us, have given evidence that a true idea of our holy religion had done its salutary work upon their souls.

Portsmouth Marine Hospital. Soon, however, Norfolk was evacuated, and Norfolk and Portsmouth taken by the North. As all that could

---

[14] A day school was also located at Saint Mary's Orphan Asylum. The Daughters of Charity had begun another school in Norfolk in 1837, but it closed after only three years and the Sisters withdrew, but returned to Tidewater in 1848.

leave before the coming of the Northern troops, had done so, our hospital was empty. The soldiers crowded into the city and great confusion followed for some days. Soon the Marine Hospital in Portsmouth was prepared for the sick and wounded, and the Northern authorities asked for our sisters to attend them.

The necessity being urgent, the sister servants here sent as many as could be spared from their houses until superiors could relieve them. Two days previous, hundreds of soldiers had arrived from the battlefield, in a deplorable condition. There was no time to be lost with regard to body or soul, for many we had cause to fear, had received mortal wounds in each. Some scarcely seemed to know who God was; some were too low [frail] to understand their own misery.

Day and night our sisters constantly administered by turns to soul and body; nourishment, remedies and drinks to the body, and as best they could, "living waters to the soul." Indeed, as far as possible, our dear sisters subtracted from food and rest, the dying and suffering state of these poor men, causing them to make all sacrifices to them even joyfully, regarding such sacrifices as only a drop or cipher compared to the crying duties before them. While they were attending to some, others would be calling to them most piteously to give their wounds some relief. Thanks to our dear Lord, many were baptized in apparently good dispositions.

In a few more days, several more sisters came to their aid from the Central House [Emmitsburg]. As if the enemy of souls wished to oppose their labors, they met with a delay on the road by being refused passports and again, barely escaped being lost in crossing a river in too small a boat for the number of passengers, but Divine Providence saved them.

With the assistance of this addition to their number, the sisters were enabled to effect more good, though Satan was always present as an obstacle in some way. Many Protestant army chaplains attended these wards and some of them zealously accompanied us from bed to bed, speaking in bland tones to the dying men, "How are you, my friend? Will you have the morning paper?" "The morning paper" to a dying man, and by a minister of the Gospel! A sister was applying cold applications to the head of a fever patient, when bursting into tears he exclaimed, "O, if my dear mother could see your care of me, she would take you to her heart."

A man of about twenty-three years of age saw a sister in a distance and, raising his voice he said, "Sister, come and pray awhile by my bed!" He was dying. Sister had just arrived at the hospital and felt as yet, untutored, but she knelt by his bed and made suitable aspirations for him in a low voice. With clasped hands he repeated all in a very loud tone, begged God to pardon him, then prayed to our Blessed Mother, his Angel Guardian and to all the angels to conduct him to heaven.

Sister said: "I will go away if you pray so loud." "O, sister," he replied, "I want God to know that I am in earnest!" Sister showed him her crucifix, saying, "Do you know what this means?" He took it, kissed it reverently, then said, "Jesus <u>hammered</u> on the cross for me! Jesus <u>whipped</u> to death for me! Will you not receive me?" Sister continued to assist him not knowing that anyone was near until presently the dying man, perceiving a companion said, "George, come here and hear what sister is telling me." She looked up and saw a wall of human beings around her, drawn by the loud prayers of the poor man. In this crowd and on his knees was one of the doctors, a Protestant, who being on his rounds among the patients, seeing sister on her knees praying, had involuntarily knelt and remained so until sister rose to prepare a table near the bed, as the priest had been sent for.

While sister was getting other things ready, the good doctor brought a table covered with a pillow case, two black bottles for candle sticks and common tallow candles already lighted, in them. The poor man kept crying out as loud as he could, "Sister, come; Sister, come."

As soon as the sister left him, a minister went to him and said, "My friend, I perceive you are dying. Let me assist you by prayer to go to heaven." The dying man interrupted him with: "Be gone from me. I would never reach there by your hands." The poor preacher, who but a few days [before] was a carpenter, turned away disappointed.

The assembled crowd was present at the last anointing and reception of the Holy Viaticum. Some asked sister to show them Scripture for these sacraments. The doctor applied to the priest for information.

The sick man died, begging God to bless the sisters and calling on angels to present his soul to God.

This was followed by several other edifying deaths, for the faith resignation of such excited others to desire the same hopes of salvation.

A wretched man, who seemed to hate the sisters, refused his medicine and tried to strike them and spit upon them when they would offer it to him. After often acting in this manner, and finding that the sister still hoped he would take it, (for his life depended on it), he said, "Who or what are you anyway?"

Sister said, "I am a Sister of Charity." "Where is your husband?" he said. "I have none," said sister, "And I am glad I have none." "Why are you glad?" he asked, still very angry. "Because," she replied, "If I had a husband, I would have to be employed in his affairs, and consequently could not be here to wait on you." As if by magic in a subdued tone he said, "That will do," and turning his face from her, he remained silent.

Sister left him but returned presently and offered the medicine to him. He took it and motioned to her to sit down. Although he seemed near death, the medicine cured him and he was very soon a true friend of the sisters, but so ignorant of religion in every way that he hardly knew he had a soul. Here again, our good Lord accepted our efforts to gain Him another soul, for the poor man with instruction, became as fervent as he had been indifferent.

A fine looking gentleman, dangerously wounded, was the object of the doctors' deepest interest and they begged the sister not to leave him alone. The sister spoke to him of God's infinite goodness, His tender Providence of the human family, etc. He listened attentively and seemed to enjoy the remarks she made. She withdrew and presently another sister approached him and inquired as to his condition, comfort, etc.

Soldiers gathered around as the Sister prayed.

He said he felt better, and much consoled in an entertainment with a pious lady of his own persuasion, (much encouraged). "Where is she?" said sister, "There," said he, pointing to the one who had just left him, "and judging by your costume, I take you to be one also." Sister replied, "Yes, we are alike in creed." He raised his eyes to heaven saying, "Thank God, I am surrounded by my own true people!" "What!" said sister, "Are you a Catholic?" Shocked through all his frame, he said "I! no, no! I am a Methodist." Later he seemed thoughtful. In the end he was baptized and died, we hoped, in good dispositions.

A young man in a dying state, said to sister, "Write to my mother and tell her that I was cared for in my sufferings by a band of ladies who were as tender to me as mothers." He asked for baptism and said soon after, "Where will I be tomorrow morning?" Sister said, "I hope in heaven, with your Heavenly Father." "Oh!" he exclaimed, "in heaven with God!" He entertained himself with God in most fervent acts and died in a consoling manner.

If we were to relate each one separately, the narratives would be too lengthy. It will do to say and to know that there were many baptisms and several conversions.

We had been at Portsmouth but about six months when the hospital was closed, and the authorities pointed out other locations. Several of our sisters were disposed in more pressing miseries and a few were bound for the Central House [Emmitsburg, Maryland]. The cars took them to Manassas, where an extensive encampment was, and in the midst of which they stopped. The sisters were told that they could not cross the Potomac [River] as the enemy was firing on all who appeared. There was a little hut there and a Protestant family dwelling in it. It was there that the Army Chaplain celebrated Mass, one of the trunks serving for an altar.

They were obliged to go to Richmond, and it was two weeks before a flag of truce could take them to Maryland.

When all were on board, an officer visited the passengers in the cabin. Among them were several Southern ladies, and some of us had also been in the South for some time. When he saw us he exclaimed, "I need not question you, sisters; all is right with you. You mind your own business and don't meddle with government affairs. Your society had done great service to the country, and the authorities in Washington hold your community in high esteem."

This officer was the judge advocate and showed the sisters every kind attention. When the papers belonging to the passengers were asked for, we offered our letters. He said resentfully, "Let me see the man who would dare touch papers belonging to a Sister of Charity! I would give him cause to regret it." Then suddenly he said, "Give me your papers;" and taking them he wrote in large letters, "Examined." "Now," he continued, "Take them. They are safe now."

While he was taking register of the names, some of the ladies looked out of humor; so on coming to the sisters he said, "O, here are faces I like to see! They are cheerful as if the peace of heaven rested in their hearts, no gloom, no frowns here."

When we reached Fortress Monroe, we wished to take the boat direct for Baltimore, but our kind friend said, "No. He did not often have the honor of having Daughters of Charity on his boat, and as we were rebels we were not over-stocked with money. On his boat we could travel free of expense, while on the other we would have to pay a high fare."

We reached Annapolis [Maryland] late for the train to Baltimore, but our kind old friend chartered a train for our accommodation, and having paid our way through, bade us farewell. We felt his kindness the more as he knew that we had been nursing the Southern soldiers. To be sure, he may have seen us also at Portsmouth serving the North. At least he knew that "party" did not influence us in our labors for the poor men. We arrived home safely.[15]

RICHMOND

INFIRMARY OF SAINT FRANCIS DE SALES

Infirmary of St. Francis de Sales. The Infirmary of St. Francis de Sales had been in operation by the sisters for the sick in general, when the war having commenced, this house was soon made use of for the sick soldiers. May 16, 1861, the first appeal was made to the sisters by the [Confederate] Medical Authorities, to admit their men for treatment. But very soon this building was too crowded for their benefit.[16] The government then took a very large house, or houses, making this a hospital. They thought their male

---

[15] Sister Mary Angela Heath and Sister Anna Louise O'Connell wrote accounts of the sisters services in Portsmouth and Norfolk during the Civil War.

[16] St. Francis de Sales Infirmary may also be known as the Catholic Charitable Hospital. Sister Rose Noyland, Sister Juliana Chatard, and Sister Ann Louise O'Connell contributed to this account.

nurses would serve their purpose, but, in a few days the surgeon and officers in charge, came to the sisters of the [Saint Francis de Sales] Infirmary and [Saint Joseph's] Asylum, begging them to come to their assistance, as the poor men were much in need of them.[17]

We went to this [Saint Ann's Military] Hospital, June 26, same year.[18] All kinds of misery lay outstretched before us. It was 10:00 a.m. but not one of these several hundred had had any nourishment up to this hour. Our first lesson received, was of patience for, in this field of suffering, scarcely a moan was heard, except that attendant on the last struggle of death. The [sufferers] poor two-fold nature, or existence, claimed assistance in an imperative voice. Our poor sisters, seemed only as means of a tender, merciful Providence, moving and suggesting to each one what to do, or what to postpone. As for reflection, or consideration, there was none. God directed, and He needed not to deliberate.

New arrivals of wounded men added much to our distress, as no more beds were unoccupied, so they were lain on the floor, and the poor sisters were happy to place even a bundle of shavings, or old paper under their wounded heads for pillows. Weary as the sisters were, they could not sleep, when indeed they were able to leave the dying men, for the heavy smell of death that seemed to fill their lodgings. They at last looked for the cause of this horrid stench, and found in an adjoining room amputated limbs of a week's standing, falling even into corruption.

Sometimes the good sister servants [local superiors] of the [Saint Joseph's] Asylum and Infirmary [of St. Francis de Sales], would send by turns sisters to aid us a little; upon one of these occasions, a man speechless and dying, gave strong evidences of desiring baptism and received it.[19] The next day another sister waited on that ward, and finding this dying man, the same efforts to aid his poor soul were made by our zealous sister; the conclusion was, the good priest was called and the dying man was again baptized after which he died. We could only console ourselves in the hope, that the Providence of our dear Lord directed the matter.

---

[17] The Daughters of Charity at St. Joseph's Asylum also provided hospitality to visiting clergy. See Rev. Joseph T. Durkin, S.J., Confederate Chaplain. *A War Journal of Rev. James B. Sheeran, C.Ss.R, 14th Louisiana, C.S.A.* ((Milwaukee: The Bruce Publishing Company, 1960), 160.

[18] Dr. Gibson requested the services of the sisters on July 26, 1861. They must have arrived soon thereafter.

[19] At this time the sister servants of the Richmond missions were Sister Juliana Chatard at St. Francis de Sales Infirmary, and Sister Rose Noyland at Saint Joseph's Asylum.

Baptisms and conversions were numerous, and it was glorious to hear the dying men invoking our Blessed Mother [Virgin Mary] so devotedly, though for the first and last time in their lives. Late one night, a Protestant doctor called us and asked if we could not do something for a wretched man, who was dying awfully. He was in great anguish mentally and bodily. We spoke of baptism to him, but to this he would say; "What do I know of it?" He seemed to be possessed by an evil spirit. A sister gave him blessed water in his drink... presently one took the relic of Saint Vincent, put it under his head, and in a few seconds a decided consent for baptism was obtained and accordingly given. He became composed, and the sisters continued making [prayerful] aspirations, hardly knowing whether he heard or understood, when presently they heard him invoking Jesus and Mary. We left him, but in the morning the nurse told us he had continued to call on the holy name of Jesus to the very last.

A poor negligent Catholic was so touched by the admonition of a sister, that he actually began his confession to her. She stopped him, and the priest was soon with him and prepared him for death. A lad was spoken to of baptism, some little instruction followed on the Blessed Trinity, the Incarnation, the Sacrament of Baptism, etc., when he suddenly cried out: "O, sister, baptize me, baptize me in the name of the Father, and of the Son and of the Holy Ghost." He occupied himself in prayer after his baptism, saying often, "My God, this is a deathbed repentance, but Oh! have mercy on my poor soul."

During August, the same year, several sisters from St. Joseph's [Emmitsburg] came to our relief, but as hostilities progressed, so also did our duties multiply. A nurse meeting with contradictions one day, cried out impatiently: "I am neither an angel nor a Sister of Charity, and will not put up with this thing."

One poor soldier seemed determined to die as he had lived, but at last told the nurse to call a minister to him. He came, looked at him, and finding him sinking, said: "Nothing can be done for this man; he is dying," then walked away. Opposite to this poor fellow, the priest was preparing a dying man for death. The other gaining a little strength, called the sister and said to her, "I heard my minister say he could do nothing for me, while my companion there has every hope in the spiritual helps he has received. Therefore, if my church can do nothing for me when I am dying, I renounce it." He was soon prepared by our holy religion for his happy exit [from this life].

Other hospitals in or around Richmond were now commenced and the government demanded sisters; but all, this side of the blockade were in Military Posts, except those engaged with our orphans, the day schools having been closed for the time. As our sisters were to be sent to these different hospitals, the number for each was small. Some continued only for some months, circumstances calling for change of place, etc. In preparing for one of these temporary labors, the head sister said, "Oh! let us not forget our little bell, for we cannot do much good unless we get our spiritual exercises." But, Alas! we were there several days before the bell was heard to sound. Mass, meditations, chaplet, reading, etc., were included in our heartfelt efforts to gain heaven for the poor wandering, but redeemed souls of Jesus Christ.

We can say that, in each and every location of the kind, there were many baptisms for the dying, conversions among the convalescent, and sincere returns of the careless Catholic. A sister would say to another; "Do you know how many have been baptized or converted?" "No, truly," was the reply. "I began to keep account, but I feared our dear Lord would be displeased, and I discontinued it." Upon our arrival at one of these hospitals, a man lay dead whose interment was about taking place. Sister said to the steward, "This man must have died in terrible agony." "Yes," said he, "He died blaspheming God, and cursing everyone around him." But thanks to our sweet Jesus, we witnessed no such horrible scenes... not another death like this occurred here.

One of our stewards was very gentlemanly in his manners, and a scholar of about forty years of age. He called himself, "Like to St. Paul, as to zeal, in his hatred of Catholicity." He said to a sister: "I admire you ladies for your great charity, but I despise your religion." Sister calmly replied: "Without our Holy Religion, sir, we would have no Charity." He left the Army sometime after, and on his arrival, his brother gave a dinner and invited friends. The conversation fell upon Catholic errors, absurdities, etc., of which, formerly, our steward had been the warmest in his bitterness, but to their surprise, he suddenly interrupted them, saying, "Gentlemen, in my presence I will allow nothing said against the Catholics; I once thought I gave glory to God by opposing that religion but, I am changed on this matter. You may think me crazy, but I watched those Daughters of Charity day and night, waiting on our sick and wounded men. Never did a frown darken their features, and I now feel convinced, that the Catholic religion alone can give such proofs of heroic virtue as I have witnessed in those sisters, and I intend to embrace their religion."

Soon after going to one of these new hospitals, the surgeon in charge said to us, "Sisters, I am obliged to make known our difficulties to you, that you may enable me to surmount them, for you ladies accomplish all you undertake. Until now we have been supplied in the delicacies necessary for our patients from Louisiana, but the blockade now prevents this, and I fear to enter the wards, as the poor men are still asking for former refreshments, and they cannot be quieted. We dislike also letting them know the straits we are in, though this hindrance may be of short duration." The poor sisters hardly saw how to aid matters, but proposed that wagons might be sent among the farm houses, and gather fowl, milk, butter, fruit, etc., etc. This was done, but in the meantime complaints had been made to headquarters, that since the sisters had come to the hospital, all delicacies had been withheld from the poor sick. The surgeon and sisters knew nothing of this until a deputy arrived to learn the truth of the charge. They visited the wards during meals, after which they entered the room where the sisters dined. They then told the Surgeon the motive of their visit. He was glad to explain to them the cause of the complaints. The deputy informed the soldiers that the good sisters were not the cause of their suffering, that their fare was always worse still, than they gave to them, for when there is not enough of what is good, they take what is worse for themselves.

A terrible engagement commencing near the city, (Richmond) this hospital being more convenient was made the field hospital, where all the wounded were first brought, their wounds examined and dressed, then sent to other hospitals to make room for others. This battle lasted 7 days, commencing about 2:00 a.m. and continuing to 10:00 p.m. each day.[20] The bombs were bursting and reddening the heavens while the Reserve Corps ranged about three hundred yards from our door. While these days lasted, our poor sisters in the city hospitals were shaken by the cannonading and the heavy rolling of the ambulances filling the streets bringing in the wounded and dying men. The entire city trembled as if from earthquakes during the whole week, with one exception of the few short hours between 10 and 2:00 o'clock. Memory is surfeited over these days, hearts overflowing with anguish at the bare remembrance of them, but, to lay the scene truly before you is beyond any human pen.

The soldiers told us that they had received orders from their generals to capture Daughters of Charity if they could, as the hospitals were in such great need of them. One night the doctors called us to go and see a man whose limb must be amputated, but he would not consent to take the lulling

---

[20] The Seven Days Battle, June 25-July 1, 1862.

dose without hearing the Daughters of Charity say he could do so. The sisters said, "it was dark and the crowd was too great to think of going." The Doctors left, but soon returned, declaring, that the man's life depended on their coming, since he would not otherwise comply. Two sisters then, escorted by the good doctors went to him, who seeing them said, "Sisters, they wish me to take a dose that will deprive me of my senses. I wish to make my confession first, and the priest is not here." Sister told him that he might safely take it and she would try and find the priest for him. She then sent for the good priest, who soon was able to put the poor man at peace. We continued our visits to him during his days of martyrdom, and we never saw evidences of greater virtue. We thanked our dear Lord for allowing us such an example of Christian patience. Another man was dying. The nurse called us up to go to him. Several doctors were around his bed. Sister spoke to him of baptism. He earnestly desired it, and after a preparation for it, sister baptized him. One of the doctors said, "Sister, do you think that will do him any good?" Sister answered him very calmly, "I think nothing. I know it will help him."

We could rarely ask them if they wished to become Catholics, for so many early objections were then recalled to their minds that they felt deterred. But simply, when death seemed near, and after the essentials were gained, we asked them if they did not wish to become Children of God in the religion established by our Divine Savior. Though many also said, "Sisters, although I have heard many terrible things against your church, yet the religion that teaches what I see you do, must indeed be a true one, and I wish to belong to it." These remarks were of very frequent occurrence.

Sometimes the poor men were brought to us from encampments of great scarcity, or from hospitals, from which the able-bodied [comrades] had suddenly retreated, and left perhaps thousands of wounded, and prisoners, who in their distress, had fed on mule flesh, rats, even the entrails of cattle, after the meat had failed to be sufficient.[21] These poor creatures on arriving among us looked like dead men, and almost without desires, at least, without voice sufficient to express them. For many such, it seemed as if the Angel Guardian of each had kept life flowing until the Saving Waters of, or words of salvation had been applied.[22]

---

[21] The bracket portion of text was omitted from the 1904 edition of this document but appears in the source document.

[22] Cf. John 3:5 "No one can enter the kingdom of God without being born of water and Spirit."

Our hospitals were often also extremely scarce of the necessities of life, but, we thanked our dear Lord that our sisters seemed not to feel their own privations if they could obtain something for the sick, wounded and starving members of our Jesus. For our own table, rough corn bread and strong fat bacon were luxuries, provided the dear sufferers were better served. As for beverage, we could not always tell what they gave us for coffee or tea; for, at one time it would be sage, or some other herb, roots, beans, etc., etc. But through all we seemed to be refreshed or supported by that invisible Bread: The Divine Will; for, some constitutions among the sisters were most weak and delicate.

As the war continued, the government made use of the Sisters' Hospital also, (St. Francis de Sales) for their soldiers. Here all things were directed by the sisters, and the government paid them so much. Here, too, our sisters could do much more for their patients. During the time their house was thus occupied, about 2,500 patients (soldiers) were admitted, of whom but one hundred died. Many, many were brought to know their duty to God and their own souls. The Blessed Sacrament was kept in our little chapel, and often a sick chaplain would share our hospitality and thus we had Mass more frequently, and the sick likewise, more instruction. No negligent Catholics rejected the kind persuasions of the sisters, who urged them to a return of their Christian obligations. Even the friends who visited them, were induced to observe their religious duties. We had also the great satisfaction of seeing our poor men enter earnestly into the Spirit of the Church, by returns of Her various festivals, in this, our own hospital.

This house [Saint Ann's Military Hospital] continued to be thus occupied until the close of the war. Every day brought some new incident before us, but, the poor daughters of Saint Vincent trusted only to the graces of their holy vocation to meet and discharge them properly.

Upon one occasion lady prisoners were brought to us for safe keeping, who otherwise must have been consigned to a common jail. Another time a female soldier was brought to us that she might be taught to know her place and character in life. The apprenticeship of this poor girl had been like a novel. One leap more, and she stands in soldiers' ranks, flushed with the thoughts of the laurels that await her. However, Saint Vincent sees her afar off. He instructs her on better things and she is soon the "humble Christian," ashamed, and tutored for heaven by the edification she continues to give.

And O, how many were taught to know the love and honor due to the Holy Mother of our Redeemer! All desired to have her [Miraculous] medal. The sisters told the soldiers, that we loved her as they loved their flag, and that if we honored her, She would protect us, as they hoped for all good from their flag. One, after his return to a far distant state, wrote to the sisters for a medal, saying he had lost his.

We may, perhaps, make some remarks on our conditions at the time the city [of Richmond] was evacuated, and the surrendering of the [Confederate] Army took place.

Notwithstanding the foresight of the authorities on the defeat, still, its arrival was of most appalling excitement. Medical stores, commissary departments and houses of merchandise were thrown open. Liquors flowed down the streets, that preventing its dangerous effects, some confusion might be spared. Stores became public property. Our poor city was trembling from the blowing up of the gunboats in the river that bounded the city on the east.

A youth was very low and not baptized. Sister said, "Did you never read in the Bible that you must be baptized before you could enter heaven?" He answered, "I cannot read." Then sister gave him some instructions. Some hours after a minister talked and prayed by him, but said nothing of baptism. Later sister asked him if he desired baptism? He did, and received it. The minister coming again to see him, the poor boy only said to him: "I do not wish you to visit me." This surprised us, for we had said nothing of the sort to him. He died soon after.

A dying man, a Protestant, was requested to make his peace with God, one evening, but he begged to postpone it for the morning. Sister said, "You are very low." "Yes," he said: "But I cannot speak strong enough now, let me wait until tomorrow." "Oh!" said sister, "Will you live till then?" "If you say a prayer to ask that I may, I will," he replied. She could not insist for fear his forced compliance might be injurious to him, so all she could do was truly to pray, as he had told her. In the morning he was able and very calmly expired.

One poor man positively refused all observations concerning his soul's welfare. Sister secreted a medal under his pillow. He soon became restless and bade the nurses remove that pillow and give him another. The nurse being a good Catholic told sister. She told him to drop the medal in the case of the other! Soon, this pillow was objected to and he would have none. Then the medal was fastened to the mattress. In a very short time he declared, he could not rest on the bed either, and would lie on floor. He died there, a little time after, as he had lived.

A Protestant minister passing around, said to a young soldier, "What is your religion, my Son?" "I have none," was the reply. "What were your parents?" "They were Baptists." "Ah! that is the true religion," he said; "These Catholics sprang from the Baptists." He then goes to the next bed, saying to another youth: "What is your religion?" "I have none," he said, "and my parents also were without any." "Well, my Son," said the good minister, "you must pray hard and hold fast to your religion, or you will lose your faith." "How can I lose what I have not got?" said the boy. But he passed on to a third one. Beginning his questions here also, the boy said with quickness: "I do not wish you to speak to me of religion," "Will you have a drink, my son, or what can I do for you?" "Call sister to me," he answered. Sister came, and the poor boy burst into tears saying: "Sister send him away, I do not care for his religion. I am a Catholic." The poor minister bowed and left them. Sister then said, "You have not told me you were a Catholic." "When I was a child," he said, "I was very sickly. My parents lived in the wild woods, and no minister lived near us. A traveling priest called one dark night at our door and asked for lodging or shelter. They expected me to die that night, and my mother finding he was a minister of the Gospel, asked him to baptize me. He did so, and the next day I was well. My mother, therefore, always told me the good gentleman had baptized me a Catholic and that was all I knew of the Catholics till I came here. But, now sister, I have resolved to live as a Catholic, so please give me a book that will tell me what I have to do." The Catechism soon became his hourly occupation, truth was making such active progress on his young heart. He soon made his confession and was preparing for communion, when he was removed to the Convalescent Corps. But we have cause to hope for his perseverance.

These, though many, are still but few of the numberless conversions, baptisms at death, and returns of the careless Catholics, our sisters witnessed in and around Richmond, in the various hospitals they were occupied in. Memory cannot retain detailed instances, but it can vouch to the pleasing fact that refusals to the spiritual assistance offered to them, were exceedingly rare, scarcely one to fifty during those days of slaughter and death.

Towards morning we thought it better to secure the Holy Mass early, for fear of what a few hours more might show forth. We were preparing for it, when suddenly a terrific explosion stunned, as it were, the power of thought. The noise of the breaking of windows in our hospital and neighboring dwellings added greatly to the alarm, as it seemed for the moment, an entire destruction. Fearing it might be the bursting of the first shells, the good chaplain thought it better to give Holy Communion to the sisters, and then consume the blessed hosts. Presently, however, we learned that the Confederates had blown up their own supplies of powder, which were very near us. Then followed the explosion of all the government buildings. We passed that eventful day with as much composure as our trust in our good Lord enabled us to do, though, from time to time, we were in evident danger of having our house, with its helpless inmates, all destroyed.

After the surrender, a Federal Officer rode up to the door, told us we were perfectly safe, that property should be respected, that he would send a guard to protect the house, etc. His visit was fortunate, for, presently a band of Negroes came and ordered our doors to be opened. The sisters pretending not to understand them were slow to obey, and this caused one to say out very imperatively; "Open dem gates, whose property dis?" Oh, said sister, "this belongs to the Sisters of Charity [sic].[23] Col. D....has been here. Everything has been attended to. All is right." He immediately passed the words to his comrades, and they rode off.

Our sisters from the various hospitals took home ward directions, with hearts and minds still more weary than their bodies.

STUART HOSPITAL[24]

The approach of the Federals placed our hospital [in Lynchburg] in imminent danger and it was decided to move the sick and the hospital stores to Richmond [in February 1865]. The Surgeon General of the Confederate Army begged that we would take charge of the Stuart Hospital in that city, which we did on the 13th of February, 1865. Father Gache accompanied us and continued his mission of zeal and charity.

We were ten in number and as usual, we found plenty to do, to place the sick in a comfortable situation, which we had just accomplished when the city was evacuated, and on the 13th of April, the hospital being dispensed with, we left Richmond for our "sweet valley home" [at Emmitsburg].

SAINT ANN'S MILITARY HOSPITAL
RICHMOND GENERAL HOSPITAL

26 July 1861

The [St. Francis de Sales] Infirmary of Richmond having completed the number that the institution can comfortably accommodate, and the sisters of the said Institution being sufficient to supply the wants of the inmates, the latter part of July found our sisters of the [Saint Joseph's] Asylum with nothing but good desires whereon to feed their zeal. We knew that the

---

[23] Daughters of Charity.

[24] In the 1904 edition, the rest of this section was included in the account of Lynchburg.

soldiers had been removed to the general hospital where they suffered for want of proper care but <u>we</u> were tied down.[25] We could not volunteer our services and the Rt. Rev. Bishop [John McGill] seemed entirely opposed to any hospital or infirmary which might prove an obstacle to the prosperity of that of St. Francis de Sales.[26]

Matters so stood when a letter was received from our kind Mother [Ann Simeon Norris] regretting that we could not aid in the noble work. Still, no formal application had been made for our services, but on the morrow of the reception of Mother's letter, Doctor [Charles Bell] Gibson called soliciting sisters most earnestly to come to the relief of the sufferers who really were such. But, how to soften the good bishop's heart! Prayers were said to the Blessed Mother and the Saints to render him propitious; and with a feeling described as akin to that of Judith when she went to "amputate" Holoferne's head, did we go to the Episcopal Palace to cut the knot that held us from our work.[27] At last a consent was obtained, and joyfully was it announced that on the following Saturday, possession would be given us. Immediately hands were busy in fashioning working aprons, and in collecting the few indispensable articles required for our migration. At last we started; twenty minutes walk brought us before a noble looking structure of brick originally intended for an Alms House.[28] It is in an unfinished state; the walls unplastered mostly, but thoroughly ventilated and free from dampness.

After some hours of tedious waiting, we were introduced to our duty. Imagine wards filled with about twelve or fourteen men, the rooms opening one into another, the house containing about three hundred patients who at that late hour advancing onto 12 o'clock had not yet broken their fast. On all sides we encountered unemptied pans and in our dismay found out it was the habit of the nurse to discharge such vessels "sans ceremonie" over the porch into the yard below.

The sight of the wounded and sick was distressing, and our first care was to provide some things to relieve their hunger. To effect this we went to the kitchen making the acquaintance of Nicholas the cook, black George and

---

[25] There were a series of twenty-eight temporary hospitals referred to by numeric designation as the General Hospital (#1-#28). This refers to General Hospital #1 (alternate name, the Alms House Hospital) located opposite Shockoe Cemetery on the north side of Hospital Street, between 2nd and 4th Streets.

[26] John McGill was bishop of the diocese of Richmond, 1850-1872.

[27] Judith 13.

[28] The Alms House Hospital was an alternate name for General Hospital #1 which the Daughters of Charity called Saint Ann's Military Hospital.

other occupants of this section of the house, who though good men and doing their best, succeeded but poorly in having an orderly kitchen. Adjoining the kitchen is the store room. Then it contained not one cupboard, but three long tables upon which were placed "petit mele," the delicacies sent by the ladies, and the bread furnished by the house. Breakfast was over. After that we looked about to see how we could manage to get things in some sort of order. One sister being detained at home later than the others and arriving at the hospital, burning with zeal to be of use to everybody, suddenly found her career of usefulness checked by another sister who possessed by the spirits of order locked up the pantry not perceiving she was in it. Another of our sisters was deprived of her nurse, who from the wards was obliged to be transferred to the "lock-up." Notwithstanding all the inconveniences, faces brightened at the fact that the sisters were going to take care of them— faces of all except the washer woman who, from a mistaken sense of duty, we suppose, <u>watched</u> instead of washed a pile of dirty sheets. Some ladies, too, were disposed to much talk, but generally they were quiet and kindly consigned to our care and the delicacies they had brought for distribution. Really, we enjoyed that day, and if fault was committed, it was that we were too generous in feeding the hungry soldiers, some of whom declared they had not had such a meal for a long time. Night came on and with it the reluctant close of our labors. Four of our sisters were to remain at the hospital at night by turns; so we who were to go home bade them goodnight and found at the door the ambulance or carriage used for the transportation of the sick and wounded soldiers, awaiting our command.[29] In we got and rode home with the expression of Saint Francis Xavier in our hearts and on our lips, "Too much O Lord, too much!"

Our sisters that night got no sleep, for the wants of the sufferers were passing and the pillow was joyfully relinquished for the vigil. The next morning was Sunday. After Mass we went to the relief of our sisters. The way we now give the meals is this: Each ward has its messroom, the food is brought there, measured out, and sent into the wards by the nurses. The second day was passed as the first, but for Sister Blanche DeLaney [*sic*, Rooney] there was a multiplication of the loaves for the supply, though slim, was found sufficient.[30] We have in this hospital our brave Southern men and the wounded men of the North, and oh! how they suffer. Some of them, whose legs were amputated, were swarming with maggots. After the

---

[29] These sisters initially stayed with the Daughters of Charity at their mission on 4th and Marshall Streets where Saint Joseph's Asylum was located.

[30] Sister Blanche Rooney went to Richmond 26 July 1861. There is no record of a Daughter of Charity by the name of Sister Blanche DeLaney.

dressing of one man's leg, I remember actually sweeping these maggots away. Yet so patient are the poor creatures, you seldom hear a complaint and they are most grateful for every little act of kindness. The poor fellow whose leg had been cut off called sister to his bedside and in a low voice, said, "You know the doctor thinks I may not live over night, therefore, I have a great favor to ask that I hope you won't refuse—I have a mother," (tears checked his utterance) and the sister said, "I understand, you want me to write to her." "Yes, tell her that her child is dead but don't tell her how I have suffered. That would break her heart." Towards night about fifty wounded soldiers - prisoners from Manassas - were brought in at once; some dying, others wounded, and until better accommodations could be provided they had to be laid on the floor where they lay, some scarcely covered. Sister called out, "Do, sister, get me something for this poor fellow's head, he has just asked me for a log of wood." The sister went out, but where to get a pillow since everyone was engaged. At last a pillow case was found and the bright idea came to the sister, "I'll stuff it with paper." She brought it to the Yankee thinking the invention suited the individual for whom it was destined. The poor fellow smiled as it was given to him. Then sister said, "Take this blanket over to that man." Poor fellow! nothing covered his shoulders but his scapulars. Another came in so dreadfully wounded in the cheek that the sister actually mistook the wound for his mouth and was presenting his nourishment there. Another came in, shot through the shin. A few words convinced us he was a Catholic. He was in danger, therefore, we made him make the acts of contrition and resignation, and prepared him for death. The priest came that night and I believe the poor fellow was anointed and died.

At last we left for bed, but when we got quietly fixed in our room, Sister Blanche [Rooney] said, "I can't sleep, there is such a smell of death." The morrow unraveled the secret for in the next room were found a pair of legs amputated the week before. Sister says it was a big trial to visit that room. She stuffed her nose and mouth with her handkerchief and threw open the window. The stench was horrible indeed. Now this inconvenience is removed, the limbs were interred at once. The other day one man was buried with three legs!!!

On Sunday we also received an addition to our number of wounded in the person of some of the Federal officers—their number soon amounted to eleven and now the garret to which they were elevated accommodates many more. When I say garret, I mean you to understand that they are fine, airy rooms, as are all the apartments of the general hospital and these rooms being the most private in the house, and the most suitable for them. The accompanying drawing will give some idea of our wards.[31] In the Officers' quarters were found Captains, Majors, Lieutenants, Sergeants, etc., poor fellows all wounded, not many of them very seriously however. One fellow blessed with a fine voice had a guitar loaned him and you may see him in the corner "whiling away the dull hours." In this ward Sister Aimee [Butterley] is stationed and it seems the employment suits her, for by the sketch she has grown very much since her arrival in Richmond. Sometimes these poor officers are rather importuned by visitors who are untiring in their questions. "Whar's you wounded? Whar's you shot at?" (meaning, what part of the body). "Shot at Manassas" was the laconic reply.

Double Baptism. As one of our sisters was crossing the porch, a tall brawny soldier cried out, "You ladies have a sight of work to do, but I tell you what you gets high pay." "None at all," was the answer. "What," said he, starting back with surprise, "You don't tell me you do all this work for nothing?" One of the nurses or hands about the place, being sadly put out about something that went wrong, explained that he was neither an angel nor a Sister of Charity, and he would not put up with it at all. I propose now, giving some attached sketches [descriptions] both of the spiritual and physical order, hoping they will contribute to your edification and amusement: The Double Baptism– on one occasion, the sister of wards T and U, being called off, her place was supplied by another who seeing a poor man whose leg had been amputated and who besides, shot through the lungs, was in a horrible condition, apparently with but few hours of life before him. Her zeal was enkindled and kneeling beside him as he lay upon a mattress on the floor, she endeavored to learn if he had been baptized or if he desired baptism. A few trembling words that she could scarcely make out; a required signal of the hand, at last assured her there was good disposition and sufficient evidence of desire for the sacrament. Accordingly when the priest came, it was administered conditionally. The medal of our Lady was placed under the man's head, and all day long the sister improved her little

---

[31] A written note with one such pen sketch reads as follows: "Genl. Rickets, U.S. Army and wife, Mr. Wilcox and three on right hand all Dorchester boys—and all prisoners at the Genl.'s Hospital, Richmond, VA, wounded at Manassas" 1861 by Roswell M. Shurstaff, ASJPH 7-5-1-2, #4. There is no Union general in 1861 by the name of Rickets but the man in the sketch was James B. Ricketts, an artillery captain at that time who eventually became a general in the Union Sixth Corps. His wife, Fanny Ricketts remained with him during his hospitalization. The artist was the sketcher for *Frank Leslie's Illustrated News* who was wounded near Hampton, Virginia, and taken prisoner. See *Richmond Dispatch*, 26 August 1861, 2 and 24 February 1862, 2.

opportunities of preparing his poor soul. In the evening she found out on her return home to state the joyous news of her success. "What!" exclaimed the sister of the ward after ascertaining the locality of the patient, "Sister, I baptized that man last night, thus with two baptisms and two medals, he made his way, I hope, to a blessed eternity."

Conversions. We have had some most consoling conversions—one, a young man who was baptized and anointed, dying two days after. His sentiments were so beautiful as the good Father spoke to him of contrition for his sins. He could not restrain his sighs and tears. It's so comforting to hear them call on our Blessed Mother, as it were for the first and last time. One night it was late but one of the doctors had come to us to ask if we could do nothing for the soul of a poor man who was dying. The poor wretch lay groaning and gasping, and to questions relative to baptism he could cry out, "What do I know about it?" He put us in mind of a possessed person. It seemed a hopeless case; again the sisters went to his bedside, this time one of us adopted the plan of giving him holy water to drink. Still though some ray of hope appeared we again left him in a most sad state.[32] The third time one of the sisters picked up a relic of Saint Vincent with the feeling that the case was a desperate one and our Holy Father must assist her. She put it under the head of the dying man; a few seconds after a decided consent was obtained for baptism which was given. The poor boy became calm though suffering much. We continued to make aspirations [brief prayers] for him, scarcely knowing if he understood them, when we were presently rewarded by hearing him invoke the name of Jesus. These two cases were among our Southern men.

In the Northern ward, a man was in danger of dying. Sister thought he was a Catholic and on inquiry found her suspicion confirmed, but like many others the man had neglected the one thing necessary. A few words from sister brought him to a sense of his duty, and so penetrated was he with the sense of his situation, and sorrow for having been such a bad boy, that he actually commenced his confession to sister who stopped him, bidding him to await the priest who came afterwards, heard his confession and anointed him. I do not remember if he received Holy Communion but the Fathers do bring the Blessed Sacrament with them and several have had the happiness of being strengthened by that heavenly food. In one of the wards you will find a colored boy. He was taken at Manassas, having been the servant of one of the Federal captains. He was shot near the lungs, the ball penetrating

---

[32] Holy Water is water which has received a special blessing and is considered a sacramental.

the back and breast. The poor boy is looked upon as a curiosity for the report got about that he was a preacher which, however, is false. Since he entered the hospital, he asked for baptism. It has been given him, also Extreme Unction. He is most assiduous in the study of his catechism, and as his health seems to be improving we already think he would prove an excellent help should he entirely recover.

The Minister's Visit. One of Sister Philip's patients, having it appears, made it a rule with himself not to let the day go by without asking for something, would constantly call her to his bedside with, "Please, sister, give me a sheet," or, "Please sister, get me some rice."[33] "Please this" and "Please that." Well one day he said, "Sister please get me a Methodist minister." Sister said for her part she knew no minister but if he would ask the doctor, one could be brought. The request was made and in came the minister who remained sometime with the patient. On going to him after the visit, sister made some remark that she supposed he was glad he had seen the minister. "O, Yes!" said he, clasping his hands. "O, yes, he promised me a soft bed."

Fearing that you may think we are too much sated with our success, I beg our sisters to recall an expression of Sister Mary Ann, "that the sisters first get a puff and then get a buff!" [34]

There is one of our Southern soldiers ill, who certainly cannot live, but some ten days or so. One morning, seeing him so sick and weak, sister asked him if he had been baptized. "No," was the answer (the man's mind was perfectly sound). "No, I am a musician, that is all I know!" The sister said that music was a delightful thing, that she had even taught it herself, but now could teach him something far better whereupon the man shook his head, for he could take a fiddle and on one string could play anything. Besides he urged that he had never harmed anyone and he believed that what he was now punished for, was for joining that regiment when he knew his constitution was illy [poorly] calculated for it. Still the sister represented the impossibility of a salvation without the sacrament and seeing the moment for conviction was unfavorable, she said, "Now you must try to think of this." The man looked at her and said, "In one ear and out of the other." It makes an impression! Nevertheless, we must not give him up, and we may yet get our poor musician at the last hour.

---

[33] Sister Mary Philip Barry (1830-1890).

[34] Possibly Sister Mary Ann McAleer (1814-1889), who established St. Agnes Hospital, Baltimore and later returned to spend the final years of her life.

The Emetic. An emetic having been ordered to one of the patients who was very ill and quite out of his head, the sister administered it and had in good preparation the basin and pitcher of hot water, but lo! the emetic had <u>no</u> <u>effect</u>. She went to the doctor and related the case. "Give another," was the answer! It was given, still the emetic had no effect. Some time passed; again the sister went to the doctor who presented a pint of hot water (down the man's throat who was out of his head). The sister went by the bedside and in spite of himself the man was obedient and drank a part. The doctors came in and stood by the bed. Again the sister stated there had been <u>no</u> <u>effect</u>; she noticed a strange expression on the doctors' countenances and one of them quietly walked away. The sister thought him rather indifferent, but it was not until one of them turning aside, asked for a clean shirt for the poor man that she realized the fact that an emetic can have two effects.

The Garret. We lost some of the prisoners from the officers' quarters. They were so far recovered that they could be removed from the hospital to another large building called the tobacco factory. They were lavish in their expressions of gratitude towards the sisters for the kind attention they had received - almost all left with the little medal and with a promise ever to keep it. They left with guards below and behind as is always the case in such circumstances. Five of them clubbed together and sent sister a check of fifty dollars for the orphans [at Saint Joseph's Asylum]. Among the number still left at the hospital there is a lady most respectably connected, a family friend of the Setons, and of Major Harper.[35] Hearing her husband had been killed at Manassas, she came on hoping to get his body, when to her joy she found him only wounded. Determined to show his fate she accompanied him to Richmond. Whilst on the way, some of the prisoners asked the conductor, "Where are you going to take us?" "To the Poor House," was the reply. "Do you hear that my dear," said the affrighted lady. "They are going to take us to the poor house." Glad enough was she afterwards to find it was a poor house only in name. Her devotion to her husband is beautiful. She is there only for him and troubles herself about nothing else, and seems to be a lovely modest woman. Her husband is Captain Rickets of the Federal Army.[36] Notwithstanding good will, nature sometimes experiences not a

---

[35] Refers to the descendants of Elizabeth Bayley Seton (1774-1821) and William Magee Seton (1768-1803) and to Major General Robert Goodloe Harper (1765-1825), who married Catherine Carroll, a daughter of Charles Carroll of Carrollton, who was cousin to Archbishop John Carroll. The Harpers were friends of the Daughters of Charity at Emmitsburg.

[36] This may be the same person who is identified as General Ricketts in the 1861 by Roswell M. Shurstaff, ASJPH 7-5-1-2, #4.

little fatigue and it would seem a most tempting time to repair this loss is during meditation. One of our sisters remarked the other day that she felt very mean, indeed, to "thank God for the graces we have received during our meditation," when she was conscious of having slept all the time.

We were all much rejoiced at the edifying sentiments of a young man who it appears was dying, when sister went to him and found that he had never been baptized. I believe she asked him if he desired baptism. "Yes," was the reply. Then a few words of instruction were given of baptism, the Incarnation of the Second Person of the Blessed Trinity, etc. "Oh! baptize me" said the poor boy. "Baptize me in the name of the Father and of the Son and of the Holy Ghost." Sister told him he should have his desire. A priest came in and thought that if the patient lived, it would be better to defer the sacrament in order to secure further instruction, but he told sister that should there be danger, to baptize him, herself. In the night she was obliged to do it. The sentiments of the poor man were beautiful. "It is true, my God," he cried out, "This is a deathbed repentance, but oh! have mercy on my poor soul."

It is most consoling to see the ease with which those men are induced to go to confession. Sometimes the priest will sit on the porch with his penitent at his side, the other boys who are preparing, walk up and down the porch as if they were taking exercises.

Having no chapel at the house, one certainly must be in earnest to go to confession under much inconvenience. In giving the Holy Communion, the good Father made use of his hat for a little altar upon which he put our Lord, for it was a cleaner place than a hospital table.

The Kitchen - Oh that I could sketch this region of the house! All good housekeepers would be in wonderment. In the first place, without exaggeration, the stove might be twice as large as it is and no harm to it. Yet, to this place are stationed the regular cooks, and besides all poultice, bits of toast, boiled eggs, warmed snacks, etc., must be cooked at that stove. Imagine the place then where the nurses, sisters and cooks were all intent upon securing their portion of the mess. Black George, when about to remove from the oven large pans of cornbread or meat will swing his arms and their contents back and forth singing out, "Clar the way, Clar the way." Then each one must look out for herself to avoid a burning. Of course there is considerable ambition manifested on these occasions in order to secure the best "pot luck." A young black boy hopped up at a pot of mush saying to one of the sisters who was about to help herself, "Fust come, fust served." "Fust come you <u>little rat</u>, what do you mean?" said the sister, "Well" said the boy, "I'll go up and tell <u>my</u> sister and she's the crossest of the gang, and I say she'll have her share of the mush."

The house is now resuming quite an orderly appearance. The wards look clean, the patients improving; the sisters' rooms are in the second story, front building, but over the entrance their sitting room and dormitory is separated by the amputation room. After an amputation, the patient is usually brought out into the large room or passage opposite. There the sisters can attend at once to him, if needed. The dormitory looks very neat - little cots with blue spreads. The walls are of the red and white peculiar to unplastered bricks, but I guess people sleep right well there. Then the sitting room has the beginning of an altar in the shape of two wooden horses, with boards put across, a little table with a tin basin, drinking cup, etc., on it. Bags of old linen, bandages, things unmarked for the hospital and a lot of chairs. Here we take our [spiritual] exercises as regularly as we can. After night prayers each sister picks up her chair and migrates to the dormitory. In the morning [she] brings the chair back again. The fare is substantial and good though we see but little milk or butter but the bread is excellent and very fresh. Old George's cornbread is hard to beat. If all goes on well no doubt, in a short time, it will be a splendid place. There is a graveyard in front of the house and one at the side. It is convenient, at the same time it renders the house much more privacy than if it were on the open street. From the windows the view commands the city of Richmond, the surrounding country.[37] Now we expect your enthusiasm will be greatly roused, and after this account many will volunteer for St. Ann's Military Hospital [in the capital of the Confederacy].

---

[37] Located on the northwestern edge of Richmond, on a hill, the adjacent cemetery was a popular spot from which to view the smoke and exploding shells from distant battlefields. On Church Hill, Chimborazo Hospital (1862-1865), provided another similar venue and was a complex of hospital wards, divided into five divisions, often referred to as Chimborazo Hospital #1, #2, #3, #4, and #5.

WASHINGTON, D.C.

In 1862, the United States Government asked for sisters to attend the sick and wounded in Washington.[1] The hospital consisted of some frame buildings and war tents. Here, as in most hospitals many hardships were to be endured, but with the one grand object kept in view, these were small, or rather, they were a cause of joy and encouragement.

Many terrible battles had filled the hospital; therefore to begin to alleviate wholesale misery, seemed a hopeless enterprise; but, He, who called our poor sisters, was there before them, and in and with Him they began.

We will not entertain you with the various inconveniences and absence of means so necessary for hospital duties, though these added greatly to our labors, distress and we hope also to our merit.

As to our little chapel, only that the Infinite Being [God] that we worship had been lodged in a stable, we would have feared for His residence among us. We had Mass on Sundays and occasionally through the week. The labors of the priests were great and trying here, and it was sometimes hard to get one, owing to the dying condition of so many thousands in and around Washington.

In one ward lay many just brought in, who were in an emaciated condition from various hardships, wounds, etc., dying before receiving any help. The sister was hastening from one to another when one using all his voice, said, "I want a clergyman!" She went to him as soon as she could; he continued to cry out until, standing by him, she asked: "What clergyman do you want?" "A white bonnet clergyman, such as you ladies have," he answered. "You are not a Catholic" said sister. "Well, I know that; still I want to see him." The priest had not left yet, and was soon with him. His compatriots looked on with wonder, for they knew he had never been a Catholic. The poor man reached his skeleton like hand to the priest, and began as follows: "In the Bible, we read," "As the Father has sent me, I also send you, etc." and, "Whose sins you shall forgive, they are forgiven;" now

---

[1] The Daughters of Charity began Providence Hospital in 1861 and soon cared for sick and injured soldiers. They also served at the following establishments during the Civil War: Cliffburn Hospital, Eckington Hospital, Lincoln Hospital, and the Stanton Military Hospital. Sister Helen Ryan (1833-) and Sister Stanislaus Roache (1831-1906) both wrote accounts of their service at Cliffburn Hospital. Sister Loretto O'Reilly (1833-1869) was called the "guardian angel of the ambulance" as a result of her ministry at Lincoln Hospital.

tell me, has that order ever been countermanded in any part of the Bible? The Father replied with a smile, "No, my son, it is the same now as it ever was and ever will be." "Well," said the man, "I have never disobeyed an order when the one who gave the order, had the authority to command; therefore, as a true obedient soldier I wish to fulfill that order in every respect."

Not being in immediate danger, as he was a scholar of considerable reading, the Reverend Father told him he would come to see him soon again, and told us to instruct him. Proper care and nourishment gave him strength, and as soon as he could hold anything in his hand, he asked for a catechism or any book that would instruct him on the White Bonnet Religion. The sister told him anything that he did not understand in the catechism, he must simply ask the meaning of.

Confession seemed like an awkward thing to him.[2] To make him be more simple [at ease] on this subject, sister said to him, "Suppose that stove was a priest; now I will make a confession aloud, and then you may see that it gives no great labor." He rubbed his hands and said, smilingly, "Well, I will be ready to see the priest tomorrow."

He made confession of his whole life and was baptized before all present in our chapel at the Mass on Sunday, "For," said he, "I do not want to be baptized behind the door," meaning privately, but wished all to know that he was a Catholic.

While he remained in the hospital, he would go from one patient to another, explaining to them what he had heard explained, or reading to them. Several Protestants attacked him on the subject of religion, but with the Bible in one hand and the little catechism in the other, he would silence them all. He got well and went into the army again, a different man. One of the sisters met him two years after and he assured her that he still firmly adhered to the Catholic religion.

A young lad, a soldier, occasionally assisted the sisters in their duties. A companion, a Baptist, asked the lad to go with him to meeting. He refused. Then the other offered him money if he would go with him. The boy grew very angry, saying, "A bought religion was no religion at all." He then came to sister and asked her for one of the little books she gave to the other boys. Sister gave him a catechism, pointing out to him what to read, and said, "Come to me tomorrow." Sister was surprised next day to find that

---

[2] In the sacrament of Reconciliation a person receives forgiveness from Christ by confessing his/her sins to a priest who absolves the individual from them. This act of personal conversion also gives praise for holiness of God and divine mercy toward sinful humankind.

he knew his task and the acts of faith, hope and love, by heart. He said that at bedtime he pulled his bed near the night lamp of the ward and studied them until he knew them. He was baptized, made his First Communion and was confirmed before he left the hospital.

One night about ten o'clock, several ambulances arrived with badly wounded men; sixty four in all, only eight of whom had all their limbs. Some died in removing them from the ambulance to the ward. Two Catholics among them called for a priest. We were at some distance from a priest and therefore there was some delay in his arrival.

The sisters were going about from bed to bed, doing all they could to alleviate the sufferings, and as they could, offering a word for the souls. Two were particularly resentful, using angry and most abusive language, telling the sisters to begone, etc. After a little while, another sister went to these two men and asked them if they wished her to write to anyone. They did; she wrote as they dictated and then read it to them, and left them. By this time, they began to reflect and believe that the sisters were indeed their friends.

The Priest arrives and goes to the two Catholics, who had called for him. When to the horror-stricken Priest and sisters, both these men renounced their faith—one declaring in a loud voice, that he was sorry he had ever been a Catholic—nothing could be done for them. The poor Priest was looking around, to see if he could aid anyone, when one of those men who had abused and driven us from them, called out, "Sister, sister, come here, come, sister; I renounce." "What do you renounce?" asked sister. "The devil and his works. Bring that gentleman in black to me. I wish to be baptized and become a Catholic!" The happy priest baptized him and also gave him the rites of the church.

While this was being done, sister went to the other cross man who seemed nearly dead. Suddenly he grasped her side chaplet and devoutly kissed the crucifix. Sister said, "Are you not a Methodist?" "I have been one," he answered, "But am now going to be a Catholic Christian. Tell that gentleman to come to me." He was baptized, asked the Father to hear his confession, and before dying received the holy Viaticum with most edifying dispositions.

One of the Catholics who gave up his religion soon became speechless and remained so till he died. The other became delirious and died so.

Of the band, eight died before noon the next day. Sometimes there would be thirty in the dead house [morgue] at one time, though two a day would be buried.

At one time our poor patients suffered from smallpox, which added much to our anxiety and labors, since their wards had to be quite remote from the others. Several died of it; one of the sisters who waited on them took it, but recovered.

Many of our sick who seemed to fear and hate us on their arrival, soon showed they had been mistaken and would even place money in our hands when they received it, and would try to find out what we would like to have, that they might get it for us. One day a poor fellow obtained a pass, and after spending the day in the city, returned at twilight, sad and fatigued. The sister of his ward asked him if he were suffering. He said, "No, sister. But I am vexed and tired. I got my pass early today and have walked through every street in Washington to buy one of your white bonnets [cornettes] for you, but did not find a single one for sale." Sister consoled him and he gave up the hope of being able to procure what she would accept.[3]

A sister approaching a man found him agonizing in violent pain, so that his face was black—really black. She saw he was dying and made a few pious remarks to him, but in his efforts to reply, he only uttered, "Too late, too late!" As he was fast sinking, she made the acts of faith, hope and charity in a loud voice, and a lengthy act of contrition with as much fervor as possible. He was attentive, and as she finished he said, "I agree to all that you have said in that prayer; yes, I agree to all that," and at this he expired. As soon as he was dead his face became as white as a child's. Sister believed then that his violent pain had made him say those terrible words, "Too late!"

Among the convalescents, there were some edifying conversions. They would read or have read to them by others, books of information on our holy religion. Among these a Colonel, who had read much, felt his mind convinced and said he would become a Catholic after he had seen

---

[3] The traditional habit of the Daughters of Charity dates to the seventeenth-century dress of French peasant women of the Ile de France and environs of Paris. Some of the early Sisters began to wear a large, white linen sunbonnet or "cornette" on their heads to protect them from the inclement weather, especially the hot sun in the rural districts. Gradually, all the sisters began wearing the cornette and it became obligatory in 1685. The large white cornette (headdress) became universally recognized as a symbol of charity and compassion. The Daughters of Charity dressed this way throughout the world until 1964 when they simplified their dress.

his family.[4] We feared for the good seed in this case, but some months after his leaving the hospital the sisters received a letter from one of his friends, stating that the colonel and his family had entered the Catholic church. His being a prominent lawyer also gave the affair a wider circulation.

Independent of what was done for individuals, thousands returned to their homes, impressed with kind feelings toward the sisters, consequently towards our Holy Faith also, which will benefit not only themselves but render in some degree our travel through the different states easier. The [military] officers, doctors and public authorities, all concurring in their unlimited confidence in the sisters must, and did have, its silent effect on all.

In all the wards printed placards were hung up with these words: All articles, donations, etc., for the use of the soldiers here, are to be placed under the care of the sisters, as also, paper, books, clothing, money and delicacies. The President's Lady [Mary Todd Lincoln] was among those who personally presented such liberalities. She showed much affability towards our sisters.

One instance more will serve to show the variety of strange occurrences our poor sisters were often exposed to, trials of best judgment as to right or wrong. A young man was dying; sister tried to help his poor soul by some suitable aspirations, but to all these he only replied, "I wish you to write a letter for me to my intended bride and after that, I will hear all that you say to me." The poor sister thinking that the soul was worth too much to stop at any terms asked him what she should say, and wrote accordingly. All the ward was attentive to hear it. When done, it was read to him. He was satisfied now to do as she advised, and being prepared for baptism died with very pious dispositions.

These are among the many, many similar occasions in which our good Lord was pleased to accept from His grateful and happy children, the spiritual and corporal works of mercy.

The sisters left this hospital early in the summer of 1865, after the hospital was closed.

---

[4] This refers to Daniel Shipman Troy, a Lt. Col. of the 60th Alabama Regiment who, along with his wife and family, converted to Roman Catholicism after his stay in the Lincoln Hospital. Troy wrote an account of his experiences entitled, "How I became a Catholic," ASJPH 7-5-2. Troy attributes his decision to the kindness of a Daughter of Charity whom he named Sister Helen Brent. There are no records of such an individual. Sister Helen Ryan was in charge of Lincoln Hospital, but withdrew from the Daughters of Charity 26 March 1869.

We will relate here some consoling facts occurring in another hospital [Stanton Military Hospital] of the same city, Washington, though its operation was commenced in March 1865, and it was closed in October of the same year.

There were two sisters engaged there. The capacity of the hospital was about six hundred. The surgeon in charge had long solicited for sisters, but there were none disengaged until now for our dear sisters were scattered wherever they could be sent. On our arrival here the surgeon and officers of the hospital were overjoyed.

Here we did not have the annoyances we had experienced in the beginning of the war since, now, our calling and costume were better known and understood.

We had a good room for a chapel, and had Mass on Sundays and benediction in the evening. Our patients were generally respectful and even kind in their dispositions to aid the sisters in any manner.

Our house was full of sick and wounded, some very low. A sister speaking to one of baptism, the poor youth said, "Sister, I have no religion, but I wish to belong to yours; for looking at you ladies caring for us poor fellows, makes one think you must have the right faith." Sister prepared him and then gave him baptism, and some hours after he died very piously. Another poor man, badly wounded, seemed animated with confidence in the sisters as soon as he saw them, and to the one who served him, he would say from time to time, "Don't leave me to myself, sister; I am only safe in your hands." He begged for baptism and after receiving it with great devotion, breathed his last, making fervent aspirations.

During May we tried to have some devotions in the evening to our Immaculate Mother. After our first decoration of her altar, the convalescent soldiers faithfully supplied her with fresh flowers, daily, and formed among themselves a little choir to sing her praises. Our Blessed Mother [the Virgin Mary] urged them to this that, she in turn might confer favors, for many among them were negligent Catholics living without the sacraments; these, she sweetly drew again to Her Divine Son. During this month one hundred Catholics returned to their Christian duties. Those of more faithful practice, also made these devotions a preparation for a fervent approach to the sacraments. When these would relate to their bed-ridden companions what they had heard and witnessed, they, too, were animated to love a Christian life more.

During this month, five were baptized. Among these was a poor man who had been discharged, but on his way home his money was stolen, and his wounded leg being tender it became too sore for him to move. Someone seeing him lying on the wayside brought him back to the hospital. His absence and hardships had caused gangrene and fears were had for his life. The sisters, alone, dressed his wounds, the nurse declaring he could not. The poor man knew not how to express his thanks to sister, but she would try to make him know that God had loved and cured him.

He said: "O, sister, I do not know how to thank the good God since I have never known how to serve him. How many thoughts I have had since I have been here! I never belonged to any religion, but how glad I would be to be instructed in your church!" The good chaplain was pleased with his fervor and by the time his wound was well, he had made his communion in our little chapel.

During the month of July, the Jesuit Fathers were giving the Jubilee in a neighboring church.[5] The soldiers hearing of it wished to attend. Some spoke to the sisters who easily obtained passes to this effect. Then these would relate to the others what they had heard and seen, so that even Protestants came for passes to attend the Jubilee! The sister gave all who wished to go in charge of a sergeant, to have good order and respect observed and to bring them safely home when all was over.

They heard all the sermons and instructions, and on the evening of the second day sister asked one if the Catholic soldiers had been to confession. "No, sister," said he, "The sergeant is no Catholic, and if we move to leave our place he thinks we are misbehaving, and he will not let us stir from the spot. He is a good man, sister, but he does not know what the people go into the confessional for. Please tell him to let us go." Sister told the sergeant and after that they had no trouble.

The good Fathers attended in the hospital to those who could not go out. The grace of the Jubilee produced much good among our poor soldiers. Many who had just come in sick or wounded received the sacraments; others who had been intemperate took the pledge.[6] One, especially, was so

---

[5] The Jesuits staffed Saint Aloysius Church, North Capital Street. The "neighboring church" may be Saint Patrick's Church. The two churches were located about a mile and a half apart.

[6] Irish Catholic children were encouraged to make a pledge not to drink alcohol until they were at least 18. The pledge was promoted by the Pioneer Total Abstinence Association of the Sacred Heart (or PTAA), an Irish organization for Roman Catholic teetotalers.

angry with himself that he begged sister to administer the pledge to him. He had not received the sacraments in twenty years. After a trial, the priest gave him the pledge and medal, and later the sacraments. He obtained his discharge and finding employment in Washington, he had the opportunity of letting sister know from time to time that he had not neglected his grace. After the war he met sister and told her that he had even lost his relish for stimulants, and that he strengthened his soul by monthly communion.

Often the poor men, when questioned concerning their future welfare, would make but one reply which was: "I have not been of your religion, but wish to become what you are. The religion of the sisters must be the true one!" "The religion of the sisters" became a common phrase among them.

A young lad, suffering excruciatingly, excited our admiration. Like a martyr in his calm courage, not a murmur or a complaint escaped him. Every evening during the octave of Our Lady's Assumption [after August 15] he recited his rosary most edifyingly.

The horrible strife of war and bloodshed having ceased, preparations were actively carried on in trying to restore order, and the poor men who were able to get home were being sent to their various destinations.

Our hospital was now filled again, from the closing of others, ours being the last to close. The poor sick were glad to be left under the sisters' care until they could start homeward. On the 1st of October 1863, the last left the hospital.

As we had had the entire charge of all the hospital goods, we made out a general inventory of furniture, groceries, bedding, clothing, etc., etc. All ended very satisfactorily and the surgeons and officers in charge expressed much gratitude and confidence in what had been done by the sisters. The first surgeon especially was at a loss to put his satisfaction into words, saying, "The Daughters of Charity were able to lessen the cares and labors of the physicians and surgeons in any hospital they might be placed in."

Here again, with our many dear sisters, we may say: Our dear Saint Joseph lulls the sharp sorrows of the harrowing anguish we had witnessed during those sanguinary months and even years.

EPILOGUE
LEGACY OF CHARITY

Love knew no bounds for the sisters. This missionary perspective enabled them to be heroic, courageous, and generous in providing emergency services during the national crisis of the Civil War. The sisters did not heed any personal cost. They were charity afire personified and did not count time, energy, or personal sacrifice. The sisters learned early in their religious formation that their vocation challenged them to love God at times of prayer and hard work. In the words of Saint Vincent: "Let us love God...but let it be with the strength of our arms and the sweat of our brows."[1] In other words the sisters vocation called for love that would be both affective and effective, whether in battlefield ambulances, wards of wounded soldiers, or isolation wards.

The Daughters of Charity went about their service with the understanding that they represented "the Goodness of God" as they ministered to the sick and wounded. True to their name, the sisters rendered competent and compassionate care "with gentleness, compassion, and love."[2]

The foundation of their service was a vision of faith that saw Christ in poor persons and the poor in Christ. This belief enabled the sisters to minister to Christ in maimed soldiers and veterans throughout the Civil War and beyond. When fatigue and stress burdened them, the sisters recalled Louise's admonition to the first sisters about being mindful of their vocation: "I beg all of you to renew your courage so that you may serve God and the poor with more fervor, humility, and charity than ever. Strive to acquire interior recollection in the midst of your occupations."[3]

Approximately 300 Daughters of Charity, based in Emmitsburg, Maryland, crossed boundaries of locale, politics, and religion during wartime for the sake of the common good in the name of their mission—to serve God by caring for "the sick poor and the wounded."[4] First person

---

[1] Conference 25. Love of God, *CCD* 11:32.
[2] Conference 85. "Service of the Sick and the Care of One's own Health," 11 November 1657. *CCD.10: 267.*
[3] L.581 Louise de Marillac to the Sisters of the Hôtel-Dieu of Nantes, 13 July 1658, *Spiritual Writings Louise de Marillac*, 600.
[4] The sister nurses represent 34% of the Daughters of Charity in the United States Province during the Civil War years. Conference 75. On Two Sisters Being Sent to La Fère, 29 July 1656, *CCD.10:161.*

accounts, diaries, unpublished holographs document the courageous and compassionate charity shown by the Daughters of Charity who nursed their dear masters during the Civil War.

The respect the sisters showed all parties did much to erode religious intolerance and bigotry, particularly toward Roman Catholics. Lt. Col. Daniel Shipman Troy, 60th Alabama Regiment (Montgomery), was one of many Civil War veterans who relinquished anti-Catholic sentiments because of the sisters' devoted and impartial care to victims from both the North and South. Perhaps such respect for human diversity may have contributed to the future recognition of civil rights for all persons.[5] Troy, an Episcopalian and son of a Mason, met the Daughters of Charity at Lincoln Hospital in Washington after the battle of Petersburg. Troy described his experiences in a memoir.[6]

> One of the first things that impressed me was that the sisters made no distinction whatever between the most polished gentlemen and the greatest rapscallion in the lot. The measure of their attention was solely the human suffering to be relieved.[7]

A fully annotated unabridged edition of the original manuscript and source document, *Notes of the Sisters' Services in Military Hospitals 1861-1865*, is being prepared for publication under the title, *Balm of Hope*. The work will also include additional memoirs, first-person accounts, official documents and correspondence related to the Daughters of Charity services during the war years. *Balm of Hope* will make the corpus of the Daughters of Charity Civil War records available to researchers, students, and the general public. Until *Balm of Hope* becomes available, *Dear Masters* is the most complete record of the Daughters of Charity response to the national emergency of the Civil War.

---

[5] For a discussion about reconciliation between former antagonists see George Weigel, "What Gettysburg Means," published in *The Catholic Review* (Archdiocese of Baltimore, 5 August 2010), 22.

[6] ASJPH 10-1-20, "How I Became a Catholic." Troy and his wife converted to Roman Catholicism 20 April 1868, at Saint Peter's Church, Montgomery, Alabama.

[7] Ibid, 16.

INDEX